ATROPOS PRESS
new york • dresden

General Editor:
Wolfgang Schirmacher

Editorial Board:
Pierre Alferi
Giorgio Agamben
Hubertus von Amelunxen
Alain Badiou
Judith Balso
Judith Butler
Diane Davis
Chris Fynsk
Martin Hielscher
Geert Lovink
Larry Rickels
Avital Ronell
Michael Schmidt
Victor Vitanza
Siegfried Zielinski
Slavoj Žižek

© 2013 by Ze`ev Maor
Think Media EGS Series is supported by the European Graduate School

ATROPOS PRESS
New York • Dresden

151 First Avenue # 14, New York, N.Y. 10003

all rights reserved

978-1-940813-07-3

Mythopoetica

Hölderlin and Bialik in a Hermeneutical Encounter

Ze`ev Maor

Table of Contents

1. Introduction 7
   1.1 Syn-opsis - Hölderlin and Bialik 9
   1.2 Biographical Notes 13
   1.3 The Course of the Research 15
2. The Breaking of the Whole - On Poetics of Crisis 25
   2.1 Hölderlin's Mythical Temporality 27
   2.2 Judgment and Being 31
   2.3 German-Hebrew Passage 35
   2.4 Bialik's Caesural Poetics 41
   2.5 In the Withdrawal of the Gods 47
3. The Poetized - Poetry and (the Question of) Mission 51
   3.1 Benjamin and the Fall of Language 53
   3.2 Heidegger between Revealment and Concealment 65
   3.3 Hermeneutical Cartography of Myth 77
   3.4 "Who Needs Poets in Lean Years?" 93
4. On Myth and Paradox 95
   4.1 Dialectics of Myth 97
   4.2 Small Genealogy of (Jewish) Historical Memory 107
   4.3 Myth as a Form of Literature 117
   4.4 Bialik and the Gap between Past and Future 127
   4.5 De Natura Dei 131
5. The Myth Carriers 135
   5.1 Bialik's Meta-Poesis 137
   5.2 Crisis and Language 147
   5.3 "Tikkun" - The Mending of the World 153
   5.4 Poetry and Invocation 157

 5.5 "Language of Sights" 161

 5.6 Poetry as (Modern) Prophesy 167

6. River and Pond - Poetry, Myth and The Political 171

 6.1 "Dwelling" - Poetry and Polis 173

 6.2 "Sechinah" - "Dwelling" in Hebrew 185

 6.3 Radical Knowing of the Unknowable 197

 6.4 "Holy Sobriety" 203

7. Conclusions 207

 7.1 Tractatus Poetico-Politicus 209

 7.2 Tradition and Speculation 217

 7.3 On Myth and Political Imagination 223

Abbreviations used in Footnotes 229

Bibliography 231

The lines of life are various,

Like roads, and the borders of mountains.

What we are here, a god can complete there,

With harmonies, undying reward, and peace.

(Hölderlin, "To Zimmer")[1]

1. Introduction

Johann Christian Friedrich Hölderlin (1770-1843) is known to be one of the greatest German-writing poets. Chaim Nachman Bialik (1873-1934)[2] is known as one of the greatest Hebrew poets of modern times. Both poets, each within his culture, is of canonic stature, and each one's poetry has brought forth a rich field of research and interpretation.

This essay creates a hermeneutical encounter between the poetries of Hölderlin and Bialik and the interpretational discourses orbiting their writing. This encounter becomes a gateway for a new reading of their work and of the critical discussion ensuing, regarding the means of movement and operation of 'myth' as poetic and political power; as inducing culture pathologies while also enabling cultural renewal at times of crisis.

---

[1] F. Hölderlin, "An Zimmern" (1812), SPF, p. 329.
[2] Also: Hayim or Haim Nahman.

1.1 Syn-opsis - Hölderlin and Bialik

At the basis of this research lies an intuitive observation regarding an essential connection and similarity existing between the respective poetics of Hölderlin and Bialik. Although there seems to be no mention in the tradition of research hinting to any influence, nor even to Bialik's acquaintance with Hölderlin's poetry, and in spite of the apparent distance between their worlds, and the different historical, geo-political, and cultural context in which each of their poetries developed, it would seem that their respective poetries are connected beyond matters of style. Rather, this connection seems to touch upon the struggle with the question of poetic mission to be found at the heart of each one's poetics.

Extensive research has been conducted on the interpretation and criticism of each of the poets separately.[3] And yet, to this moment - as far as we know - there has been no theoretical and interpretative encounter placing together, for the purpose of comparison and critical study, the poetries of these two protagonists of culture, who reflect and represent the preferences of their cultures as well, by virtue of their public acceptance.

Hölderlin and Bialik sing their private and individual poetries, while at the same time singing for their people, as prophets agonizing over their missions. Their poetries seem to react, each within the circumstances of its time and place, to the transformation of the ongoing crisis at the basis of modernity; the crisis of tradition and the divesting of myths of their historical authorities; a crisis which seems to still be pulsating, perhaps even more so, in our times. Within this context, the poetic reaction of the two poets to crisis, with its philosophical and political aspects, seems worthy of examination.

Hence, the basic research question touches upon the existence of a poetic and conceptual connection between Hölderlin and Bialik, and upon the characterization of the assumed connection. To put it concisely: Is there a connection between the poetries of Hölderlin and Bialik? And if there is, how can it be conceptualized? The hypothesis seeking corroboration in this paper is this: Between the poetics there is a connection touching upon their common subject, each dealing in its own way with the question of the 'idea' of poetry and the mission of the poet under circumstances of the 'crisis of modernity'; and that the interpretational encounter between Hölderlin and Bialik may, at least, enrich the understanding and interpretation of their poetries, honing the view of the connections, and the differences in the way the two traditions (the German-Western and the Jewish-Israeli) cope with this crisis. A second-order hypothesis will be: The encounter between Hölderlin and Bialik invites, as well, a critical poetic-political study of the questions regarding the place of past myth in contemporary culture.

---

[3] The writings of Hölderlin and Bialik have yielded extensive elaborate research that cannot be fully mentioned here. However, chapters 2 and 6 present cartography of the literature and interpretational discussion central to our subject, regarding each of the poets.

Syn-opsis - Hölderlin and Bialik

The term 'synopsis', in connection to its Greek origin, well-indicates the main method of this essay: "to see together" - as it wishes to place the texts, poets and interpretations in mutual connection, and to create a fertile discussion.

The research opens with a close synoptic reading of childhood poems, from which - as assumed, the similarity and connection between Hölderlin and Bialik is revealed, at the heart of their respective poetics and their reflexive ars-poetica writing. One may draw an analogy between, on the one hand, the process of secularization and disillusionment of Hölderlin's period at the end of the 18th century, in the transition to Enlightenment, and - on the other, the awakening from the promises of the Enlightenment and its slogans in Bialik's period. Both poets may be read as singing the essence of their times as the song of the whole and its disintegration; the poetry of the shattering of belief and the crisis of disillusionment.

The question of the ideal of poetry, as too the question of the poet's mission under conditions of multi-dimensional crisis, rocking the old foundations of thought and the definitions of identity and identification, turn out to be the focus around which is woven the poetry of both poets, each under its particular circumstances, as well as their theoretical writings. The poets' stance (or to be more precise: movement) regarding these questions is examined here both in their poetic and their theoretical writings, in addition to the main controversies of the contemporary dominant interpretative discourse. In this context, works of the following writers will be addressed: Martin Heidegger, Walter Benjamin, Maurice Blanchot, Theodor Adorno; as well as those by Avital Ronell, Jean-Luc Nancy and Philippe Lacoue-Labarthe dealing with Hölderlin; and by Baruch Kurzweil, Eliezer Schweid, Ziva Shamir, Ariel Hirschfeld and Assaf Inbari dealing with Bialik.

Examination reveals that both in the case of Hölderlin and in the case of Bialik, as read by the interpreters, the controversial issue regarding the way in which the mission of the poet is perceived, as well as the mission of his poetry - is the issue of 'myth' of the past and the question of its delivery into our times, beyond the shattering of the authority of its transcendental origin. Study of the interpretational and critical fields of the two poets' poetries shows a polarized, dichotomous cartography between two opposing approaches regarding the myth. On one side, there is the re-mythological interpretational approach imbuing the myth with privilege-rights, identifying with its power and the yearning, one way or another, for its return. On the other side, as its dialectic opposite, there is the de-mythological position warning against its subjugating power, wishing for release from its shackles, and for its eloigning from the contemporary poetic-political discourse.

The hermeneutical encounter shows the poets as embodying the crisis of tradition of their respective cultures in their writings (and no less, in their circumstances of life) - in other words, the problem of delivering into the present a myth from the past, at times when the very delivery is questionable. By means of the synoptic reading of their writings, and by intersection of the poets' concepts (such as 'Dwelling'=Wohnen of Hölderlin, and 'Shechinah' of Bialik; and, respectively, 'Holy Sobriety'=Heilige Nuchternheit, and 'Blima'), it will be claimed here that the outlines are marked and emphasized of a reading born of the encounter (and which does not necessarily occur when each poet is read on his own, or within the framework of the interpretational field surrounding him). This reading reveals that the intersected concepts of the poets serve as mechanisms of judgment, and constitute a poetic (and political) approach of 'gap', between the withdrawal of the mythic and the possibility of its future presence. This is basically a textual approach, attaching major significance to the historical continuum, viewing myth as a type of literature, and averting the focus of the historical interest from the question of its transcendental validity to the conditions of its possible, or unfeasible, delivery. This is a poetics that sings the crisis of tradition as part of the continuum of the tradition itself, thereby conducting a move of breaking up of the sequence and restoring the continuum simultaneously. This poetic approach, discovered here to be close to, or even common to Hölderlin and Bialik, is actually a poetic-political response of the poets, each according to his own way and circumstances, to the crises from which their poetries are derived. As shall be claimed here, their common approach reveals the illusion of the binary opposition between de-mythologization and re-mythologization as a complete view of the world. It presents possibilities, which seem vital to our times, of "modern" thought regarding the idea of 'tradition'; thought that wishes to go beyond the accepted dichotomy towards renewed understandings of the potential of myth in (post) modern culture.

Within the framework of this essay there is no pretension, or possibility of encompassing or exhausting the vast fields of knowledge surrounding the works of Hölderlin and Bialik. The essay creates an encounter (as a particle collision, if you wish) between the writings of the poets, following the repercussions of the event; it does not, however, wish to eliminate or push aside the research work conducted up to the present, but rather to be supported by it, and - through debate - to add outlines of one other reading, by which it presents the possibility of new questions.

The first hypothesis, regarding an assumed connection between the poetries of Hölderlin and Bialik, is corroborated already at the beginning of the research, from a reading of their childhood poems. The study then goes on to focus on the characterization of the poetic connections between the poets, through questions that guide the process of examination from one chapter to the next. This research approach combines two modes of reading-writing: the first is methodical - analyzing artistic and poetical means within the text, while the second is based on the former, expanding the analysis and the interpretation with an inter-textual approach, weaving the interpretational space around the text and through it.[4] This hermeneutical approach views the text as a multi-layered object, through whose signs the hidden dimensions are hinted at, and in which the potential connections bubble up. This type of reading may be likened to the process of unraveling a woven cloth, and then weaving it anew[5] or as digging at an archeological hill.[6] This is a process in which one may view the texts as "conversing" with one another in cultural, historical and literary contexts.[7] Thus, additional meanings are created and the field of meanings and interpretations expanded. The positioning of the texts one upon another, or side by side, appears, therefore, as a means of creating new from the old, and new with old, through an ongoing creative process.

---

[4] In connection with the hermeneutical research approach, according to which the text has been created for the interpreter and his process of reading. J. Kristeva. *Language: The Unknown; An Initiation into Linguistics* (1969), trans. A.M. Menke (New York: Columbia UP, 1991), pp. 241-253.
Also see: J. Kristeva, *Black Sun: Depression and Melancholia* (New York: Columbia UP, 1989).
[5] See: R. Barthes "le neuter" (The Neutral): Lecture Course at the College de France (1988-1978), (New York: Columbia UP, 2005).
[6] See: A. Azoulay, Once upon a Time: Photography in the Footsteps of Walter Benjamin (Bar-Ilan: Bar- Ilan UP, 2006).
[7] See: (Kristeva, 1989).

Syn-opsis - Hölderlin and Bialik

The existence of a "true" conversation between the texts, namely, a dialogue, which does not entail subjugation of one text to another, or expropriation of one for the other, obligates a fundamental principle (although somewhat arbitrary) - that the texts of the two poets should be studied in such a manner that they will both gain from this dialogue.

1.2 Biographical Notes

Hölderlin: Born in Schwab; studied with Hegel and Schelling; an ardent admirer of the French Revolution; a despairing and disastrous lover who wrote his best poetry in his 30s, and then fell into the twilight of mental illness, living out the rest of his life in the home of Zemmer the carpenter, under the observation of his admirer, in a little tower overlooking the Neckar River. And Bialik: a rural child from Rady near Zhytomyrin in the Volhynia region of the Russian empire (now Ukraine); a yeshiva student who left his religious Talmud for the Enlightenment; public leader, culture entrepreneur, publisher, one of the leaders of the Zionist movement and reviver of the Hebrew language, who built his home in Tel-Aviv, and in his lifetime was recognized as the "national poet", becoming an authority father figure of modern Hebrew culture.

It would seem that the life circles of the protagonists of this research are very distant; however, in spite of these differences, one may discover quite a few points of similarity: Both grew up in religious homes, threw off the shackles of tradition and left its boundary to expand their education. Hölderlin was the son of a monastery administrator, his mother was the daughter of a priest, and he himself was meant to become an evangelist priest, having been sent for that purpose to various evangelist learning institutions in Württemberg, and to university in Tübingen, and then to Jena, where he was exposed to revolutionary ideas and events of his period. Bialik grew up in a traditional-religious Jewish family; studied in the Jewish 'Heder' till he was 17, when he left home for the Volozhin Yeshiva in search of the new ideas of Enlightenment of his period.

There is also a certain similarity between the two on the subject of the early death or absence of the father: Hölderlin's father died when he was a baby, and seven years later he was again orphaned, this time from his beloved step-father. Bialik's father died when he was seven, and since his family was poor he was turned over to his strict religious grandfather's care. In order to illustrate this similarity, we shall mention Hölderlin's biography by Jean Laplanche in which the psychoanalyst analyzes Hölderlin's madness as related to his growing up with no father.[8] Or the humiliated character of Bialik's father, appearing in his poems as a martyr fallen into a world of sacrilege, and how Bialik's power of creation dwindled in the second half of his life, and he was then paralyzed by the depression that had harbored from his youth.[9]

There is also a similarity between the two protagonists in the dimension of the socio-political circumstances of their lives, in other words, in the fact that both of them, despite the hundred years dividing them, are at the heart of periods of formative political changes, shadowed by crises and revolutions.

---

[8] J. Laplanche, *Hölderlin et la question du père*, Paris: PUF, 1961; *Hölderlin and the Question of the Father*, trans. Luke Carson (Victoria, BC: ELS Editions, 2007).
[9] A. Holtzman, *Chaim Nachman Bialik* (Hebrew), (Tel-Aviv: Shazar Center, 2009), p. 38.

Bibliographical Notes

During Hölderlin's adolescence the French Revolution overturned European politics. Its slogan "Freedom, liberty, brotherhood", as well as Rousseau's writings at its basis (and of considerable influence upon the young Hölderlin), sent tumultuous waves across Western thought. At the turn of the century, Napoleon - riding the crescent of the revolutionary wave - had swallowed portions of Europe and was almost at the gates of Berlin. In Hölderlin's surroundings the German Romanticists were divided about the events: There were those who viewed the revolution as a titanic liberating power, while others saw the French Titan as pure evil.[10] One way or another, in his surroundings, German nationalism gathered strength,[11] and soon enough the events knocked on his door when his friend and benefactor Isaac von Sinclair was arrested in February 1805 in the Duchesse of Homburg, by demand of Friedrich the second of Württemberg, and interrogated for treason. Hölderlin was also under investigation, only to have his case dropped when doctor and pharmacist Müller of Homburg testified to his madness.

Bialik's life story also illustrates his tumultuous times: A child who was torn from his village to the town of Zhytomyr, due to his family's poverty, and from there as an adolescent to the Volozhyn Yeshiva, which he also left, for Odessa (in 1892), where he joined a group of Zionist writers and poets led by Ahad Ha'am.[12] There he married Mania (nee Averbuch) in 1893, and started to deal in the wood trade, until losing his money. Following the pogroms of Kishinev (in 1903)[13], Bialik wrote two of his best known works: "On the Slaughter"[14] and "In the City of Slaughter"[15], which were chopped down and changed by demand of the censor. The Russian Revolution (October 1917) put the town of Odessa under the rule of the Bolsheviks, and in 1921 - with the personal intervention of the writer Maxim Gorky, and a special directive of Lenin, Bialik was given permission to leave the USSR with a group of several Jewish writers. He moved to Berlin, where he dealt with publishing books in Hebrew and with Zionist activity, until moving to the 'Land of Israel' (Mandatory Palestine) in 1924, and to a house especially built for him in Tel Aviv.

Bialik had, in his life time, the stature of a culture hero, while Hölderlin was barely recognized during his life, with his poetry almost forgotten (although Nietzsche kept his memory going). It was only at the beginning of the 20th century that he was rediscovered, and gained his known stature, specifically thanks to Norbert von Hellingrath, of the poet Stefan George's circle, and later due to the interest that Heidegger and Benjamin found in him.

---

[10] See: J.M. Coetzee, *Hölderlin, The Poet in the Tower*, NYRB e-edition, October 19, 2006, http://www.nybooks.com/article/archives/2006/oct/19/the-poet-in-the-tower/?pagination=false
[11] See: J.G. Fichte, *Reden an die deutsche Nation* (1808) *Addresses to the German Nation*, trans. G. Moore (Cambridge: Cambridge UP, 2008).
[12] Ahad Ha'm is the pen name of Asher Zvi (Hirsch) Ginsberg (1856-1927), one of the founders of Zionism, founder of the branch of the spiritual Zionism, and one of the most important figures to define the secular-national Jewish identity.
[13] Pogrom - riots and murder of Jews under the auspices, and encouraged by, the rulers; took place in 1903 in Kishinev, Bessarabia (now the capital of the Moldavian Republic); 49 Jews were murdered, hundreds wounded, and thousands of homes and shops were looted and destroyed. The pogrom was a turning point, followed by an increased immigration to the USA, and to the Land of Israel. This pogrom convinced Theodor Herzl to propose the Uganda Plan at the 6th Zionist Congress, as a solution for the dire situation of Russian Jewry.
[14] C.N. Bialik, "Al Ha-Shechita" (Hebrew), 1903 -BYP
[15] C.N. Bialik, "Be-Ir Ha-Harigah" (Hebrew), 1904 -BYP

The Braking of the Whole

1.3 The Course of the Research

The return to childhood - as the memory's tracing of one's primary experience of discovery - is well-known as a recurring theme in modern art. A reading of the poem "In My Boyhood Days",[16] and parts of the epistolary novel "Hyperion",[17] and synoptically in Bialik's poems "Zafririm"[18] and "Zohar"[19] as well, illustrates already in Chapter 2, "The Breaking of the Whole", that - both for Hölderlin and for Bialik - the childhood experience is a formative element of the poetic perception and the poet's mission.

The childlike state appears in the poetries of both poets as a primal pre-lingual condition, offering the child - protected by his innocence - an experience that is both direct and elusive-concealed, of a natural unity flickering and disappearing; a condition of inspiration (as in magnetic induction); a moment of dwelling under the wings of the gods, then past and gone with only the recollection echoing on. Childhood as a concept embodying its loss as well is presented by the poets through their personal experiences, while at the same time appearing as an expanding comprehensive symbol of the "childhood-of-man" or "childhood-of-the-nation".

Study of these childhood poems shows Hölderlin and Bialik as singing from the heart of the same rift, personal and historical, multi-dimensional, focusing on the pendulum of disillusionment, or awakening from the naïve being, to a ripped reality of missing source and broken whole. For both poets the essence of childlike wholeness and the memory of the moments of flitting access of the disappearing wholeness are likened to events with the power of anointing the child to poethood, following the model of the prophets. The image of the poet, as a child who had grown up in the laps of the gods until manhood, or as a child playing with the mythic morning creatures until abandoned by them in youth, appears as one devoted to preserving and conveying the mythic charge from its withdrawing source unto the present. After discovering the similarity between the poets, at the base of their poetic mission and in the conceptual-historical crisis from which it grew, and after their poetic childhood is presented as that which had prepared the poets for their modern prophecy, the question raised by the study is: How can prophecy (or prophetic poetry) be formulated in a world void of gods? Or in other terms: Do, and how do, the two poets propose a model of (poetical) adulthood in a post-metaphysical world?

---

[16] F. Hölderlin, "Da ich ein Knabe war" (1798-1800) SPF, p.27.
[17] F. Hölderlin, *Hyperion oder Der Eremit in Griechenland* (1797), *Hyperion or the Hermit in Greece*, trans. R. Benjamin (New York: Archipelago Books, 2008).
[18] C.N. Bialik, "Zafririm" (1899), translated as "Imps of the Sun" in *Selected Poems*, trans. R. Nevo, (Jerusalem: Magnes Press, 1981), p.15.
[19] C. N. Bialik, "Zohar" (1900), BYP.

The discussion in Chapter 3, "The Poetized", derives from Hölderlin's poem "The Poet's Courage"[20], as expressing the question of the poet's mission and his poetry, under the crisis conditions elaborated on in the previous chapter. In its various versions, the poem is examined through two fields of interpretation: The first focuses on the dominant readings of Walter Benjamin and Martin Heidegger of Hölderlin's writings, where their perceptions of the language and the art are established. From here on, the study broadens to a second interpretational level, where we survey and examine the view-point of Maurice Blanchot and of contemporary readers of Hölderlin, such as Philippe Lacoue-Labarthe, Jean-Luc Nancy and Avital Ronell. The various readings and accumulated view-points reveal that the question of the paradoxical existence of myth, in an age that does not recognize its transcendental origin, is the central motif of the controversy in the interpretational arena. The mapping of the outlines of the controversy yields a hermeneutical cartography organized around the two polar approaches, or opposing interpretational trends, which we may call 're-mythologization' on one hand, and 'de-mythologization' on the other. The re-mythologization pole is marked by Heidegger's reading that presents Hölderlin's poetry as the embodiment of the ideal of poetry, bearing a foundational quality, since it renders an opening for the appearance of 'being'. The poet appears as one who exists within the rift caused by the hidden faces of the gods; the one who as yet converses with them and announces their absence/return. The poet, therefore, is the 'Demigod', preserving the divine fire for Man, transferring the ontotheological abundance into his hands, thus granting him his place in the world. This approach sides with myth, seeing it as an essential element of significance and history. In this context the poet is perceived as the hero of his culture who also prods, as does the prophet with his people, to bravely enter into a new mythology.

Counter to this direction, and as its dialectic opposition, is the second interpretational direction, presented by Benjamin and his followers, oriented toward 're-mythologization'.[21] This approach, in the spirit of Lacoue-Labarthe's reading of Benjamin reading Hölderlin,[22] nowadays popular in the critical research of literature and supported by the readings of Nancy and Ronell,[23] emphasizes the status of the poet as a failing prophet, and his mission - as the abandonment of myth, and generally of any "mission". According to this interpretation, Hölderlin's courage is that of remaining sober in the face of Romantic enthusiasm over a new mythology. Hölderlin's poetry is perceived as expressing the poem's divesting of its mythic authority; and in its absence, the poetic condition is described as a condition of non-mission and non-action; a state of infinite attentiveness and openness, as a state of "stupidity" (Ronell), and of total submission to relations. Hence, following Benjamin, the poetry will also become one that disintegrates itself in its movement towards prose.

The image of the poet, the nature of his mission and destiny are found in this chapter to be the response presented by Hölderlin's poetry (and the course of his tragic life) to the crisis that gave birth to it, and was early on

---

[20] F. Hölderlin, "Dichtermut" (1800-1801) - "The Poet's Courage" (first version) in Selected Poems and Fragments, trans. M. Hamburger (London: Penguin Books, 1998), p.99.

[21] We should mention here, in spite of the putative interpretation, that Benjamin's approach to myth is both unequivocal and ambivalent: on one hand, his rejection of myth is broadly delineated here, but on the other hand - one cannot ignore the messianic dimension and the desire for redemption to be found in it.

[22] P. Lacoue-Labarthe, Poetry's Courage, in The Solid Letter: Readings of Friedrich Hölderlin, ed. A. Fioretos (Stanford UP, 1999), pp. 74-93.

[23] Blanchot's interpretation appears in this context as interestingly eluding the duality that the dialectics of the myth presents in the field of interpretation. His reading-interpretation of Hölderlin preserves a tension that keeps his approach from being mapped onto the outlines we've described, so that it flickers between the poles. That said, there does seem to be a tendency of a direction which, for reasons to be mentioned further on, seems closer to that of Heidegger.

identified by it. It would seem, however, that each of the two poles established as the possible alternate interpretations of the image of the poet is problematic and insufficient in itself. On the one hand, there is the re-mythological interpretation represented here by Heidegger, which sees the poet as the prophet who, through his language, preserves and revives the people's connection with the withdrawing source. The poet's fate here is that of a martyr: Exposed to the danger of the divine saturation, the poet restores the people to their history, until he is defeated and beaten by madness. The weakness of this approach is that it actually embodies (as described by Benjamin) a 'Romantic' yearning for the 'absolute', and as such entails the choice dangers of myth - its subjugating power; its latent survival (in the seemingly secular institutions); and its non-accidental historical tendency (as described by Lacoue-Labarthe) to be actualized as proto-fascistic 'political theology'. On the other side there is the de-mythological approach, represented by Benjamin and supported by the readings of Adorno, Lacoue-Labarthe, Nancy and Ronell, declaring itself as the position of 'sobriety' vis-à-vis myth. This sobriety stretches into an effort of purifying from myth, so that the poetry is relieved and freed of its fetters and messages, in favor of attentiveness and total openness. This approach, aspiring to "release", actually internalizes Benjamin's perception of his contemporary reality (and also Benjamin's interpretation of Hölderlin's approach to his own times) as the experience of a 'fall' to a damaged reality where language - already lacking the mythic element, is in exile from the world. It seems that the weakness of this approach is in its tendency to swiftly transform into a melancholy state (a matter not at all foreign to Benjamin) as a pathological reaction to loss, by way of refusing in principle any alternative object.

This approach, then, empowers passivity, neutralizing the possibility of action, and leaving, with no response, the question of shifting to a politics of justice. Hence, this approach, although seeking - as mentioned - to be released from myth (while the possibility of that happening is not at all clear), turns out to echo in its process the same known Cartesian meditation, which in its striving to reason within the foundations of consciousness, asks to be purified, and to divest itself of any prejudice. Thus it seems that the de-mythological approach has run the risk of falling into the temptations of another kind of 'absolute'.

In view of the cartography of the field of interpretation of Hölderlin's poetry, organized in a dichotomy between advocates of the myth and its opponents, it seems that the discussion's progress at this stage requires two directions of examination: The first will touch upon the concept of 'myth' itself, placing the dialectic controversy regarding it in a historical context; and the second will deal with an examination of the place and status of 'myth' in Bialik's poetry.

Chapter 4, "Myth and Paradox", traces the genealogy of the concept of 'myth' and surveys its transformations with cross-reading of chapters from the history of Western philosophy (as the context of Hölderlin's cultural foundation)[24] with parallel chapters in the history of Jewish thought (as the foundation of Bialik's poetics)[25] - a survey from the horizons of an inherent paradox to be found in the approach to myth from a perspective that is necessarily

---

[24] Starting with the Greek and Hellenistic philosophers, then Della Mirandola, Spinoza, Kant, Nietzsche, the German Idealism with emphasis on Schelling, Lévi-Strauss, Erich Fromm, Carl Jung, Ernest Cassirer, Emile Durkheim, Georges Sorel, Max Horkheimer, Theodor Adorno, Roland Barthes and Marshal McLuhan.
[25] A survey splitting up from Spinoza, and going through Nachman K. Krochmal, Samuel Hirsch, Gershom Scholem, Martin Buber, Franz Rosenzweig, Hermann Cohen, Leo Baeck and Leo Strauss.

modern, and itself embodies the crisis in the mythological consciousness, reflected in the secularization process. Tracing the movement of the concept of 'myth' in the Western and Jewish intellectual history raises several issues regarding the dialectical tension within it: One such tension stretches between the perception of myth in the eyes of its believers as a story whose significance tells truth, and the perception of myth (already in ancient times but much more strongly in modern times) as a fable; as a beneficial fiction, or a functional story with a historical core. A different tension deals with the dialectics between myth and the historical present, in other words, viewing myth from the perspective of the researcher's current times, rather than belonging to the past that is examined. Additional dialectic tension is expressed in the repeated darting back and forth across history between seemingly opposing cultural trends of 're-mythologization' and 'de-mythologization'. This movement to and fro also creates ironic dynamics according to which whatever was done with the declared intention of 'de-mythologization' in one period, may be perceived as the act of 're-mythologization' from a later perspective.

The discussion in this chapter, with the help of the works of David Ohana and Robert S. Wistrich[26], and of Eliezer Schweid[27], forms a presentation of myth from a contemporary view point, as one of the most sophisticated in cultural creations - to be precise: A type of literature, a founding text delivered from period to period while given to re-reading and re-interpretation. Myths (as too their deconstructions), beyond being justifications for an enslaving status quo and even murderous fanaticism, also turn out to be a generating motivating factor of critical elements in social existence, such as participation, identification, commitment, etc. Myths and their ways of delivery in culture convey accumulated historical information about the poetic and philosophical ways of coping with fundamental questions of human existence, and the ways in which a nation, or a group, or a set of individuals, wish to organize their unique collective memory.

There seems to be a difficulty here in denying the fact that myths are regenerated and will be regenerated for reasons of what seems to be a theoretical and historical necessity. In other words - that a significant perception of reality, capable of granting people general orientation and marshaling their required energies for a purposeful enterprise of historical dimension, is not possible without myth. Myth is revealed here to be the 'meaningful', if only for the fact that the approaches wishing to divest themselves of myth find themselves - perhaps of necessity - in that which exceeds meaning (and as may be expected, will shift into new meanings).

The crisis of the gods' withdrawal or the "hidden face" of the god, as experienced by Hölderlin and Bialik each in his own way, is aligned by super-positioning with the basic crisis of contemporary culture and politics, which may be seen, on the one hand, as the difficulty in accepting this comprehensive explanation that myth provided people for so long a time. On the other, as the dialectic pole of this view, it is connected with the fundamentalist myths gathering forces in an interpretative version that is mimetic, insular and enforcing. The (theological-political) dangers encompassed in myth on the one hand, and what may be seen as its necessary presence as a condition for cultural renewal, on the other, raises questions about the very possibility of delivering a founding idea over the course of time.

---

[26] David Ohana and Robert S. Wistrich ed., *Myth and Memory* (Jerusalem: Van Leer - Hakibbutz Hameuchad, 1996), pp. 11-37.
[27] E. Schweid, "Myth and Historical Memory in Jewish Thought" in David Ohana and Robert S. Wistrich ed., *Myth and Memory* (Jerusalem: Van Leer - Hakibbutz Hameuchad, 1996), pp. 41-72.

Or, in the words of Hannah Arendt: How is it possible to deliver the experience, concepts and culture of a past tradition into the future without dragging along all the accompanying problems?[28] According to Arendt, this is a political question - a matter which returns the course of this study to the question of the (poetic-political) status-function of myth in Bialik's poetry.

Chapter 5,"The Myth Carriers", traces the movement of myth in Bialik's poetics, through joint analysis of "Shirati" (1900)[29] and "Zohar",[30] two poems that were originally parts of a long lyrical poem that was divided by the poet for publication. In the poem, Bialik's poetic source is illustrated as springing from what may be called 'threshold being', dwelling in the gap or fault between 'twin worlds'. On the one hand, old and crumbling, yet conveying a forgotten truth, while on the other - new, sparkling, freeing, promising, yet also misleading and full of nothing. If the field of interpretation of Hölderlin's poetry contained a dichotomous cartography as mentioned, then study of the field of interpretation of Bialik's poetry evokes a similar tension (albeit more extreme and varied) between de-mythological attitudes interpreting the poet's mythic experience as an inner personal one,[31] and the approach viewing Bialik's poetry as mystical poetry reporting on transcendental revelation.[32] With the aid of research by Ziva Shamir[33] and Eliezer Schweid,[34] Bialik's dialectic poetics is revealed to be an attempt at developing a response from within the crisis state of the traditional language. This response is drawn as sober poetics according to which one must not try to throw out the old, in the Nietzschian sense, but rather build the new by blending it with the old. Thus Bialik points to a direction and way of a quasi new solution, which is also the transformation of an old idea: 'Tikkun'. For this purpose he presents a 'new poetry' in his writing, in the form of personal and collective myth, melting within it and weaving together a variety of layers of mythic material from the past, re-activated in order to occur as an 'event' in the present. The blending of traditional myth material experienced through the prism of personal experience, in itself perceived as "typological", and thus as prophetic - according to Schweid[35] - places Bialik's entire work, and particularly its parts of myth, in the broader context of the traditional Jewish literature, as its dialectic continuation.

Hence, the consciousness of faith crisis enters myth as a central event of dramatic 'fall' to an abyss of disappointment and despair. Moreover, the story of the 'fall' is what generates in myth the transformation of the power of traditional religious experience into national experience (such that the Zionist idea is posited as the mythological continuation of Jewish destiny). These are then the means with which myth was validated and its reliability restored in modern consciousness, or in other words - thus traditional myth was regenerated and repositioned as revolutionary national myth.

---

[28] H. Arendt, Between Past and Future: Six Exercises in Political Thought (New York: Viking, 1961), p.17.
[29] C.N. Bialik, "Shirati" (1900), BYP.
[30] C.N. Bialik, "Zohar" (1900), BYP.
[31] See: A. Hirschfeld, "Bialik's HaBrecha: I - as a World" (Hebrew), in *Jerusalem Studies in Hebrew Literature*, vol.24 (Jerusalem: Mandel Institute, 2011).
[32] See A. Inbari, "On the Language of Revelation" (Hebrew), in *Hadarim* 14, ed. H. Yeshurun, Tel Aviv, winter 2002.
[33] Z. Shamir, "To Compile Sparkles Amidst the Broken Vessels", in *Sadan: Studies in Hebrew Literature*, vol. 4, ed. A. Holtzman (Tel Aviv UP, 2000), Pp. 75-113.
[34] E. Schweid, "The Language of the Renewed Prophecy", in *Prophets for Their People and Humanity* (Hebrew), (Jerusalem Magnes Press, 1998).
[35] Ibid.

Hence, study of Bialik's poetry presents a theoretical possibility or a certain response to the dialectics of myth - a response which locates itself beyond the dichotomy discussed in the interpretation of Hölderlin's poetry, between those who deny myth and those yearning for it. Bialik's poetry, through its poetic and linguistic means, presents an action of 'delivery' of myth (Jewish, in this case) as a renewed interpretation positioning itself as part of the historical continuum, while at the same time disrupting and restoring it. This is a poetics of 'awakening', located in the gap between the enslaving intoxication of a burning desire for the absolute - and the tempting misleading illusions of freedom. It is a poetics that is, in itself, a political act.

The question of myth and its delivery, raised in the discussion on Hölderlin's poetry, is thus examined as well in this chapter on the reading of Bialik. The discussion clarifies both Bialik's poetic-political steps, and the connection between his 'awakening' and Hölderlin's 'sobriety'. The question at the end of this chapter touches upon the possibility that Bialik's poetic perception opens the way for a new reading of the place of myth in Hölderlin's poetry, beyond the dichotomy characterizing the dominant interpretational discussion.

In continuation of the process clarifying the connections between the poetic and the mythic in the poetries of Hölderlin and Bialik, and in the interpretational field surrounding them, Chapter 6 "On River and Pond" intersects several of the poets' central concepts, reading one in terms of the other, thereby seeking to present a poetic-political approach that seems to be common to both poets. Hölderlin's poem "The Rhine", and the fragment "In Lovely Blue", are the point of departure in this chapter for studying the concept of 'dwelling' as it appears in Hölderlin's writing, and develops in a Heideggerian interpretation. If the 'poetics', or the poetic language, were previously seen to be perceived by the two poets as the foundation, the 'lebensraum', or the means of the historical movement of myth, presented as a type of literature - then the discussion of the concept of 'dwelling' in this chapter clarifies (by the concept of 'polis') the status of the 'poetic' as the founder of 'the political'.

Bialik's poems "Alone" (1902),[36] "The Pond" (1902)[37] and the essay "Revealment and Concealment in the Language"[38] were the point of departure for discussing the concept 'shechina' in Bialik's poetics - a concept that constitutes an appropriate translation of 'dwelling' into Hebrew, while indicating (mythic) expression of the divine. Examination of the connotations of 'shechina' sharpens the distinction between two poetic-political steps in Bialik's poetry: The first is the methodical use the poet makes of myth, by taking the concept of 'shechina' with its train of connotations, and re-operating it as an authentic prophetic myth, blending the poet's crisis of his individual being with the miserable historical fate of the people. The second deals with Bialik's perception of the experience of revelation, as a dialectic linguistic experience of revealment and concealment. In the essay "Revealment and Concealment in the Language",[39] Bialik presents the mythic concept of 'blima' (the traditional interpretations of bli+ma give it the meaning of: 'no real in it') as the region that is totally unknown to man, and is blocked to language in principle. And yet, surprisingly, it is suggested, hinted at, and peeks out to the one searching for it. The language of poetry (as that of

---

[36] C.N. Bialik, "Levadi" (1902), in *Songs from Bialik: Selected Poems*, trans. A. Hadari (Syracuse: Syracuse UP, 2000), p. 23, stanza 1.
[37] C.N. Bialik, "Habrecha" (1902), BYP.
[38] C.N. Bialik, "Gilui Vekisui Balashon" (1917), (Hebrew), in *Literature*, (Tel Aviv Dvir 1977).
[39] Ibid.

the mystics) is merely an additional concealment, only it is a primary concealment with the power of suggesting that which it conceals. For the poet, this unified perception is the basis of a sober poetics of 'gap', attentive to a hint from the abyss in any detail seen and in any sound heard.

The river, in Hölderlin's poetry, as the history or the process of creation, is - in its course, a continuation from the source onward, to the future, to a comprehensive balance embodied in an apocalyptic wedding ceremony, a speculation of reconciliation of man with gods, where instead of appeasing the gods, the scales of fate will be balanced if only for a short while. The poet, in the image of Rousseau, is the one who, as a Dionysian priest, bestows the language of purity (pure in German is Rein). The poet has of the divine tongue, granting of the holy plenty. In his poem "Half of Life"[40] Hölderlin presents the concept of 'holy sobriety' which, in the spirit of Bialik's poetics, appears in the reading as the yard-stick of judgment, and as the element divesting myth of its authority (in the way of 'sobriety'), while not denying its vitality that grants man a place (in the way of 'holiness'). Thus myth is placed in a new context of holy-sober. Denial (as in Heidegger's case) of the divesting dimension of sobriety is the danger that lurks in total devotion to the historical power of myth, a devotion that made it possible to stretch the interpretation of Hölderlin's poetry downhill toward the 'absolute', as far as advocating a 'new mythology'; and on the other hand, denial of the dimension of 'holiness' of myth and its rejection seem to lead to melancholy.

The concepts discussed, intersecting in the poetries of Hölderlin and Bialik, appear then as mechanisms of judgment, embodying an approach of 'gap' between the lack of myth and its return, and as those who expose the illusion of a binary contrast between de-mythologization and re-mythologization as a complete picture of the world. Both Hölderlin's poetics, stretched between extremes as a heroic attempt to deliver a Greek past into a German present and to blend idolatry polytheism with Christian monotheism for an idyllic future in 'Hesperia', his Schwabian homeland; and Bialik's poetics which re-activates myth's materials of the past to deliver them as an 'event' of the present, as the labor of 'tikkun' within the rift between the old and the new - both poetics sing the crisis of traditional myth, as part of its own story continuum, thereby constituting a disruption and restoration of the succession simultaneously. Hence, both poets may be read as placing in their poetries a view point or even approach existing beyond the dichotomy between the advocates of myth and its deniers, a poetic-political approach which is mainly textual, and attaches major importance to the historical continuum which diverts and transfers the center of gravity from the question of the factual validity of delivered myth, to the ways of its delivery and to the interpretation; in other words, shifting the source of myth's validity from that which is derived from the past, to that deriving from the present. This approach sees myth as a poetic-political factor of regenerative quality, and the poet's image as a modern prophet bearing the failure of his mission to his people, as the lightning-rod of history.

The question arising towards the summation of the encounter between the poets is based on the founding connection between the poetic and the political, and is the continuation of the noble failure of the Hölderlin poetics and the successful failure of the Bialik poetics. In other words: Given the cultural vitality of myth on the one hand, and

---

[40] F. Hölderlin, "Halfte des Lebens" (1803-1804), SPF, p. 171.

the dangers lurking in the political theology on the other, is it possible - after Hölderlin and Bialik, to consider the continuation of the presence of myth as a regenerative factor[41] in contemporary culture and politics?

In Chapter 7, summing up this essay, it seems that the initial hypothesis of the research, about the existence of a conceptual connection and poetic similarity between Hölderlin and Bialik is sufficiently corroborated, since there is considerable similarity in their basic questions regarding the poet's mission and the purpose of the poetry, issues at the very core of their poetic writing and ars-poetica. The hermeneutical encounter between Hölderlin and Bialik may be seen in this essay as opening a discussion on the question that appeared as fundamental to both poets' poetic mission, namely - the question of myth and the possibility of its delivery beyond the modern crisis with transcendental authority.[42] The images of the two poets appear from the encounter as ones who, in their writing, present an alternative to the dichotomy between what was described as 'de-mythologization' and 're-mythologization' of culture, or between what may be termed (in a creative generalization) "liberal rationalism" and "romantic fundamentalism" - an alternative that is embodied in a poetic-political approach. This approach, characterized here by its closeness to the idea of the 'traditional', carries out the mission of the meandering continuity of myth, through interpretation and poetic re-activation, from the past to the present culture.

While the concept of 'traditional' in its common use represents one pole of the dichotomy vis-à-vis renewal, then - following what has so far been characterized in the approach of Hölderlin and Bialik, one may view the concept as an affirmative product of the dialectics based on movement along the linguistic-textual-interpretational continuum of expression, movement through which myth appears as a (certain type of) literature, bearing as well the keys for renewal of culture from its crises.

According to this meaning, tradition is everything that grows from the inner life of the creation in constant acts of interpretation, canonization, forgetfulness and remembrance. What turns it into one entity is its continuum within and around its sources. Tradition is connected to the idea of delivery.[43] In delivery, the recipient's attitude is a priori that of loyalty or faithfulness. This attitude is not an imitation of previous generations but rather a willingness to suggest an interpretation and to fight for it.[44] Hence, 'tradition' appears as a quasi 'language' into which man is born, in and through he grows, becoming a member of the community, becoming acquainted with the world around him, and constituting his subjectivity. Tradition, forever contemporary (as opposed to its image as a matter whose content and meanings are sealed) is simultaneously that which enables grasping reality and interpreting it, and also that which sets the boundary and the horizon of those same perceptions and interpretations. Due to its institutional and symbolic

---

[41] The term 'regenerative' is presented here as a biological metaphor describing myth's possible movement in culture. Regeneration indicates a process of renewal while maintaining a dynamic connection to the source, as a blemished genetic code that operates faithfully to its origin yet has internalized in its movement also reaction to trauma. This term is also, as shown further on, a polemical response to the challenging thoughts of Wolfgang Schirmacher in the concept of 'homo generator'.
See: W. Schirmacher, "Homo Generator: Media and Postmodern Technology" (New York, 1994).
[42] Kristeva claims that the poetic language is what enables change and rejoining of the fragmented subject. Poetic language not only shatters meaning but also goes beyond it, enabling the creation of new meaning. Poetic language grants passion to suppressed urges, not by refining them, but by giving them renewed meaningful form.
See: J.Kristeva, *Revolution in Poetic Language* (New York: Columbia UP, 1984), pp. 163-164.
[43] In Hebrew the word 'mesirah', translated as delivery, and the word 'masoret' - tradition, stem from the same linguistic root.
[44] Buzaglo, 2008, p.13.

structures, tradition forms the social, cultural and political reality, and imbues it with meaning, while being far from a closed, eternal, unequivocal dictate, since its deliverers are also its interpreters.[45]

Hölderlin and Bialik may be seen from the encounter as those who sing the crisis of tradition, and agonize, each in his own way and circumstances, over the paradoxical difficulty of myth existing in an era that does not recognize its transcendental source. Through the perspective of Heidegger[46] the 'poetic' appears as the founder of the 'political', and through Arendt's[47] - the very definition of the 'political' connects to the question of the possibilities of delivery of the past inheritance in the present. The encounter between the two poets, who appear in their writing as having agonized over the question of the delivery of myth, is - in the conclusion of the essay - an opportunity to ponder over the political relevance of their poetic approach, and the possibilities of its application to urgent contemporary questions. Hence, in the conclusion of this essay we shall attempt to speculate as to the possible transformation of poetic 'myth' into a regenerative element of our contemporary culture. The speculation about the possible contribution of re-activating poetic myth in contemporary politics (without denying the risks involved in such a step) is described in outline, in the context of the Israeli-Palestinian conflict - in itself a 'tragic laboratory' of relations between myth and politics.

---

[45] Y. Yadgar, "Masortiut", (Hebrew), *Mafteakh, Lexical Review of Political Thought*, vol. 5, summer 2012.
[46] M. Heidegger, *Hölderlins Hymne Der Ister* (1942), trans. W. McNeill & J. Davis (Bloomington & Indianapolis: Indiana UP, 1996), pp. 79-83.
[47] H. Arendt, *Between Past and Future: Six Exercises in Political Thought* (New York: Viking, 1961).

You Greeks always remain children

(Plato, "Timaeus")[48]

In my boyhood days / Often a god would save me / from the shouts and from the rods of men; / Safe and good then I played / With the orchard flowers / And the breezes of heaven / Played with me.

(F. Hölderlin, "In My Boyhood Days")[49]

So, God in his mercy gathered me up under the shelter of his wing, and let me sit silent at his footstool and play quietly with the fringes of his throne and the edge of his mantle.

(C. N. Bialik, "Aftergrowth")[50]

2. The Breaking of the Whole - On Poetics of Crisis

The childhood being that Hölderlin presents in his poem "In My Boyhood Days"[51] is described as a private experience in essence, one which posits the individual dimension of experience as the point of departure for mutuality and participation. This childhood, with the grace of god, has found a region-shelter at least for the time being. There, quietly and safely, the child can play with both the natural and the sublime. Beyond the space of divine shelter, as if biding its time, there is the world of the people and their shouting. There, for the laws of people, the sublime is defeated with only the protected being of the child saved, as long as there is the possibility of conjoining the natural (as the woodland flowers - Blumen des Hains) and the divine (as the breezes of the heavens - Lüftchen des Himmels) into one unity.

---

[48] Plato, *Timaeus*, trans. Benjamin Jowett (Middlesex: Echo Library, 2006), 22b, 48.
[49] "Da ich ein Knabe war" (1798-1800). SPF P.22.

[50] "Safiah" (1909) in H. N. Bialik, *Aftergrowth and Other Stories*, trans. I. M. Lask)Philadelphia: Jewish Publication Society, 1939), pp. 39-40.
[51] F. Hölderlin, "Da ich ein Knabe war" (1798-1800), p.27.

The Breaking of the Whole

It is clear already from the first stanza of the poem that the childhood being appears as a remembrance, or a story that's past, and as such, is caught in a complex tangle of temporal connections - since in essence, childhood is temporary and finite (at the end of the poem the child is already a man), and is also in itself a time requiring grace. It is almost of necessity that childhood be lost in time, at least in order to be perceived as such, that is - as a generalizing concept. From the distance of time, echoing as well the poetic distance from the being, childhood appears as a recollection, as a witnessing or yearning for a primal being, whole and lost.

Hölderlin's Mythical Temporality

2.1 Hölderlin's Mythical Temporality

So you made glad my heart

Father Helios, and like Endymion

I was your darling,

Holy luna.[52]

In the primary language of plants that grow toward the light, the joy of childhood is described as a response (to the plenty of Father Helois) and as a giving (to the love of the moon) to the heavenly. The heavenly bodies are depicted both as natural parents and as gods. The description of the parents lacks features of a biographical nature, a lack which strengthens the abstract dimension of the poem. This is a childhood which is individual but not at all personal, in other words - the childhood of man.

Helios, the sun (Hyperion in Homer's "Iliad and Odyssey"), and Endymion, lover of the moon (who was put to sleep so she could gaze at him), as the parents of the child, place the system of poetic connections in relation to Classical Greek culture, or to be exact - in relation to the magical spell the myth of the unity of the Greek epos and society had cast upon the variety of expressions of the German culture. These names, conveying an associative-cultural value, seem to have been given to their subjects later than the childhood experience described, as stated by the narrator in the poem:

True, at times I did not

Evoke you by name yet, and you

Never named me, as men use names,

As though they knew one another.[53]

---

[52] Ibid.
[53] Ibid.

The names seemingly came from the regions of people and their language that presumes to know, since the narrator's knowledge of the gods in the poem precedes the act of naming; it is fuller than his knowledge of the language of his own kind, and is silent like the Aether.54 The childhood appearing in the poem is then the world of immediacy and primal touch, pre-lingual, with the natural and the sublime connected in complete unity. It is a world of pre-articulative knowledge about holiness and nature as distinct from one another yet bound together. Moreover, and at the same time, this time of childhood is described from the horizons of a different time, later on, to which the man returns as a remembrance of his childhood. It is a recollection of separation based on the almost inevitable transformation of the child to a man. The immediacy of contact with the childlike reality, and the reflection in the form of witnessing, naming, etc., take place side by side as components of yearning, creating unrelenting tension between immediacy and reflection. The remembrance binds the immediacy into dialectics which places man's life on an 'eccentric path' where non-reflective unity, which precedes judgment and language, structures the element of existence; but since we cannot remain there, it becomes something we aspire to with our free spirit.55

I grew up in the arms of the gods.[56]

On the one hand, this may be read as a lament, on becoming a man, one of the world of the people with their laws and shouting, a lament of the fatal loss (in the deterministic sense) of the childhood that was quiet and safe in its unity. On the other hand, it may be read in the sense of growth: The becoming of a man who learned to love, a process empowered by its divine base to possibly attain a different fate (from that of the people mentioned before). Perhaps this is how the narrator is singled out, distinguishing between man's childhood and his private fate, which too is non-personal but rather mythic, and has been destined from the outset to be different, by virtue of the grace bestowed upon him. The fate of the narrator in the poem is that of one devoted to the change, or in other words: This growth in the arms of the gods seems to have anointed the child for poethood, as though his fate against fate has been determined, amidst the crisis he is in, to be a rift within the rift.

The epistolary novel "Hyperion" opens as well with a description of childhood and the immediacy of being connected to it, as a whole that has broken:

---

[54] The Aether in Greek thought is the fifth element; the pure air breathed by the gods; an infinitely thin substance found everywhere, and the breath of the world.
[55] See: J.A.Gosetti-Ferencei, *Heidegger, Hölderlin, and the Subject of Poetic Language: Toward a New Poetics of Dasein* (New York: Fordham UP, 2004), p.198.
[56] F. Hölderlin, "Da ich ein Knabe war" (1798-1800) SPF p.27.

Peace of childhood! Heavenly peace! How often I stand still before you in loving contemplation and attempt to fathom you! But we have concepts only of what was once bad but has been made good; of childhood, of innocence we have no

concepts. When I was still a serene child, and knew nothing of all that surrounds us, was I not then more than I am now, after all the troubles of my heart and all the reflection and struggle? Yes! The child is a divine being so long as it has not been dipped into the chameleon colors of men. The child is wholly what it is, and that is why it is so beautiful. The compulsion of the law and fate does not touch it; in the child is only freedom. In the child is peace; it is not yet at odds with itself. Wealth is in the child; it knows not its heart, nor the destitution of life. It is immortal, for it knows nothing of death. But this, men cannot bear. The divine must become like one of them, must learn that they, too, are there; and before nature drives it out of its paradise, men coax and drag it out into the field of the curse, so that it, like them, shall slave away in the sweat of its brow. But beautiful, too, is the time of awakening, so long as we are no awakened at an untimely moment.57

The serenity of childhood is heavenly, and can only be faced in silence. We crave to imagine it, but can only attain it damaged and mended. The child appears as a pre-human creature, almost divine, free of the restrictions of law and fate. His being is whole (and peaceful), and his ignorance of death places him on the threshold of immortality - no less. In the childhood description in "Hyperion" one may see an explicit expanded version of the idea of childhood in "In My Boyhood Days", as described by Paul de Man:58 The boy's connection with nature is characterized by spontaneous simplicity which is highly valued in "Hyperion". Nature is organized with a simplicity that ties the boy in to a complete wholeness. This wholeness is the point of departure for the 'eccentric path' man's life takes from simplicity to complexity of the consciousness, both in its general and particular sense.

The concepts of childhood and innocence of Schiller59 appear here, not abstractly, but rather as a personal experience. The concept of 'Bildung' with its variety of derived meanings60 is identified with separation by Hölderlin, the initiative act of the consciousness as that which, by virtue of its action, destroys the primal connection with being. Thus, it is made clear that separation from the unity is the price paid for man's activity. In this context we also notice that the very naming of the totality constitutes a distancing from it, as a claim that knowledge destroys the original unity. Similar perceptions about the childlike primacy and its loss are to be found in Rousseau, whom Hölderlin held

---

[57] F. Hölderlin, *Hyperion oder Der Eremit in Griechenland* (1797), *Hyperion or the Hermit in Greece*, trans. R. Benjamin (New York: Archipelago Books, 2008), pp.14-15.
[58] See: P. De Man, *Critical Writings 1953-1978*, ed. L. Waters (Minneapolis: University of Minnesota Press, 1989), pp.198-213.
[59] F. Schiller, *On the Aesthetic Education of Man in a series of letters*, ed. & trans. E.M.Wilkinson & L.A. Willoughby (Oxford: Clarendon Press, 1982).
[60] See: W.H. Bruford, *The German Tradition of Self-Cultivation: Bildung from Humboldt to Thomas Mann*, (London: Cambridge University Press, 2010).

to be the distinct representative of the image of the poet; or in Wordsworth ("The Child is the Father of the Man")61 - as a theme progressively established in modern art. Nevertheless, childhood for Hölderlin is not only something to remember with elegiac nostalgia, but rather - as pointed out by de Man - there is a purpose to the eccentric path that aspires to restore the unity and rehabilitate it. The eccentric path of life appears as a struggle between loss of the

harmonious original unity and the urge of the free spirit of man to overcome any obstacle in its way. It is from the real that the need springs, in itself not arbitrary but rather based on the law of gradual growth (in the Hegelian style), to be carried beyond the being of separation. Through his actions man strives to and directs the rehabilitation of the unity. The 'Bildung' then faces the future while taking an urgent stance of moral demand.

---

[61] W Wordsworth, "My Heart Leaps Up" (1802), in *Poems by William Wordsworth*, (New York: Ginn & Co., 1897), p.409.

Judgment and Being

2.2 Judgment and Being

The path of movement of human consciousness, as described by Hölderlin, passes then from naïve immediacy, through the distance, to the future recovery of the unity. The perception regarding this movement, which appears in Hölderlin's poetic writing, may be further honed if it is also examined in relation to his theoretical and philosophical preoccupation with the pre-judgment experience, and in the context of the theoretical field of his times.

In his contemplative writing, Hölderlin is seen to have established a unique approach in relation to his social and conceptual circle. J.G. Fichte (1762-1814), whose lectures Hölderlin attended at Jena University, developed his criticism of Kant's claim regarding the existence of the 'noumena', or 'things as they are', and not only as they are perceived by the categories of human comprehension. Fichte disagreed with Kant about the importance that the latter attached to the 'thing in itself' as detached from the ideal being. He claimed that the source of everything cannot exist separately from the constituting "I" in which its freedom is expressed. In other words: The "I" does not operate as result of things being as they are, but rather the things are as they are, due to the way in which the "I" operates. For Kant, perception is connected to sensing; intellectual intuitive perception is in the realm of the gods. Fichte, on the other hand, sees the "I" as the source of regulation of itself, the place where ideals and actions intersect due to the will - a will in itself resembling the divine will. In other words: The divine element operating in man is not the ability of reflection but rather the "I" giving direction to his being.[62]

According to this approach, the status of the "I" also entails moral implications. Man, as perceived by Fichte, is a wanderer between two worlds, internal and external: The action is that which is revealed, and the concealed is the will, which is the leading force. Victory of the will is victory of freedom, since only the will grants meaning to nature's lack of meaning. Hence, through the victory of the will, man can attain the state of a hero, which enables him to take part in eternity and to connect to the divine element that had constituted him. At this point, there is a connection between man's finite status as a mortal and the divine eternity - a connection existing in the world of the spirit. According to Fichte, man dwells in the lap of the omnipotent reason, where - through epistemological idealism in which the object originates from the consciousness - man activates his existential ability to overcome the schisms separating the object and the subject, thus ensuring his place in the absolute. Fichte, in his method, abandoned the idea of the 'noumenal' world that exists separately from our perception of it, claiming that the consciousness is based on nothing but itself. This idea became a prominent characteristic of the German Idealism, and an essential layer of comprehending the philosophies of Hegel and Schopenhauer, although they both rejected Fichte's claim that the consciousness is a sufficient basis for being.

---

[62] J.G. Fichte, *Introductions to the Wissenschaftslehre and Other Writings (1797-1800)*, ed. and trans. D. B. Hackett (Indianapolis: Cambridge, 1994), pp. 119-133.

F.W..Schelling (1775-1854) expanded Fichte's work while lending it a different dimension, whereby the subjugation of the object to the "I" is a path leading to organic unity between the object and the subject.[63] Schelling supported the assumption of a world existing outside the consciousness and viewed this world as embodied in nature, which encompasses all things that are objects of the consciousness. There is tension between these two factors, 'consciousness' and 'nature', with the absolute containing them both - the divine. The identity of the absolute is the sum total of all the potentials, hence substance and spirit, ideal and real, object and subject, are one.

The absolute resides in the essence of the human soul, for it is simply the capacity to see the universal in the particular, the finite in the infinite, the two combined into a loving thing. This, for Schelling, is intellectual intuition, and is the key to the identity of the absolute and to understanding the divine. Nature, according to Schelling, is also the spirit developing dialectically (in a Hegelian style), whereby each stage of the development brings it closer to blending into the "I" unto unity. Schelling calls this method "Transcendental Idealism", in which nature is revealed spirit, and spirit is concealed nature.

The theological aspects of Schelling's writings may also shed light on the theological foundation of Hölderlin and his partners in the intellectual debate of their times (Schelling, Hegel, and Hölderlin were fellow students at the Theological Seminary in Tübingen). For Schelling, the divine represents a complete entity that by virtue of its very being serves as a 'background', anchoring spirit and nature into a complete identity. Each intelligence is perceived as a component of the divine. Through assimilation into the divine, the history of the world reflects the spirit (an idea appearing in Hegel). The attaining of the divine is enabled by the infinite which loves the finite infinitely. Man, according to Schelling, differs from god, who is the origin of the ideals, since man is not the reason for himself. In spite of his ability to go beyond his place, man is in a miserable finite existence in a disharmonious world where evil exists. It is a melancholy world, whereby the melancholy is the everlasting human yearning for the divine, a yearning that never forgets. This yearning is based on the tension between the identification of man with god, and on the other hand, his separation from him. The solution for the tension is not to be found within the boundaries of logic, which concentrates on the unattainable, but rather in a positive direction through eliminating the unattainable - the divine revelation expressed in the holy trinity. This solution, of unifying contrasts in a dialectic balance, is asked for, since the contrast is the reason for needing the unity. Hence, the confrontation between bad and good, and between the particular and the universal, must exist in order for it to be annulled in that same unity. That is why the absolute includes three potentials: the negative, the positive, and the unity.

Within this contemplative climate, Hölderlin develops his approach, as seen in "On Judgment and Being",[64] which speaks of the basis of reflexive consciousness of the "I", which should be perceived beyond the distinction between the subject "I" and the object that it assumes. Hölderlin calls this basis 'absolute Being', and it is - to his mind, the foundation of any judgment. The original unity of the subject and object in Being is what constitutes a

---

[63] F.W.J Schelling, "Zur Geschichte der neueren Philosophie" (1833-4), in *On the History of Modern Philosophy,* trans: A. Bowie (Cambridge: Cambridge University Press, 1994), pp. 3-23, 94-134.
[64] F. Hölderlin, "Über Urtheil und Seyn" (1795), in H.S. Harris, *Hegel's Development: Toward the Sunlight 1770-1801* (Oxford: Clarendon Press, 1971), pp. 515-516.

separation through judgment, which is itself understood to be the division between the subject and the object, a division which makes the subject and the object possible.[65] According to Hölderlin, it is not possible to hold on to knowledge about Being, and primary unity is the basis for any judgment. Subjectivity cannot be the primary principle of philosophy, since it will always be defined in relation to the object. In this fragment of Hölderlin, one sees Kant's influence in that the existential dimension of his approach entails an inescapable being of schism, a reality of man's alienation from the wholeness, from immersion into the world, up to a constant sense of dissatisfaction. Hölderlin therefore attempts to rehabilitate the unity, by indicating the element of the original unity found at the basis of the consciousness. However, unlike Hegel and Schelling, his partners to the theoretical mission of his times in restoring the Kantian rift, Hölderlin places judgment as that which incessantly undermines unity, in fact turning it into the object of remembrance and yearning. This approach, with characteristics which may be called (for lack of a better term) 'relational', turns out to be an enriching thought whose traces are found in the works of Hegel and Schelling; and it is what Dieter Henrich has described as Hölderlin's unique contribution to the theoretical debate of his time.[66]

Hence, the primal unity appears in Hölderlin's poetic as well as theoretical writing, as the basis for inevitable separation, and is the basis of the judgment which underlies subjectivity. The immediacy of the childlike being of the world exists side by side with the annulling and separating reflection. This tension between unity and freedom recurs in Hölderlin's poetics. It is found at the root of his philosophy and even the root of human fate itself.[67]

---

[65] Ibid, p.516.
[66] D. Henrich, *The Course of Remembrance and Other Essays on Hölderlin*, ed. E. Förster (Stanford: Stanford University Press, 7992), pp. 31-71.
[67] See: P. De Man, *Critical Writings 1953-1978*, ed. L. Waters (Minneapolis: University of Minnesota Press 1989), pp. 198-213.

2.3 German-Hebrew Passage

The basis for the declared theme in the poem's title "In My Boyhood Days" is presented to the readers already in the first stanza, which is a quasi exposition of the temporal state described, whereby god sheds his grace upon a child, saving him temporarily from the world of the adults. This space of shelter is also the space where the child's diversion from himself takes place, responding as he does to something outside himself. We should note that the described contact does not indicate assimilation or blending into the whole, or to a mystical otherness that constitutes the whole except for the "I" diverted toward it and surrendering. Rather, this contact is presented as play, with two dimensions that are unique to this activity: First, a lack of purpose outside the very action; and secondly - participation or mutuality, as shown by use of the connector 'with' ('mit' in German). The dimension of participation is further emphasized, it seems, by the child's playing with the woodland flowers, and even more so, with the breezes of heaven (Lüften des Himmels) - an element which is natural (the breezes), like the flowers the child plays with, while at the same time including a mythic-transcendental essence (the heavens) that is playing with the child. In the poem "Hyperion's Song of Destiny",[68] learned by the hero from his mentor in his blissful ignorant days of youth, a similar expression appears, and with similar meaning:

Holy spirits, you walk up there
　in the light, on soft earth.
　　Shining god-like breezes
　　　touch upon you gently,
　　　　as a woman's fingers
　　　　　play music on holy strings.[69]

The blessed spirits are gently touched by those same breezes of heaven, free of fate, like a baby, in contrast to the long-suffering human beings who fall as the blind, hurled to the unknown.

In the poem "In My Boyhood Days", as in "Hyperion's Song of Destiny", and as in the respective 'Lüften des Himmels' - 'breezes of heaven', and 'Götterlüfte' - 'god-like breezes', an element of 'heavenly' quality - 'divine' - is in contact, playing, with the blessed; those immersed in a childlike state, those who have attained the grace of contact

---
[68] F. Hölderlin, "Hyperions Schicksalslied" (1799), SPF p.25.
[69] Ibid.

protecting them from human fate. To sharpen this presentation of the matter, in both of these poems Hölderlin describes contact with breezes whose origin is as if heavenly, at the basis of the childlike being. In "Hyperion's Song of Destiny", these breezes appear as extensions of the gods, touching the blessed lightly, as the fingers of a musician. In "In My Boyhood Days", these breezes, originating from the heavenly, are engaged in playing with the boy among the woodland flowers. In both poems, in the same context of the immediacy of being of the childhood world (since the boy is in contact with the gods that encompass him as a breeze, and as the Aether), the idea of the original unity of man with the gods and the world is embodied - where, at the core of the unity, the elementary tension of the Hölderlinian poetics pulsates, returning to childhood as a remembrance from the downhill of time, confronting the being of unity with the separative reflection.

Tracing these expressions of Hölderlin and the way they appear in the translations of the two poems into Hebrew,[70] we see that in both of them the element of breeze was translated as 'zafririm'. Thus, 'breezes of heaven' was translated as 'zafrirei shamayim' and 'god-like breezes' as 'zafrirei eilim'. If we deliberate on the meanings of the Hebrew word 'zafririm', the choice made by the translator in both poems, we see that the Hebrew concept in its use here is actually a new one coined by Bialik. Furthermore, this is the very concept that brings about the encounter, in the translation, between Hölderlin and Bialik - a concept vital and fundamental to Bialik's perception of childhood as well.

The Hebrew concept originated in the tradition of Kabbalah literature. 'Zafrir' (in plural 'zafririn') is the name of one of the imps or devils appearing supposedly in the morning, a bad morning spirit, similar to 'Lilith', who reigns at night.[71]

In his poem "Zafririm"[72] (1899), Bialik re-activates this word, or ancient myth, describing what at first seems to be an innocent childhood experience of a boy awakening from his dream to a dance of spirits or morning imps, and a quasi-revelation; it is the experience of waking up to a clear morning and the dance of morning spirits tempting but also misleading and deceiving. The imps invite-seduce the child to go out to them, to glisten with them in nature and in all the physical expressions of the world, while he in turn invites them to wallow under his sheet, to dance upon his skin and soft flesh, down into the depths of his soul until filled with pleasure and overflowing, bursting again into an ecstasy which it is difficult not to describe as orgasmic. There the god is present.

A drowsy haze of pleasure seizes me,
in every vein and tendon runs delight,
my heart's brim full, a well of flowing light.

---

[70] Translated by Shimon Sandbank, canonic translator into Hebrew and recipient of the 1996 Israel Prize for translation of poetry:
See: Frederich Holderlin, *Selected Poems* (Hebrew), trans. S. Sandbank, (Tel-Aviv: Hargol, 2005);
F. Holderlin, *Hyprion or the Hermit in Greece* (Hebrew), trans. S. Sandbank, (Tel-Aviv: Babel, 2003).
[71] From the Aramaic translation of the High Priests' Blessing, Numbers, 6:24, and Psalms 121, traditionally by Yehonatan Ben Uziel.
[72] C.N. Bialik, "Zafririm" (1899), in *Selected Poems*, trans. R. Nevo. (Jerusalem: Magnes Press, 1981), p.15.

German-Hebrew Passage

How sweet it springs!
I shut my eyes and blink and God! Light streams.[73]

Ziva Shamir, analyzing Bialik's poem,[74] describes a personal childhood experience of a boy awakening from his dream, and drawn alone from the world of the adults outside to a happy childlike game with the morning lights, glistening and shining their light upon a variety of physical manifestations of the world: nature, body, objects, wheat tips, bird wing, child's laughter and tear, brass button, and poem's rhymes. The light of the imps shines, reflects and glistens from all the manifestations of an enormous wholeness, with the stanzas ending in blinking and rolling of the eyes, in the mentioning of the god's name and ecstatic rinsing in the light, as assimilating and uniting into that very light - hinted at those imps with abundance of physical and spiritual love.[75]

The narrator of the poem may be seen as quasi child recollecting recent experiences, and a quasi elderly man indulging in the distant days of childhood. We shall, however, wish to be more precise with this interpretation, and to note a sharper division existing in the poem between the first narrator of the poem, telling the childhood experience based on seduction or recurring invitation of the child, with hinting and winking, to the game of the imps; and on the other hand - the narrator appearing at the beginning of the last stanza, who presents what seems to be the remembrance of the adult of the lost wholeness of his childhood. And those same imps that had tempted him in his childhood he now invites into his bed and soul: "Come to me, you imps of innocence",[76] as if the power of remembrance and yearning were enough to bring it about. This stanza too, which seems to be about past remembering, ends in the same ecstatic cry of the name of the god as revelation and rinsing in the light.

Bialik's imps appear then as flickering spirits of the morning, as sprays of light glistening and shining over every physical presence, as luminal entities, revealed flashes of the sparks of a secret smoldering in the material world, joining into an abundance of rinsing light that may fill one till one can fill no more, till one merges with the light, with god. The innocent childhood is the primal basis "till the break of day" for playing and dancing with the imps, however, the day is destined to begin, and in its light the seducing imps will abandon the child, just as childhood abandons the narrator-poet.

Similarly to what we found in Hölderlin, the primary childhood experience represents a whole unity which, from the moment it appears shining, is separated from the narrator by virtue of the separative time, giving itself again as remembrance, as a retrospective glance of an adult of his childhood. However, this remembrance is not merely nostalgic, desiring, yearning for that which has gone, never to return. This remembrance has, as well, the power enabling a quasi re-activating of the remembered event, with the fullness of it recurring in the same light.

---

[73] Ibid.
[74] (Shamir, 2000), pp. 75-113.
[75] Ibid, p. 86.
[76] C.N. Bialik, "Zafririm" (1899), in *Selected Poem*, trans. R. Nevo (Jerusalem: Magnes Press, 1981), p.15.

How sweet it springs!
I shut my eyes and blink and God! Light streams.[77]

Bialik then presents a re-activation of the concept of 'zafririn' from the Kabbalist demonology in Hebrew literature - as a reaction to the concept of 'zafirus', the light western wind of Greek mythology, abundantly found in humanistic poetry, and in its classical-romantic transformations (in itself a cultural source common to Hölderlin and Bialik) - imbuing the concept with new personal meaning. While the concept of 'zafirus' deals with lightness and airiness, the concept of 'zafririm' casts upon this lightness demonic and mysterious meanings from the Kabbalah. Bialik's imps, as Shamir shows, are not only light and pleasant morning spirits ('zafra' in Aramaic: 'morning'), merry wind or ray of light dancing in the morning hours, but rather morning devils as well.

If we return from Bialik to reading again in Hölderlin, we see that just as with Bialik's 'zafririm', so do Hölderlin's 'breezes of heaven' and 'god-like breezes' hold a clear connection to the Greek 'zafirus'. However, while Hölderlin uses the concept, as we have seen, as an original name of what he considers to be a forgotten source of his culture, Bialik uses this source largely as a response to the presence of the Greek concept, to transform and blend it into an ancient Hebrew origin.

These imps, as described by Shamir, these quasi nature-representatives, quasi transcendental creatures, flickering between the worlds, revealing and concealing, and confusing the child's mind, inviting-seducing him to divert from his place - they are as well the heroes of the drama taking place in Bialik's poem "Zohar" (1901):

In very youth long on life`s sea was I cast,
 And ever I languished for calm secrecy;
I panted for light from the world's body vast,
 And something I knew not, like wine surged in me,
I searched hiding-places. There gazed I, meseemed,
 I met the world`s eyes; there my friends were Revealed
To me, and their secrets I grasped as they gleamed
 And close in my still heart their voices I sealed.[78]

---

[77] Ibid.
[78] C. N. Bialik, "Zohar" (1900), BYP, translated as "Light" (also known as "Radiance"), by B. Beinkinstadt, in *An anthology of poem translations: From the Hebrew and the Yiddish*
(Cape Town: City Printing Works, 1930), pp. 34-44.

As in Hölderlin's "In My Boyhood Days", so too Bialik's poem "Zohar" presents the childhood days of the poet as an individual experience of secret mute connection with a sublime unity. The poem embodies the joyful childlike experience in nature. At its heart is the child's journey in the company of his friends the imps in a space washed with radiance. At the beginning of the poem the imps seduce the child to join their dance, while at the end their parting from him is grim. As the mythological plot unravels, the poem emphasizes a concrete reality, thanks to the detailed precise description of the plants, animals and people inhabiting the stations of the journey: the grass, wheat field, a pond.[79] The experience of the journey itself encompasses various layers, and holds the familiar tension (to readers of Hölderlin as well), starting with the intoxication of the harmonious merging into the wholeness of the surroundings, up to the sobriety that adulthood expresses, entailing the knowledge that "silent the song of light, evermore done."[80] In this poem, the imps themselves are not of an innocent light character, and something of their original demonic essence is revealed, since their seduction and temptation of the child conceal a proposal to surrender to the dark enchantment of death.[81]

In that same individual, illuminated, silent - pre-lingual - experience, suddenly appears - in the image of the 'pears of Kol Nidrei', the 'seven-spot ladybird'[82] - the echoes of culture, giving names to things, those names used by the children of the Beit Midrash (religious school) identifying nature through the prism of the language of tradition. What does this resemble? Perhaps the way in which Hölderlin, while playing with the woodland flowers and the breezes of heaven, hears the silence of the Aether, greets father Helios, and likens himself to Endymion before Luna. And similarly to Bialik, who uses the language of the Beit-Midrash in order to look at the pears and beetles, so does Hölderlin place himself in his network of relations with the elements or the heavenly bodies, using their Greek (and later Roman) names. In their descriptions of the primary encounter with their world, both poets then use the mythological names of whatever they hold and declare as their culture, thereby interpreting and distancing themselves from the experience. Hölderlin relates to this in "In My Boyhood Days": "True, at the time I did not evoke you by name", in order to show that the experience is described from a place already beyond it; and in both poems, "In My Boyhood Days" and "Zafririm", it turns out at the end of the poem that one is speaking of a contemplation and description in retrospect.

---

[79] A. Holtzman, *H. N. Bialik* (Jerusalem: Shazar Center, 2009), p. 101.
[80] C. N. Bialik, "Zohar" (1901), in) Beinkinstadt, 1930), p.44.
[81] (Shamir, 2000), p.86.
[82] The Pears of Kol Nidrei - the wild pears ripening in the autumn around Yom Kippur (The Day of Atonement). Kol Nidrei is the prayer said at the beginning of Yom Kippur, and includes the declaration of annulling the promises and oaths of the praying public.

In The Withdrawal of the Gods

2.4 Bialik`s Caesural Poetics

Yet sounds in my soul their melodious strain-

But they to the near wood have fled: from afar ,

A soft glance of solace upon me they bent ,

Which hinted: "Till morn," then they flew beyond ken.

- -

It fell on a day-when, I cannot recall,

Once more did I see them-why know I not, then

For me full of pity were they, when they went,

All vacant and void was their gaze, naught it spoke.

At morn the warm light me from slumber awoke

And dazzled my eyes, burnt my lips with its fall . . .

I gazed through the window – and lo, there was the sun

Long, long waited I-no more did they appear.

And silent the song of light, evermore done. [83]

    The end of the poem reveals that the imps that seduced the poet-narrator to leave his home and go out with them to the fields, did not but grant him, according to Shamir, short-term temporary hedonistic joy, from which he awakens and sobers up, in an awakening one may call 'traumatic'. Nevertheless, he is grateful to his deceiving, immoral and uninhibited friends, for the temporary experiences of a debauchery, knowing that the best of his visions have derived from them. The end of the poem implies that the fantasies and dreams are not nonsense and vanity, as customarily thought in the old-fashioned Judaism described in the first part. Only the dreams do not last forever, and

---

[83] C. N. Bialik, "Zohar" (1900), in)Beinkinstadt, 1930), p.43-44.

the moment arrives when one must sober up and face the literal reality - a sobriety appearing here as an awakening from a dream.[84]

Shamir discusses the poem "Zohar" as part of a lyrical poem divided by Bialik into two parts. One part, the short one, laden and somber, is "Shirati" ("My Song", 1900)[85] (containing about one third of the complete poem, and to be discussed further on), and the poem of light and joy is "Zohar". The latter describes the entire poem, before its division, as a tertiary structure indicating directly or indirectly the three stages that the "I" underwent, both personal and national, from the period in which it was part of the ascetic collective being, closed within its tiny cubicle of holiness, up to his awakening from the dream, both pleasant and threatening, induced upon him by his friends the imps in their radiant journey. These are three distinct stages in the dialectics that took place in the life of the "I" narrator, the private and the national, in the historical time of transferring from the being of the Jewish ghetto, of the books and the dead letters, to the external world of Western culture and the Zionist solution.[86]

With the awakening from the experience of the imps, the narrator disappointingly and happily discovers that the song of the 'zohar' (the 'radiance') has forever ceased:

But deep in my heart is its echo hid, in

My eyes preserved I its vast splendor unequalled:

My life`s sweetest dreams in this grate world of din,

From its source are drawn-even my visions most dear,

And pure are they, blessed from its spring, whence they welled.[87]

In the awakening from the childhood dreams to the burning light of realistic and sober truth, Bialik merges ("And dazzled my eyes, burnt my lips with its fall. . .")[88] the story of the blinded Samson with the story of Moses, who according to the legend became hard of speech following the burning of his lips with an ember. Through this conjoining, according to Shamir, Bialik connected the most Helenistic figure in the Bible, Samson the monk, who excelled in his courage, strength and looks, and who tied his fate with that of a woman of the Philistines (originating from the Greek isles), to the Hebraist figure of Moses. This Hebraist-Hellenistic synthesis (as opposed to the

---

[84] (Shamir, 2000), p. 85.
[85] C.N. Bialik, "Shirati" (1900), BYP.
[86] (Shamir, 2000), p. 96-97.

[87] C. N. Bialik, "Zohar" (1900), in (Beinkinstadt, 1930), p.43-44.
[88] Ibid.

surrendering to the Hellenistic innovation to be found in Tchernichovsky, for instance)[89] is, according to Shamir, the element by which Bialik constitutes the innovation of his poetry.[90]

Here we should note that while Shamir emphasizes the dimension of the synthesis between Hellenism and Hebraism, which Bialik was undoubtedly preoccupied with (and through the very difference between the cultures), we shall wish to emphasize the dimension of the tragic fate and the failure embodied in the two stories of mission: Samson's mission which ended in "May my soul perish with the Philistines", and Moses', ending with his seeing the Promised Land and not entering it. The 'stop' ('blima') put to both of them, one in his strength and courage, and the other in his leadership, appears as an internalizing of a rift, or rupture, between the mission and the possibility of its realization, similarly to the yearning for the days of childhood that are inaccessible except in remembrance of that vanished unity of the world and god blended one into the other. This matter is shown in the poem "Zohar" as well, in the poetics of structuring the poem so that a hyphened portion or graphic caesura breaks the continuum, at the end of the description of the poet's journey with the imps and their melancholy parting from him, with the reading picking up after the caesura, to describe the time of remembrance retrospectively of that same event; a remembrance that cannot overcome the distance and the imps' abandonment, with only the sound of the experience of wallowing with them still echoing as a live source of the current visions.

The caesura in Bialik's poem appears as a multi-dimensional one. In addition to the formal dimension of the poetics, namely - the graphic and sound caesura of the text, the theme of the poem with its variety of meanings centers around the caesura line of the childhood ruptured and drifting in time from the adult, who in his remembrance yearns for it and grieves over its loss, while also drawing strength for his life from the remembrance itself. It is also possible to locate here the crisis of innocent faith reaching sobriety that hides the face of god, and the rift of the tradition and the dwindling world of the Jewish 'Heder', which in its misery ceases to be meaningful, the more the boy is exposed to Western culture and ideas of the new times. It seems that around the rift lines of the lost childhood, Bialik - in a way that Shamir contends is characteristic of his poetics and singles it out - built an abundance of personal, national, biographical and symbolic rifts and splinters from which the power of the poet's mission and uniqueness grows.

We can also easily identify the mirroring of the Bialik caesura in the Hölderlin one ('die zasur'). For Hölderlin, in the "Remarks to the tragedies of Oedipus",[91] the concept of caesura indicates the reversal of a tone as well as a reversal of time, with the end re-establishing the beginning, a connection that seems to have been lost. This moment of reversal is described by Hölderlin as a rift, rupture, tear, actually enabling the tragedy to go on in the framework of what he calls 'the law of calculation', an anti-rhythmic disruption that operates as balancing the continuation of the representation - that which Hölderlin terms 'the pure word' (das reine wort).[92]

---

[89] Shaul Tchernichovsky (1875 –1943) was a Russian-born Hebrew poet.
[90] (Shamir, 2000), p. 86.
[91] F. Hölderlin, "Anmerkung zum Oedipus" (1804), in *Essays and Letters on Theory*, trans. and ed. T. Pfau (New York: University of New York Press, 1988), pp.101-109.
[92] Ibid.

The concept of the caesura has undergone various developments in the hands of Hölderlin's interpreters. De Man has tried out different names for the 'discontinuous element' characterizing the temporal structure of the Hölderlinian poetic form.[93] Adorno's 'parataxis' is another possibility.[94] In these interpretations the concept of 'incomprehensibility' operates, like the tragic victim. It cannot be represented, and it does not belong to the historical level of action. The caesura is the close point to the paradox, and as such - it is a mechanism of criticism annulling hierarchy. It is the silence of the subject, the place where the poetry breaks, where it is beyond thematization and perception, and even beyond 'the event'; it is beyond theory and poetry. It is what poetry becomes (as described by Adorno), when it does not have the ability to speak for itself.[95]

In his essay "Parataxis", Adorno shows, from the point of departure whereby 'the whole' is 'the untrue', how the parataxis structures characterizing Hölderlin's later poetry radically disrupt the thetic logic which ruled in German Idealism, and in particular - Hegel's Speculative philosophy. Traditionally, the parataxis has been perceived as a grammatical system of coordination and serialization, which does not operate relations of subjugation. Adorno applies the term to the recurring opposites of the predicative logic common to Hölderlin's later hymns and fragments, and he re-interprets parataxis as 'constitutive dissociation', in other words - as an anti-idealistic linguistic strategy undermining the hierarchy. According to Adorno, precisely as the mechanism of reversing-the-order works in disrupting hierarchical relations, so may the parataxis divert theological drift or speculative thought. Only through exposing the numerous effects created by the parataxic structure of this poetry, to Adorno's mind, will the critic-interpreter of Hölderlin's later poetry perceive what is purely poetized in this poetry.[96]

By using the term 'parataxis', Adorno actually expropriates a concept presented by Walter Benjamin in his essay "Two Poems by Friedrich Hölderlin",[97] while asking to legitimize the strangeness, otherness and the sublime somberness of Hölderlin's later poetry, but also the content of its truth, which to his mind had misled traditional systems and methods of literary analysis. This too, according to Adorno, is what happened in the case of Heidegger's a-historical and anti-philological interpretation, which overlooked the aspects of aesthetic form. According to Adorno's method, only an immanent analysis tracing the de-limitation powers of the analyzed material can research the way in which the strangeness of this poetry transcends subjective intentions.

To understand the gap between the external layer of Hölderlin's poetry and the undermining critical power concealed in it, Adorno returns to Benjamin's work (this time to his essay on Goethe from 1922) to distinguish between Sachgehalt (material content) and Wahrheitsgehalt (truth content). The former refers to the revealed

---

[93] (De Man, 1989), pp. 198-213.
[94] T.W. Adorno, "Parataxis on Hölderlin's Late Poetry" (1964) in *Notes to Literature: Volume 2*, trans. S. W. Nicholsen (New York: Columbia University Press, 1992), 109-149.
[95] J. A. Gosetti-Ferencei, *Heidegger, Holderlin, and the Subject of Poetic Language: Toward a New Poetics of Dasein* (New York: Fordham University Press, 2004), pp. 61-99.
[96] (Adorno, 1964), pp. 109-149.
[97] W. Benjamin, "Zwei Gedichte von Friedrich Holderlin (Dichtermut - Blödigkeit)" (1914-1915), in *Selected Writings Vol I*, ed. M. Bullock & M. W Jennings (Cambridge: Harvard University Press, 2000), pp. 18-36.

composition of the poem, the aesthetic dimension where myth is present, while the second refers to the deeper meaning remaining concealed under the mythic surface.[98]

The concept of the caesura in Hölderlin actually demonstrates the rift line around which the Hölderlinian mythology is organized, namely - the unmendable rupture between 'gods' and 'mortals', a rupture which his poetry yearns to mend. The rift in the contact between man and gods appears in Hölderlin also as an expression of the crisis of the tradition detached from the preferred closeness of Western culture, which he calls 'Hesperia', of the Classical Greek heritage - a matter that he expresses distinctly in "Hyperion", which extols ancient Greece and sharply criticizes Germany of his time.

---

[98] See: B. Hanssen, A. E. Benjamin, ed., *Walter Benjamin and Romanticism* (New York: Continuum, 2002), pp. 741-147.

2.5 In the Withdrawal of the Gods

According to the Hölderlinian mythology, and in connection with the ethos of the German culture of Hölderlin's times, what was unique to the Golden Age of ancient Classical Greece was the dwelling of mortal man in the lap of the immortal gods. In this view, in the Classical Greek world there was true closeness and a shared life between man and the gods, who lived and operated amongst men, were involved in their lives and granted them of their abundance, or of the rod. Hölderlin's caesura is hence formulated as a failure of the gods as well, for disconnecting from man, abandoning him to his fate, and failing to return. In this crisis of man's detachment from the source of the plenty, Hölderlin was one of the first to identify the basic crisis of modernity.

Unperceived at first they come, and only the children surge towards them,

Too brightest, dazzling, this joy enters in, so that man is afraid,

A demi-god hardly can tell yet
who they are and name those who approach him with gifts.

Yet there courage is great. His heart soon is full of their gladness

And he hardly knows what is to be done with such wealth,

(...) such is man; when the wealth is there, and no less the God in person tends him with gifts, blind he remains, (...)

(stanza 5)

But my friend, we have come too late.

Though the gods are living, over our heads they live, up in a different world.
Endlessly there they act, such is their kind wish to spare us,

Little they seem to care whether we live or not.

For not always a fragile, a delicate vessel can hold them,
only at times can our kind can bear the full impact of gods.

Ever better our lives is a dream about them. (...) (stanza 6)[99]

---

[99] F. Hölderlin, "Brot und Wein" (1801-1800), SPF p.151.

Hölderlin's poetry, hence, sings the crisis that man is in - that of sobriety from the distancing childlike wholeness; the crisis of the withdrawal of the gods from a world that cannot contain their abundance; the crisis of the withdrawing origin of modernity. The 'origin' appears here in the sense of the thing by itself, the whole - accessible with no mediation, influencing and infinitely giving of itself. That was before it assumed a succession of references, representations and metaphors, impeding and concealing it. The source is not only whatever was in the past; the source is that which was and no longer is. The loss is built into the source, it is its fate.[100] Hölderlin's caesura indicates the rupture from Classical Greek culture (in itself not only characterized by Olympian-Apollonian serenity but also, and particularly, by tragic Dionysian depths),[101] which is also the moment of birth of modernity, appearing therefore as a synonym of exile.

As we've seen, Bialik's poetry - of considerable resemblance to Hölderlin's, also sings the crisis of awakening from a childhood sheltered under the wings of god; a crisis of faith in the Jewish tradition, whose language, in view of modern secularization, lost its ability to connect between the origin and the present time of the poet; at the same time also the crisis of the promise of modernity doomed to disappoint.

"So, God in his mercy gathered me up under the shelter of his wing,

And let me sit silent at his footstool and play quietly with the fringes of his throne and the edge of his mantle."[102]

In "Aftergrowth", Bialik's multi-facet romantic poetic prose, he presents the yearning for the childhood being and the primacy of the encounter with nature, and the primal world view, virginal and innocent. As in Hölderlin's "In My Boyhood Days", the childlike wholeness constitutes a quasi alliance with the gods, and the child's soul seems to be charged with unique strength. This is an alliance, as in the prophetic model, between the divine plenty and the one singled out and anointed, through the experience of contact with it, to poethood.

Both poets, in the span of a hundred years between them, present poetics singing from the heart of the rupture of what they perceived to be the historical continuum of their respective cultures. Through the rupture (as shown by the concept of the caesura) we may again see the continuum appearing as a succession from an origin of past mythical qualities, delivered through the course of time unto the present. The experience of the loss, as losing the whole grip of the original unity, accessible in the past and now gone, is common to both poets, and may be seen in this discussion as the foundation from which both poets formulate their poetic mission according to the prophetic model, of the

---

[100] D. Pimentel, "The Gift of Place" (Hebrew), *Bezalel History and Theory Protocols*, vol. 10 (October 2008).
[101] Hölderlin prods his contemporary rationalists to study the 'holy pathos' of the Greeks, thereby preceding Nietzsche.
[102] C. N. Bialik, "Safiah" (1909), in *Aftergrowth: and Other Stories*, trans. I. M. Lask (Philadelphia: Jewish Publication Society, 1939), pp. 39-40.

messenger conveying the plenty from the origin to man. After having expounded the similarity between the two poets in this chapter, of the basis for their poetic mission and the conscious-historical crisis from which it had grown, and after having presented their poetic childhood as that which prepared the poets for their modern prophecy, one may ask, in the way of summary: From within the rift of a world devoid of divinity and the mythic authority of tradition, what may be the possible message of prophecy or poetic mission? In other words: What is the model of 'maturation' that the poets offer those awakening to a post-metaphysical world, one with no winning method?

Who wants poets at all in lean years?

(F. Hölderlin, "Bread and Wine")[103]

For Hölderlin, the poet matters more than poetry.

(Jean-Luc Nancy, "The Calculation of the Poet")[104]

3. The Poetized - Poetry and (the Question of) Mission

In research tradition, Walter Benjamin is considered one of Hölderlin's most important interpreters. His first significant essay "Two Poems by Friedrich Hölderlin"[105] is a fundamental text for pondering the poet's work, as well as an opening into understanding Benjamin's theory of art criticism, and his perception of language. While reading Benjamin's writings, and especially his work on art criticism, perception of language or history, one realizes Hölderlin's enormous impact upon him. Suffice to mention some of the issues dealt with in this essay, such as 'judgment' as a power separating between language and the world; the lament over the whole lost, never to return; and the ambivalent connection to myth. We will not be surprised if we find the interpreter and interpreted immersed one in another, more than pretensions of critical analysis imply.

---

[103] ("Wozu dichter in dürftiger zeit") "Brod und Wein" (1800-1801), stanza 7, SPF p.151.
[104] J.L. Nancy, "The Calculation of the Poet", in *The Solid Letter: Readings of Friedrich Hölderlin*, ed. A. Fioretos (Stanford: Stanford UP, 1999), p. 44.
[105] BSW - vol. 1 (1996), pp. 18-36.

Benjamin and the Fall of Language

3.1 Benjamin and the Fall of Language

The eccentric path of Benjamin's life and thought, as expressed in his literary work, seems to lead from disappointment with philosophy to the searching for content and answer of another kind. Between 1916 and 1919, Benjamin may be seen as a mystic, and subsequently as more and more of a Marxist. His search for redemption is ever present in his contemplative work, even as it becomes secular in nature. However, at the core of his conceptual movement there is always the 'word' as the key to redemption: "Divine Language" in 1916; "Restorative Language" in the 20s; and "The Words of God as the Basis for any Linguistic Theory" in 1938.106

The search for redemption seems to be motivated by the present's lack of wholeness, so that Benjamin fluctuates in it between hopeless sadness and utopian hope - theological or Marxist - until despairing of them both. As part of the intellectual climate of the early twentieth century, language was one of the mainstays of Benjamin's work. His efforts in this arena were devoted to developing an alternative to the heritage leading from Descartes through Kant to German Idealism, a heritage based on the perception of language as representing conscious states of the subject.

In his essay "The Origin of German Tragic Drama"107 (a teacher-qualification essay turned down by the University of Frankfurt in 1925), which may be seen as a quasi key to his thought, Benjamin formulated his most crystallized thought about language, describing it as the locus of essences constituting the basic coordinates of being. 'Name' for him is the basis of these essences. In his "Critique of Pure Reason", Kant claims that the experiencing subject is the source of the conjunction that constitutes our experience. In contrast, Heidegger claims, through the idea of transcendentalia, that conjunction occurs in the world itself, and is not a product of the subject and his consciousness. Benjamin, however, by considerable affiliation to Heidegger, while differing from him, wishes to show the elementary conjunction of the world as embedded in language itself.108

In his essay "On Language as Such and on the Language of Man",109 Benjamin discusses the lack of wholeness characterizing language in its present state, with a rift between the word and its meaning, a rift formed by the deterioration of man's power to perceive reality intuitively and directly. Benjamin distinguishes between three types of language: 1. Divine language, expressed in the biblical phrase "Sayeth the Lord"; 2. Man's language before his fall from the Garden of Eden, where man named the animals, thereby defining their essence; 3. Language after the fall, the language of our times, bearing the sin of Babylon, and the confusion of languages. The divine language created the world, but man - emphasizes Benjamin, was not created by speech; god did not create man from the word, and did not give him a name. He did not wish to subjugate him to language, but rather - language is god's gift to man. This

---
[106] See: M. Sluhovsky, "The Beauty of Failure" (Hebrew), *Amirot*, February 2012.
[107] W. Benjamín, "Ursprung des deutschen Trauerspiels" (7921) *The Origin of German Tragic Drama*, trans. J. Osborne (London, New.York: Verso, 2003).
[108] See: A. Noor, "Introduction" (Hebrew), in W. Benjamin, *The Metaphysics of Youth*, trans. D. Dotan (Tel-Aviv: Resling, 2009), p. 11-54.
[109] W. Benjamin, "über sprache überhaupt und über die sprache des menschen" (1916) in BSW (vol. 1, 2000), pp. 37-46.

creativity, free of the divine essence, became knowledge. Man has the knowledge that moves in the same language in which god had created. God created man in his image; he created the knower in the image of the creator.[110]

The language of the Garden of Eden, where names were given to animals, is described by Benjamin as a language that itself mediates, but is still ideal and not arbitrary. The name man gave the animal indicates its essence. Since both man-nature and knower-known have a common divine source, even if their creation was different - through language there is an immediate unmediated connection between man and nature, and when man gives a name to nature, nature speaks back to him.

The third language speaks in the stage that followed the sin of eating of the Tree of Knowledge, and the expulsion from the Garden of Eden to the reality of our times. Benjamin sees his current reality as the fall to the damaged cursed being, a world view entailing depression and melancholy. The fall caused the desecration of the eternal purity of the names. Due to the sin and the expulsion, the words lost their primary power of expressing reality, and became merely means of communication. Our language lacks the mythical dimension enabling intuitive knowledge of the world, hence - language is in quasi exile and no longer has the power to achieve the knowing of the world. Language has therefore fallen to the mediating function of chattering, and thus has man lost the ability to know nature, with nature itself destined to silent sadness. After the fall, which turned language into a mediating factor, the foundation was laid for a myriad of signs leading to linguistic confusion. Eating of the Tree of Knowledge grants the power to discern good from bad, in other words, the power of judgment that distances man from the primordial language. From here the path is short to rebelling against the divine declaration "This is very good", a rebellion that breaks the unity that has characterized the creation of the world by god. This then, according to Benjamin, is the first flash of rational thinking, of discerning and separating, at the basis of existing language. This is also the step that pushes man into a world of doubts and dualism. By virtue of creating a distinction between things, the seed is planted for the existence of multiplication and confusion, and an overabundance of the language, since an abundance of names is the deepest lingual reason for melancholy. Through an ontological discussion of the Platonic dialogues, Benjamin presents language as a system of connections that frequently changes, enveloping man and conveying all knowledge. In "The Arcades Project",[111] language is described as a locus of dialectic images, which are the focus of his later discussion of history. The dialectic image is the meeting place of the present moment with the conflict pulsating in it, and the tension between contrasts that every historical situation conjoins; in other words - a moment of the past redeemed through remembrance and action.

Benjamin's preoccupation with language is also connected fundamentally to the ontological-historical discussion on determining poetry as a work of art. In "The Work of Art in the Age of Mechanical Reproduction"[112] Benjamin presents his approach regarding the religious status of the work of art, which has gone, never to return. The duplicated secularized work of art is no longer experienced solely subjectively, but rather is accessible to the multitudes, which

---

[110] Ibid.
[111] W. Benjamin, "Passagen werk" (1927–40), in *The Arcades Project*, ed. R.Tiedemann (Cambridge: Harvard UP, 1999), pp.871-873.
[112] W. Benjamin, Das Kunstwerk im Zeitalter seiner technischen Reproduzierbarkeit" (7991), in BSW (vol. *3*, 2000), pp. 101-134.

increases its influence but also brings about the collapse of the religious 'halo' of the work, and its mythical value is eroded.[113]

In 'Two Poems by Friedrich Hölderlin"[114] Benjamin analyzes the poetic language in relation to myth, and as we shall expand further on, identifies poetry with the dimension of sobriety, poetry free of any mission, and which bravely rejects the mimetic as well as the mythical. Benjamin's perception of the meanings and forms of the concept of 'myth', as it operates in the Modern age, is a key to understanding his metaphysical writings, which present a dialectic tension between two dimensions. On the one hand, there is sober modern secularity charged, in view of events of Fascism, with sharp criticism of the idea of progress. On the other hand, there is the soul-less Marxism, namely, that which lacks the theological dimension developed by Benjamin in later years in "Theses on the Philosophy of History",[115] where he proposed a messianic addition to historical materialism. In his essay on Hölderlin, one also sees the shifting of the work of art from the realm of the psychological or biological subject. This approach is presented programmatically and explicitly in "The Task of the Translator",[116] where the emphasis is shifted from the subjectivity of experiential lyricism, with its biographical approach, to the historical philosophical dimension of the orders of being. This is also expressed in his radical declaration that no poem is intended for any reader.[117] In "On Language as Such and on the Language of Man"[118] Benjamin characterizes his approach to the phenomenon of language in relation to the explanation given in Genesis. Benjamin states there that in principle his approach follows that of the Bible, in that it posits language as an extremely elementary mystical reality which cannot be explained, and can only be viewed in its various transformations.

In Benjamin's writings about Kafka there is a polarity of mystical yearning for ancient days, and of hope that from the collapse of tradition a new kind of beauty will grow. One may learn from his studies of Kafka about his approach to tradition and history, which is also important to understanding his writings about language, as well as his interpretation of Hölderlin's poems. In the world revealed through Kafka's works, Benjamin finds a mirror of the modern world where the individual is in the hands of a vast anonymous bureaucracy characterized by alienation, resulting as well from the scientific and technological revolution of the twentieth century. People of the modern era seem in a new being that they cannot comprehend, trying in vain to decode the secret laws governing their lives. Past experience does not help them find their way any longer in the world. Conversely, wisdom of the past, created by the accumulation of experiences passed from generation to generation can hardly be understood anymore, and if it still

---

[113] S. Moses, *Walter Benjamin and the Spirit of Modernity* (Tel-Aviv: Resling, 2003), p. 83. Moses claims that this matter exemplifies the ambivalence inherent in Benjamin's thinking, and his dialectic thought darting between the mythical and the materialistic.

[114] BSW - vol. 1, (1996), pp. 18-36.

[115] W. Benjamin, "Über den Begriff der Geschichte" (7941), in *Illuminations: Essays and Reflections*, ed. H. Arendt, trans. H. Zohn (New York: Schocken Books, 1968), pp.253-264.

[116] W. Benjamin, "Die Aufgabe des Übersetzers" (1921), ibid. pp. 69-81.

[117] Benjamin is extreme in his objection to the process of 'empathy' which Johann Goethe emphasized, confronting him with the perception of criticism. (Noor, 2009), p. 19.

[118] BSW (vol. 1, 2000), pp. 37-46.

exists - its voice gets to us in a muffled whisper, as the last echo of the lost truth. Only the rumor of the real things has remained from the stable world view of the past.[119]

In "Theses on the Philosophy of History"[120] Benjamin intended to prove that the historical materialistic approach is actually based on concealed theological ideas. The bulk of the text sharply criticizes the concept of 'progress', described as infinite repetition of those same known patterns which cannot bring about a qualitative change of reality. On the other side, he depicts the utopian revolution, as well as the messianic one, as offering redemption of another kind, namely - a sudden leap out of the historical time continuum. Both utopian revolutions are described as wishing to explode the historical continuum, and carry mankind toward a new richer reality. In order to diverge from the compulsory historical time continuum, it is necessary to revive the experiences hidden in the past. Benjamin exemplifies this through the holidays (Passover, for instance) which to his mind break the secular time succession, and introduce into the caesura another time of remembrance. According to this principle, every revolution is based on the revolutionary ideas preceding it, and by quoting from previous attempts, redemption is granted to the failed past. Hence redemption is not the result of a developmental process, but rather, conversely, it appears suddenly, in the flash of remembrance.[121]

On the basis of Benjamin's perception of language and history one may learn about his approach to literary criticism. Every important literary work is seen by him as an allegorical structure reflecting a specific moment in the historical process of the deterioration of tradition. The critic's role is to decode the linguistic signs indicating the process. Benjamin refers to authors of restorative position, such as Proust, who with their nostalgic point of view aspire to return to a lost paradise. In his essay "On the Image of Proust"[122] Benjamin mentions the recurring theme, the yearning for the past, the search for past happiness. This is the elegiac form of happiness: the eternal repetition, the eternal restoration of the first original happiness. According to Benjamin, this happiness is to be found in the child's ability to grasp things in their original unity; the child knows how to discover the mysterious resemblance between things that are seemingly discrete and detached from one another. This is Proust's secret: he yearns for a world where everything is distorted, in other words - he returns to a state of imagination, a state that reveals the true surrealist face of reality.[123]

Benjamin calls the experience returning us as a bolt to the past 'remembrance' ('Eingedenken'). In this concept he does not refer to the usual action of the mind of reconstructing the past, but rather to a quasi mystic immersion through which the artist re-conquers the past as it really was. In the remembrance experience only segments and fragments are

---

[119] See: (Moses, 2003), pp. 9-18.
[120] W. Benjamin, "Über den Begriff der Geschichte" (1940), in *Illuminations*: Essays and Reflections, ed. H. Arendt, trans. H. Zohn (New York: Schocken Books, 1968), pp.253-264.
[121] (Moses, 2003), p. 20.
[122] W. Benjamin, "Zum Bilde Prousts" (1929-1934), in *Illuminations*, ed. H. Arendt, trans. Harry Zohn (New York: Schocken Books, 1969), pp. 201-215.
[123] The same yearning to return to the primary unity also characterizes several of Baudelaire's poems. The poet of the modern city describes the 'breaking of the halo' as the central experience of the artist lost in the tumultuous large city. Conversely, and as a form of compensation for the broken halo, he creates a complementary experience for himself, with which he succeeds in re-sensing the existence of those concealed and enriching connections between the dispersed parts of reality that restore the lost unity to the world. Baudelaire's 'Correspondances' lead the artist back to that same primary state, where he knew that the perfumes, colors, and sounds respond to one another.
See: (Moses, 2003), p.16.

awoken from the past; however, these segments are the only evidence we have of the existence of previous life that took place and is gone. Perhaps this is what led Benjamin to view these splinters and fragments as indications of truth.

In "Berlin Childhood around 1900"[124] and in "Moscow Diary",[125] Benjamin is clearly interested in rediscovery of the child's world. In an early note connected to "The Arcades Project"[126] he describes his perception of the role of childhood: To immerse in the new world in the symbolic space. The child's experiencing of the world is presented as the moment preceding awakening or sobriety from the mythical world of the merchandise. Benjamin's thought regarding that experience is part of his theory of the 'threshold', with childhood as a state of pre-transition to maturity that appears as awakening. In another fragment of his early notes to "The Arcades Project", Benjamin describes his 'awakening' as a teleological moment of the old succumbing to 'death till further notice', awaiting the second when he can subversively escape his pursuers. This too, in his opinion, is the case with the dreaming collective whose children are the right incentive for its awakening. The fact that the adult had always been a child, as well as his ability to observe the way in which children experience the world - contribute to the Benjaminian recognition of the necessity to awaken from the dream world of myth.[127]

The idea of 'waiting' ('wartend') is another way to describe the 'threshold'. In a fragment among the preparatory notes to "The Arcades Project" Benjamin writes about the need to develop a 'metaphysics of waiting'. The dialectic view that Benjamin is studying reveals itself both in the idea of childhood and in the idea of waiting: It is necessary to dream the dream in order to awaken from it. The idea of 'death till further notice' till that very awakening, enlightenment, recurs and finds its place in the discussion of myth in the essay "Fate and Character"[128], where Benjamin determines that man is never totally immersed in the illusions of the myth, in which he is, as being mere life, life such as it is. This attitude claims that life is always more that mere life, even if its better part remains concealed from sight. This dialectics is possible if the dream is intensively dreamt. In connection to his attraction to surrealism and Dada, Benjamin writes about the dialectics of intoxication, the loosening of the "I" through intoxication that is presented as an enriching and reviving experience, enabling people to avoid circles of influence.[129]

Searching and tracing the primacy of the experience bring Benjamin to meditate on childhood memories. He is aware of the spell that the world, as it appears to the child, casts upon authors and poets, yet he is wary of hallucinations of unity with nature, or the innocence of childhood as a harmonious pre-cultural merging with the world. From his earliest essays about Romantics, and his doctoral dissertation onward, he is preoccupied with the view of this period of life in literature, art, and philosophy. In his analyses of the various genre forms of narrative representations, Benjamin identifies the secular form in which the first awakening from myth takes place in legends. In

---

[124] W. Benjamin, "berliner kindheit um neunzehnhundert", *Berlin Childhood around 1900*, trans. H. Eiland (Cambridge and London: Harvard UP, 2006).
[125] W. Benjamin, "moskauer tagebuch" (1926–1927), *Moscow Diary*, ed. G. Smith, R. Sieburth, trans. G. Scholem (Cambridge and London: Harvard UP, 2006).
[126] W. Benjamin, "Passagen werk" (1927–40), in *The Arcades Project*, ed. R. Tiedemann (Cambridge: Harvard UP, 1999).
[127] See: (Noor, 2009), pp. 22-27.
[128] "Schicksal und Character" (7979), in *BSW (Vol 1.* 1996), Pp. 211-217.
[129] W, Benjamin "der sürrealismus: die letzte momentaufnahme der europäischen intelligenz" (1929) (Surrealism: The Last Snapshot of the European Intelligentsia) in: BSW (vol. 1999), pp. 217-221.

his essay on Robert Walser[130] Benjamin confronts this genre with that of the positive religions, which he contends have not confronted myth in a simple unequivocal way.[131] Being simple and unequivocal, however, are the very traits that characterize the secular form of the legend. Benjamin claims in "The Storyteller"[132] that this narrative form is what teaches children - as it had taught humanity in the past - to confront the world of myth and to grow beyond it. Through legends children learn the trickery and daring they need in order to overcome myth, as does humanity in general. Benjamin writes that the liberating magic of the legend does not stem from admitting nature in as a mythical participant, but rather by indicating that the legend is an accomplice of the liberated man. The mature person only senses this partnership at times, in moments of joy, but the child encounters it first of all in legends, and that is what directs him to happiness.

The mission of raising past memories from childhood is to discover the liberating spell in the child's experience, so that through his acquaintance with it he may learn the trickery that enables mankind - from the view point of the philosophy of history - to struggle with myth. Perhaps it is in this sense that Benjamin speaks about the possibility of this attempt leading to redemption. Benjamin's analysis of Kafka's story "The Silence of the Sirens"[133] uses the interpretation of the philosophical historical threshold between myth and legend as a paradigm of liberation. This analysis provided the seed for expanding the subject of enlightenment and myth in Horkheimer and Adorno's essay "Dialectic of Enlightenment".[134] Benjamin writes about Ullysses as standing on the threshold separating myth from legend. Wisdom and trickery have laid traps in myth, and its influence has ceased to be irresistible. The legend is a statement about a victory won. The action of disruption by wisdom and trickery are what Benjamin emphasizes in his questioning of myth, a step he reinforces relating to Kafka, who make use of legends (or sagas) only to transform them. Similarly to Kafka, Benjamin searches for insufficient childlike means which may bring about redemption.

The romantic impulse aspires to unimpeded access to the absolute. Thus Benjamin, in "The Origin of German Tragic Drama"[135], characterizes the ways in which the child perceives the world, before they have been dulled by the heavy weight of exploitative logic; not yet restricted by the categories dividing the world. The child communicates with the world as a whole, an experience from which the 'sublime' glimmers out. Benjamin's interpretation of childhood employs the terms of his philosophy of history, namely - the terms of the philosophical historical analysis of the relation to the mythical spell-bound view of the world, from which man, as man, tries to extricate himself. From Benjamin's point of view, in childhood there is no approach to the world that is innocent, but rather it is an encounter with the spells of myth - the world in its misrepresented and distorted version of itself, occurring such that the child has resources at his disposal to fight this mythical world. The theory of the 'threshold' ('Schwelle') developed by

---

[130] "über Robert Walser" (1929) in: BSW (vol. 1999), pp. 257-261.
[131] See: (Noor, 2009), pp 22-27.
[132] "Der Erzähler" (1936), in BSW (Vol. 3, 2000), pp.143-166.
[133] W, Benjamin, "Über Kafka" (1934), in *Illuminations*, ed. H. Arendt, trans. Harry Zohn (New York: Schocken Books, 1969).
[134] M. Horkheimer, T. W. Adorno, "Dialektik der Aufklärung" (1944), *Dialectic of Enlightenment, Philosophical Fragments*, ed. G. S. Noerr, trans. E. Jephcott (Stanford: Stanford UP, 2002).
[135] W. Benjamin, "Ursprung des deutschen Trauerspiels" (1928), *The Origin of German Tragic Drama*, trans. J. Osborne (London, New York: Verso, 2003).

Benjamin sees the childhood experience as the chance to become acquainted with the mythical world, to understand it and go beyond it.136

Benjamin's remembrance of his experiences of the world as a child seem close to Proust's steps, which indicate a dialectics of happiness, as characterized by "The Image of Proust".137 In Proust Benjamin finds two types of desire for happiness: one, a sublime heavenly form, and the second - a melancholy elegiac form of happiness; or as Benjamin describes it: The infinite restoration of the primordial original happiness - the form of happiness that Proust searches for, and from which proceeds his being in remembrance.

In his essay on Proust, one sees the beginning of the Marxist dimension gathering strength in Benjamin's writings. He continues, in the essay, to develop the concepts that had previously preoccupied him: redemption, melancholy, and mending. In Benjamin's opinion, Proust weaves his story with the knowledge that he will never attain perfection, because of the imperfection of the present, which is the result of the collapse of the primordial world. Every present and reality, as such, cannot be mended and completed. There is no cosmic perfection, nor is there personal perfection; there is only 'L'imperfection'. Hence, Proust's definition of happiness: "The eternal return, the eternal reconstruction of the original first happiness". It is a circular experience of time, known from Jewish messianic thought, as well as from Nietzsche's motif of eternal return, and the compulsive nature of neurosis in Psychoanalysis. Benjamin contends that for Proust, the precise return to the past makes it become present, and eliminates the dimension of time. There is a difficulty in experiencing, since there is a difference between the event and the experience. The encounter between a present experience and a past one is a one-time event, and is not that of slow studious memory. It is 'remembrance' and not 'memory'. The experience of the past within the present is the ignoring and destroying of the concrete existing present, which makes way for the past. This is a dialectic action - a destructive and constructive action simultaneously. For the first time Benjamin emphasizes the destructive element: Something must be destroyed for the truth to appear or be revealed; and he emphasizes the instantaneous revelation, which is not the result of historical development. This is revelation as a most personal act: "Even at the center of Proust's work, there is loneliness that pulls the world downward, to be swallowed in the vortex", and there is no place there for the other. This is revelation that creates a new world, reconstructs a lost past - however, these are a totally private past and world. Redemption appears as a possibility while denying the very idea of historical development. At the moment of revelation, which creates a private schism in the present, it is the past that rushes in - and not the future.

Isn't everything alive already in your blood?
Doesn't Fate herself keep you in her service?

---

[136] See: (Noor, 2009), pp. 28-30.
[137] W. Benjamin, "Zum Bilde Prousts" (1929-1934), in *Illuminations*, ed. H. Arendt, trans. H. Zohn (New York: Schocken Books, 1969), pp. 201-215.

Wander defenseless, therefore,
   Through life and don't worry!

Whatever happens will be sacred to you;
   Be expert in joy! For what could
     Harm you, heart! What could
        You suffer, where you must go?

(...)[138]

This poem, seven stanzas of 4 lines each in classical hexameter, appears in three versions as part of Hölderlin's ongoing process of rewriting. The first two versions bear the mentioned name ("Dichtermut"), while the last, dated to the period following his trip to France, is called "Blödigkeit" - a complicated word usually translated as 'timidity' or 'awkwardness'. The motif is identical in all three versions: a task or mission of the poet requiring a complex quality of courage.

In "Two Poems by Friedrich Hölderlin"[139] Walter Benjamin analyzes the first and last versions of the poem, of the three (deliberately ignoring the middle one). As presented by Benjamin, the purpose of the essay is critical in nature, or what he calls "the aesthetics of the poetic art", organized around the search for 'das Gedichtete', usually translated as dictamen, or 'the poetized'. For Benjamin, this concept, originating in Goethe, marked the direction to the inner pattern (called by Goethe the 'content'= 'Gehalt'), the mission, the essence, or the 'Idea' of the poetry.[140] According to Benjamin, access to the poetized may be gained through a method. He uses a Kantian, or post-Kantian language of the a-priori, whereby the poetized is not the reason for the poem, and is not whatever enables its interpretation, it is not in itself poetic. It is the prerequisite of the possibility of the poem. The poetized is described as a special sphere, whose image changes from poem to poem, and which embodies the mission of the poem and its prerequisites. The sphere is the result of the examination, while at the same time being its object. It is no longer comparable to the poem; it is simply the only thing that examination of the poem can unequivocally determine. In this sphere, the special unique realm is meant to open, containing the truth of the poetry. This truth, which is claimed by the most serious of the artists regarding their work, should be understood as the actual, the way in which the present mission of their art is realized.

Hence, the poetized is described in its general form as the synthetic unity of the spiritual and tangible order. This unity attains its particular image as the inner pattern of an individual work. The poetized is a border concept for two reasons. In relation to the concept of the poem, the poetized is differentiated, as a category of aesthetic examination, from the

---

[138] F. Hölderlin, "Dichtermut" (7117-7111), "The Poet's Courage" (first version,(SPF, p.99.
[139] BSW - vol. 1 (1996), pp. 18-36.
[140] P. Lacoue-Labarthe, Poetry's Courage, in *The Solid Letter: Readings of Friedrich Holderlin*, ed. A. Fioretos (Stanford: Stanford UP, 1999), pp.74-93.

scheme of form and material - it preserves the basic aesthetic unity rather than separating it, embodying in itself the immanent necessary connection between them. The unity of form and material is shared by the poetized with the poem itself, as one of its essential characteristics. The poetized is built according to the basic law of the artistic organism. As a border concept, as the concept of its mission, it is not differentiated from the poem, neither in a simple way nor in any principled characteristic. For its over-openness, its over-ability to let things be determined one way or another, the poetized is the slackening of the functional cohesion ('funktionelle verbundenheit'), and not because of any quantitative lack of determining, but rather due to the potential existence of determinations.

The poetized appears then as the definition of the border of the real and spiritual unity of the poem, while it is also a border concept for another functional unity of the idea of the mission, of which the poem is its solution. According to Benjamin, for the creator, this idea of the mission is always of life appearing as the place of the other functional unity - the poetized turns out to be the space of transference from the unity of life to that of the poem. In the poetized, life is determined through the poem and the mission - through its solution. The poetized does not dwell at the base of the individual atmosphere of the artist's life, but rather at the base of the woven connections of life determined by art.[141]

The categories in which this sphere, the intermediate sphere between the two functional unities, may be perceived, are not yet formed, and could perhaps lean mostly on the concepts of myth. It is the very slim achievements of art that relate to the immediate sense of life, while the more substantial ones relate to the sphere close to the mythic sphere: to the poetized. It is from the nature of the poetized - its being an area between two borders - that its method of presentation is born. There is no evidence regarding fundamental elements, as the poetized has no such elements, only evidence to the degree of cohesion of the real and spiritual elements. In this evidence it must be clear, claims Benjamin, that the crux of the matter is not in the elements but in the relations.[142] He further adds that revealing the purely poetized, the absolute mission, must remain a methodical purely-conceptual purpose, otherwise it ceases to be a borderline concept and becomes either poem or life. Hence, it is possible to give reasons for the judgment of a poem's value even if one cannot prove this kind of judgment.

When the wave smashes a courageous man under,
   Where he truly dares to go,
      And the voice of that singer
         Falls silent as the hall turns blue (…)[143]

---

[141] BSW - Vol 1, (1996), pp. 18-36.
[142] Ibid.
[143] F. Hölderlin, "Dichtermut" (1800-1801), "The Poet's Courage" (first version) SPF, p. 99.

In the first version of the poem "The Poet's Courage", Benjamin identifies inner unity between god and fate as the mark of myth, necessity being an almighty goddess[144] who only gains in strength from the struggle with her. The object of the poem for Hölderlin is fate - the death of the poet. He expresses, in the poem, the origin of courage in the face of death. It is the center from which the poetic world of death originates. Existence in this world is meant to be the courage of the poet. Contrary to the claim that the poem is the vessel of the writer's psychological and biological traits, Benjamin develops the idea of a world achieving skin and bones in a poem. Furthermore, he adheres to the stance whereby the greater the distance between the poem and the content of the factual psychological biological existence of the poet, the greater is the poem's ability to create its own world. The poetized, das gedichtete, or the world that the poem has created, is the object of poetic analyses, on the one hand, and of philosophical historical contemplation clarifying its place in the order of things, on the other.

The mythical-earth aspect of life, according to Benjamin's method, needs to undergo transformation of form, which retroactively reveals the connection between myth and the human realms, now liberated from their submission. This is his contention expressed at the end of the essay on Hölderlin, when he writes that "clarifying the poetized does not lead to myth - but rather to the mythical connections formed in the work of art in a single image - neither mythological nor mythical, and not totally comprehensible". The movement from the earth-mythical aspect of life onward to the realms of liberated humanity begins in the transformation of form occurring in the poem. This is the movement that Benjamin describes at the end of his essay, when the legends that distant themselves from earth turn their faces toward mankind.

One of the central terms in Benjamin's essay on Hölderlin is the 'caesura'. In his essay "Goethe's Elective Affinities",[145] Benjamin returns to this concept, developing it into a dominant category in the field of the theory of literature and the philosophy of history. The term 'caesura' indicates the moment of suspension when a turning point occurs in history, opening it to something else. Benjamin writes about 'caesura' that something enters the poet's words from beyond. It will not be exaggerated to claim that this moment of extreme otherness is what Benjamin tries to fathom in his entire writings.[146]

The 'dictamen' is then courage. The poet's courage, claims Benjamin, is mythological Topos, and this is the way Hölderlin relates to it in the first version of the poem; Topos of a heroic poet mediating between gods and man. The artist appears as a demigod, who withstands many dangers to complete his mission. Benjamin criticizes the simple recurrence of the Topos, which he claims weakens the first version of the poem. In addition, man's relation with the gods (or the poet's relation with the god that serves as his role-model) does not escape the conventional; and the essence of faith as well (death and existence) is not perceived - hence the poem is too weak to give form to the world. In the second version, Blödigkeit, the 'mythologem' of decline and wane is left out, and together with it the mediating hero is abandoned. According to Benjamin, it is the relinquishing of the mythological in the second version that

---

[144] Ananke, the goddess of force, constraint, and necessity in Greek mythology, from daily needs to actual shackles and slavery, also mentioned in connection with family ties, love, and friendship.
[145] "Goethes Wahlverwandtschaften" (1922), in BSW - vol. 1 (1996), pp. 211-217.
[146] (Noor, 2009), p.17.

paradoxically strengthens the mythic. The 'dictamen' appears in its truthfulness. The essence of courage is achieved only by the crashing of the mythological, only at the precise point of failure. Here Benjamin speaks of 'disposition' (Umstezung) of the mythological. To his mind, the dictamen of the first version only knows courage as a quality. Man and death opposite each other are motionless, lacking a common world; the relations of the poet to death are mediated by the divine which owns death mythologically. The duality of man and death can only be based on the causal sense of life. This duality ceases to exist the moment the dictamen pulls itself into a deeper connection, and creates shapes (gestaltete), or draws itself a spiritual principle - courage.[147]

Hence, courage is self-abandonment in face of danger threatening the world. Within it is concealed a particular paradox, which for the first time, allows for the structure of the dictamen in both versions. The danger is there for the courageous, but the courageous does not consider it, since if he did, that would be cowardly. However, if it weren't for the danger, he would not be courageous. This strange relation is resolved so that it is not the courageous who is threatened by the danger, but rather the world. Courage is the sense of life of the man giving himself to danger, so that in his death he expands the danger to engulf the world, while at the same time overcoming it.[148]

The world of the dead hero is now mythic, in other words - in danger. This is the world of the second version. The spiritual principle has become the governing one: the heroic poet and the world have become one. The poet no longer has to fear death; he is a hero since he lives in the focal point of relations. The principle of the dictamen in itself is the supreme sovereignty of relation. This means then that Blödigkeit becomes the authentic position of the poet transposed in the middle of life. Nothing remains for him but the motionless experience, total passivity which is the essence of the courageous, nothing but totally giving himself to relations.[149]

Benjamin's philosophical approach may be characterized as based on explicit rejection of Phenomenology, which acquired status as one of the central forms of philosophy at the turn of the century. Benjamin's concept of 'dialectic image' exemplifies the basis for this rejection. The concept, whose matter focuses on the flash lighting the past precisely at its moment of disappearance into the present, counters the methodical return to the 'essences' ('Wesenheten') that Phenomenology presumed to remove from the phenomena. When Benjamin speaks in "The Arcades Project" about these essences, there is a connection to the way in which Husserl presents them in his Phenomenology. Benjamin distinguishes between the 'dialectic image', bearing central function in his later work, and the essences of Phenomenology - by stressing the fact that the 'dialectic image' has 'historical index'.

---

[147] (Lacoue-Labarthe, 1999), pp. 14-90.
[148] Ibid, p. 86.
[149] Ibid, p. 90-92.

3.2 Heidegger between Revealment and Concealment

The central philosopher except for Husserl to work within the tradition of Phenomenology in Germany of the 1930s was Heidegger, and indeed, his writings constitute a concentrated effort to expose the structure of historical understanding. Benjamin, however, claims that Phenomenology's effort of saving history was made in vain, since Heidegger's idea of history remained abstract. Benjamin does not develop his criticism in detail, but one may assume that he sees the analysis of the 'Dasein' and the existential structures of its being as occurring, if not far from the concrete historical experience, still not in its domain; and this in spite of Heidegger's claim that he anchors the name 'Da' of the 'Dasein' in the situation lived, and from which all of its meanings is derived.[150] Benjamin's attempt to emphasize the distance between himself and Heidegger is a matter requiring response, since there are several aspects of their thought with more than a superficial connection between them, for instance: shifting the centrality of the knowing subject; the criticism about Husserl's concept of 'internationality'; centrality of the idea of 'decision' in their early work; the attempt to clarify the lack of instrumentality of the language; and more.[151] Hence, we shall examine Heidegger's writings while focusing on his perception of the role of the poet, through the connection and tension between his thought and Benjamin's. Lacoue-Labarthe's essay conveniently juxtaposes Benjamin's and Heidegger's respective readings of Hölderlin, and may sharpen our understanding of their different approaches to the connection between poetics and myth.

In his lectures on Hölderlin's "Hymns" during the winter semester of 1934-5,[152] Heidegger developed his thought in declared connection to Hölderlinian poetics. In a step that may be called 'anti-Platonian', distinguished revolutionarily from the tradition of metaphysics up to his times, Heidegger regards art not as mimesis of the truth, but rather as its place of appearance - 'aletheia'. Art is unique in that through it, the truth of beings is revealed; a uniqueness indicating the connection of art to being, origin and meaning. Seeing language as the origin of the constitution of the world and history, Heidegger turns to the paradigmatic arena of linguistic occurrence, namely - poetry, finding in Hölderlin the model of an authentic poet, whose poetry deals with the revealing, constituting power of poetry.

Heidegger reads Hölderlin's poetry as that which deals with the essence of poetry. The poetic action is described as conveying a constituting quality, since it opens an aperture for the appearance of being, and is a discourse with the

---

[150] (Noor, 2009), p.37.
[151] Ibid.
[152] M. Heidegger, "Hölderlins Hymnen Germanien" und "Der Rhein", *Freiburger Vorlesung*, Wintersemester 1934/35 , ed. S. Ziegler (Frankfurt a.M.: Vittorio Klostermann, 1980).

gods. The poet is perceived as exiled to the space of the gap between the gods and mortals, his mission to deliver the divine plenty to men in order for them to have place and history. In this mission the poet seemingly dares to penetrate and enter the 'foreign', in spite of the fire approaching him - the danger of the gods' forceful plenty, the danger of burning in the divine lightning of fire; or in other words, the danger of madness.

In the discussion on "The Origin of the Work of Art"[153], Heidegger asks about the actual work of art, its essence and quality, as well as the nature of art actually realized through its work. These questions mark his tendency to overcome the traditional aesthetics and metaphysics, giving ontology a renewed basis. Heidegger's perception of the history of aesthetics is examined in relation to Nietzsche's thought. According to Heidegger, when Nietzsche sees art as superior to truth, it must be understood as a reversal of the accepted Platonic position of truth above art. Heidegger sees Platonism (if not Plato himself) as responsible for this approach. In spite of the distance kept by Plato between art and truth, Heidegger finds that in the Phaedrus dialogue, Plato treats 'beauty' as that through which 'being' is revealed. Hence, claims Heidegger, in relation to Plato the breach between beauty and truth is positive, since it is the basis for revealing being, creating a quasi alignment between beauty and truth. He adds however, that this breach is eradicated in Platonism, reaching fearful dimensions with Nietzsche.[154] Modern philosophy's perception of aesthetics as contemplations of man's feelings about beauty emphasizes man's place. That is why the concept has been understood the last few hundred years as a type of observation. Modern aesthetics sees the work of art as the embodiment of beauty, evoking the creator or spectator's feelings. Heidegger maintains a view similar to Schelling and Hegel about the connection between art and truth. However, shifting man from the center lessens his place in relation to the aesthetic appreciation, and presents the work of art as conveying the truth; hence, it is the focus in which being is revealed. In this step Heidegger wishes to eliminate the remnants of subjectivism and anthropocentrism present in his early perception in "Being and Time",[155] thereby applying the Phenomenological approach and letting things show themselves through themselves.

Heidegger presents the work of art as world-constituting, as revealing the truth of beings. The work of art, when born, reveals the opening of the aperture in which it rises and appears. The work of art, therefore, is the creation of a world and an occurrence of truth. This ability is not the result of mimetic power, but rather stems from the work of art being a reproduction of the general essence of the thing presented in it.

The shifting of human existence from the center and placing the work of art in its place allows the illumination of the thingness of the beings; the power of revealment is made possible thanks to the nature of the connection between the artist and his work of art, and between it and being presented through it, which is not an instrumental connection. Works of art in general, and masterpieces in particular, stand on their own, and are not connected to other beings, including the artist who had created them. The only aspect of the artist's intention preserved in his works is that they were created by him in order to exist independently of him. Thus, the works of art have a special connection to that

---

[153] M. Heidegger, "Der ursprung des Kunstwerkes" (1936), in: *HBW*. Pp. 139-212
[154] A. Mansbach, *Existence and Meaning: Martin Heidegger on Man, Language, and Art* (Hebrew), (Jerusalem: Magnes Press, 1998), pp. 81-82.
[155] M. Heidegger, *Sein und Zeit* (1927), trans. J. Stambaugh (New York: State UP, 1996).

presented through them. This matter is exemplified by Heidegger through a painting of Van Gogh.[156] The painting sheds light on the farmers' shoes and through them reveals the world of the farmer, the paths of the field, the dampness and treasures of the earth - thus the thingness character of the shoes is revealed. The essence of the connection between the work of art and that presented in it is creation of a world. Masterpieces create worlds to a comprehensive being; this is the element of their power to reveal truth, identified in the last part of "The Origin of the Work of Art"[157] as 'primordial poetry' (Urpoesie), gradually becoming a concept with a central role in Heidegger's approach to language.[158]

The world-revealing power of works of art also has a historical dimension. The temple enables the god's presence within it. This presence of the god is itself the space and delineation of the place as a holy site. The temple is world-revealing to individuals, and to a whole community fed by the history it makes present, and the tradition it delivers. The work of art also accentuates the entire 'earth', all the meaningless beings found beyond man's world. The stones of the temple are in themselves meaningless and impenetrable, with only their templeness becoming clear. Heidegger's concept of 'earth', reminiscent of Aristotle's 'material cause', expresses the impossibility to reveal all aspects of the beings. In this context Heidegger contends that many aspects of the beings cannot be controlled by man, and only few may be known. Whatever is known is left inaccurate, and whatever is controlled remains uncertain. Hence, the concept of 'earth' is perceived as indicating the irrational.

The concept of 'earth' serves Heidegger to overcome the 'subject', and traditional metaphysics. The priority of the subject in metaphysics derives from reduction of being to presence, hence to rational, so that the existence of 'earth' beyond presence weakens the favored status of the 'subject'. Nevertheless, 'earth' is what enables the presence, the rational. The concept of 'world' indicates the ordinary, accepted, rational - connected to the earth through a rift ('Riss') which does not destroy them, only delineating and restricting them. The irrational component determines the boundaries of the rational, and vice versa. Thus the limitation of anthropocentric analysis is clarified (as in being and time), as having no possibility of discovering the boundaries of the rational. Beings are perceived as instruments whose applied purpose is emphasized, while their materialness disappears into usefulness.

The work of art embodies the thingness of being, revealing the earth aspect belonging to each being. 'Earth' does not become clear and comprehended as a result of its prominence in the work of art; when we wish to give it shape 'earth' withdraws back; when we wish to claim ownership, it drops from our hands. Basically, it closes into itself, averting any attempt to penetrate it. Being highlighted means being presented naked, as incomprehensible. Heidegger exemplifies this through the stone whose weight may be quantified in terms of weight, yet this utterance, albeit very precise, will always remain a number, while the weight itself is beyond us. One may also penetrate the stone and shatter it to pieces, but even then it will not reveal its internal side. In this case, the stone will revert immediately to the

---

[156] M. Heidegger, "Der ursprung des Kunstwerkes" (1936), in HBW, pp. 139-212.
[157] Ibid.
[158] (Mansbach, 1998), p. 83.

same opacity of the weight of its fragments and chunks. Thus, too, does the radiant color withdraw and disappear when we analyze it in rational terms of wave length.[159]

Heidegger uses the concepts of 'world' and 'earth' as an alternative distinction to those of 'material' and 'form' in the traditional dictionary of aesthetics. 'World' is the comprehended space; the meaningful surroundings; the residence of man. 'Earth', on the other hand, withdraws and objects to any attempt of man to penetrate it, give it shape, own it. Hence 'earth' is an expression of alienation, of otherness; it is the opposite of the world and all that is ordinary, accepted and familiar.[160]

'World' and 'earth', as presented by Heidegger, are totally different from one another, and yet are bound by a connection expressed in their counter positioning, and in each one's undermining of the other in a constant struggle which is their very essence. This is not a struggle of destruction and annihilation, but rather the delineation of the boundaries of the opponents. Delineating 'world' and 'earth', the struggle symbolizes the rift between them. The rift is not an abyss, but rather the inner affiliation of the opponents. From within this rift, by virtue of the conflict and mutual play of enlightening and concealing, beings immerge and the truth of the rift is born - the origin of the meaning. Although the rift is the common grounds, one cannot view it as a uniting principle, but rather as a conjoining difference. Here enters, into this context of the rift between 'earth' and 'world', the concept of the truth as Aletheia (from Greek - negation of forgetting; remembrance). Each thing exists due to its revealment, which occurs by its very presence in the open domain. This presence, neither created nor constituted, immerges and is made possible thanks to the withdrawal and revealment. In every being that we encounter we discover the strange contrast of presence, so that it is at the same time withdrawing and hiding. The 'clearing in the forest' (Lichtung) where being appears is at the same time its hiding place.

The nature of 'earth' entails that the essence of beings may be revealed from a certain aspect, if there is a shifting that conceals other possible aspects. Hence, every situation of truth, every immergence, involves concealment. This concealment is inevitable in order to enable any revealment - this is a character of being. Therefore, one must not simply identify 'world' with the revealed, and 'earth' with the concealed. The nature of the truth, of the revealment, is imbued with refusal, in the double meaning of prevention (Versage), and camouflage or pretension (Verstellen). The refusal or camouflage is not a shortcoming from which to be released. If this were so, then truth would cease to be it itself. This duality of revealment and refusal is inherent in the element of truth. Truth in essence is non-truth. Let us clarify that this does not mean that truth is not truth, nor does it indicate a dialectic relation between revealment and blocking. The intention is that truth as 'aletheia' always exists with its other, which is not its opposite. Hence, the open place is not as a stage where beings appear to the beholders, but rather it is an 'event' occurring as a struggle in the swaying of the pendulum of revealment and concealment.

---

[159] Ibid, pp. 84-87.
[160] Ibid.

The importance of the work of art, in the framework of the discussion on the meaning of being, is clarified when it is placed beside the question of man and the problem of authentic existence. The way of authentic existence is described in "Being and Time"[161] as possible only after the collapse of the meaning of the ordinary world known to all, whereby the authentic selfness is revealed naked. This revealment is the result of three moments that make man (Dasein) transparent to himself: toward death, anxiety, and the call of the conscience. Although these provide the basis for authenticity, they are not enough to peel man of his non-authentic existence and completely reveal his realness. This situation fits the general Heideggerian motivation which searches for a place beyond subjectivism. The presentation of authenticity as a mode of human realizable existence would turn man into a subject determining himself and the world, from within himself. However, the lack of possibility to realize the authentic existence, presents Heidegger's basic ontology with the problem of perceiving the authentic mode of existence as the way of revealing being.[162]

A partial solution to the problem is to be found in the concept of the 'hero'. Only the hero, who is actually the hero of culture, can be authentic and reveal being, thereby initiating history. He provides a past to men, which they may project into the future, together with the entire community. This solution raises two additional problems, one dealing with the question of continuity of revealing being - how it is preserved throughout history; and the second: what prevents us from seeing a subject in the hero?

The discussion in "The Origin of the Work of Art"[163] offers the beginning of a solution for these issues: the work of art is given a role similar to the hero's. Its revealment is authentic. As in anxiety, the work of art is devoid of non-authentic residue. It itself is authentic. Anxiety keeps man from assimilating into the others. The daily routine collapses, and man ceases to understand himself and the world in the way interpreted until now. The thing we fear has no character of any being, it is no-thing. Anxiety reveals the non behind all phenomena. The work of art acts in a similar way, located in a defined system, as in the case of the Greek temple, radiating light that illuminates, reveals and grants new meaning to its surroundings; hence, it is world-constituting and delineates its boundaries. Man's choice may be directed by well-known works of art, and by adopting the past of a hero as his own past.

What then enables art to generate truth? And to works of art to be conveyors of meaning and constitute a world, thereby maintaining authentic continuity? Heidegger uses the concept of 'poetry' ('poesie') in the common sense of a measured rhythmic poetic work; and the concept of 'primordial poetry' (Urpoesie, Urdichtung'), in the sense of an element found in every work of art, and the basis of the entire realm of art.[164]

---

[161] (M. Heidegger, 1927).
[162] (Mansbach, 1998), pp. 47-41.
[163] W. Benjamin, "Ursprung des deutschen Trauerspiels" (1921).
[164] Poesie, from the Greek poiēsis: making, fabrication, production, poetry, poem, which in turn comes from poiein: to make, to do. Aristotle (in "Nicomachean Ethics") distinguishes poiēsis , "making", which essentially has an end-product, a poiēma – from praxis , "action" – which does not. Poesie has a narrower meaning than poiēsis, applying especially to verse in contrast to prose. Dichtung, from dichten , "to invent, write, compose verses", which sounds Germanic but comes from the Latin dictare , "to say repeatedly, dictate, compose". This has a wider meaning than Poesie or poetry. It applies to all creative writing, including novels, not only verse. The verb has the flavor of "to dispose, order, shape". Heidegger uses

'Primordial poetry', according to Heidegger, enables the works of art to create a space where beings reveal themselves. This is the stage of creating an opening (das Offene) where beings are. Primordial poetry enables the blending of beings into the world, and creates connections with other beings, thereby building up meaning. Primordial poetry is inherent in the process of creation, but since the only thing preserved in the work of art from the connection with the artist is the artist's intention that the work exist on its own merit, the poetry is no longer dependent on the artist, and belongs to the entire work. Poetry is the occurrence of truth in the non-concealment, and thus it enables each masterpiece to generate truth.[165]

Heidegger also calls the 'primordial poetry' 'primordial language' (Ursprache), and claims that language itself is poetry in its essential meaning, in other words - primordial poetry. Similarly to what Benjamin calls 'the language of things', this is language of pre-separation between the sign and the referent; it is neither external nor later than the thing whose name it calls, but rather belongs to it in essence. This is language that belongs to the thing more than to the speaker, and in which the speech and the thing are one and the same. It is the language of being, or the language of god, of pre-falling to human language. Thus Heidegger sees the essence of the work of art as the essence of language. Primordial poetry is the element of language that explains its role and action.

Language too, as the work of art brings beings out into the open, revealing them and enabling their presence. Authentic language is the vessel of poetry, creating a world by imbuing meaning to things. The spoken and written language is a distinct phenomenon of openness, of the location of poetry, which enables the meaning. Poetry is made of the basic materials of language, words and sentences. Hence, primordial poetry, in Heidegger's opinion, is revealment of the concealed, and not a fable or invention of events. It is intended for revealing being. The creation of the world by poetry constitutes the open space where all the objects appear.

Heidegger sees in each of the arts a special primordial poetry, but since the role of language is to preserve the original essence of truth, and the essence of language is primordial poetry, one must see - in the work of art whose medium is language - direct access to revealing beings; when it is explicitly expressed, the revealment is more complete. The power of the works of art reaches its full potential when a lingual statement accompanies the work. Any art that enables the truth of beings to be revealed is in essence poetry. Constituting a new world by the Greek temple, for instance, is more comprehensive if it is accompanied by the myth enveloping it. Therefore, the essence of art is primordial poetry, and the essence of primordial poetry is its being a lingual semantic element through which being is revealed, and truth determined.

Hence, language is poetization. The utterance causes the revealment of being of the beings, and revealment of being in general. This occurs since language is the stage in which 'world' and 'earth' immerge, and it takes place in the area of tension between them. The tension between 'earth' and 'world' - between that which can be meant and that

---

dichten and Dichtung in a narrow and a wide sense: In the wide sense, dichten means to invent, create, project, but it is distinct from "untrammeled invention" From the inventive [dichtenden, creative, projective] essence of art, it happens that art in the midst of beings clears an open place in whose openness everything is other than before.: see: M. Inwood, ed., *Heidegger Dictionary* (Oxford, Blackwell 1999).
[165] See: (Mansbach, 1998), pp. 92-99.

which cannot - is what enables meaning. It is in this respect that language occurs between the beings and 'being'. The act of creating and the act of the interpreting guards reveals the historiness of primordial poetry. Works of art in general and poetry in particular constitute a new beginning that redefines history. Primordial poetry is the initial element that reveals the historical basis of man (and his historical community).

According to Heidegger's perception, language as a vessel for poetry is historical in essence. In the lingual works of the people, such as legends, sagas, and traditions, the elementary components are preserved that were once world-constituting. In the context of a new interpretation of the works and their becoming a tradition, through which they shed their light upon the future, people may start a new beginning and discover the truth, which grants them in the present, and will grant them in the future, their particular place in history. Myth is the fabric of meanings that includes poetry, with which a new era in the history of a people begins. Myth shapes and organizes the past as a tradition that men adopt and project onto the future. Hence, "History…if it is anything, it is mythology."[166] Myth reveals the historical meaning of a people, since 'myth' means to express, cause to appear; therefore, "Myth… and logos express the same thing."[167]

For the community, language is a composition of truth. It is the revealment of being throughout history, occurring due to the poetic element. The temporal dimension of language, its history, corroborates the claim that the perception of truth as the compatibility of statement and fact assumes the occurrence of an event (for instance, the Mount Sinai event), in which the community adopts the past, turns it into a challenge, and attempts to realize the potential inherent in the community and in the tradition adopted. This is an event of truth which enables the community to create its history, and imbue the future with coherence and direction. The beginning of the event also conceals its end. Language is an occurrence of projective utterance, where a historical world becomes a people, and 'earth' is preserved as that which remains sealed. Hence, the projective utterance prepares that which may be said, while at the same time bringing forth into the world that which cannot be said as such.[168]

Heidegger turns to the poet in order to examine the power of language. The poetry of Hölderlin, whom Heidegger considered the utmost poet, is described as dealing with the revealing and constituting power of poetry. To his mind, the contribution of poetry to revealing itself, is in its being a constituting action of the power of the word, and within it. As to preserving its revealment, Heidegger adopts Hölderlin's words of the conclusion of the poem "Remembrance" ("Andenken"), that "…Poets establish that which endures."[169] In other words, the language of the poet and the authentic language preserve beings as such. Language preserves beings throughout history, thereby maintaining revealment. The determining and preserving are conducted through the name. The act of naming (Nennen) reveals

---

[166] M. Heidegger, "Einführung in die Metaphysik" (1935), *Introduction to Metaphysics,* trans. G. Fried and R. Polt (New Haven: Yale UP, 2000), p. 115.
[167] M. Heidegger, "Was Heisst Denken?" (1951-52), "What Calls for Thinking?", in HBW. pp. 341-343.
[168] (Mansbach 1998), pp. 92-99.

[169] F. Hölderlin, "Andenken" (1803-1805) "Remembrance", SPF, p. 251-252.

beings: when language first called out the name of being, it brought being into utterance and appearance. Naming extracts beings from within their entity. The utterance is a clarifying projection through which revealment occurs. The projection is in essence poetization, expression of primordial poetry.

The name turns beings into part of man's world, serving him, blending in with his world, and merging into his history, that of the community, and of the people. This then is the constitution of beings as meaningful phenomena through the primordial element, not by granting existence to beings, but rather by recognizing them as existing. Poetization constitutes the open space by turning beings into accessible to man; through them man relates to the world around him, and to himself. It constitutes the world in which man lives and from which he attains his meaning. Hence, the poets' words create the basis, in the sense of an underlying assumption in the foundation of man's being. Daily language is poetry whose revealing power has eroded. It is worn and forgotten poetry.170

Important lingual works can withstand the tendency of daily language to forgetfulness, since they preserve the tension between revealment and concealment; between 'world' and 'earth'. However, since authentic existence is not detached from daily existence, it is not possible to become detached from daily language in authentic speech. Although daily language is poetry that has became trite and incorrect language, it plays an important role in shaping authentic language. Poetization draws its origins from a vague meaning of things at the background of man's daily speech, in other words: sagas, epic poems, traditions and legends.

In this fashion the primordial element of daily language is regenerated, becoming a new truth for the community. Tragedy, for example, taking its strength from Homer's poem, not only carries out something familiar, but also actualizes events belonging to human thought. Originating in folk speech, the work of art processes man's words in such a way that its own words fight the final battle between the holy and the non-holy, between sublime and inferior, between courageous and cowardly. Heidegger's meaning is that the entity of being is revealed through language. When we give a name to a particular being it becomes non-meaning. It is not the case that language grants existence to beings, but rather that language turns them into phenomena, whose entity is revealed by man. However, without language, beings have no possibility of being present. Hence, according to Heidegger there are no mere beings, only meaningful ones. This is the background for understanding his statement that when we go to the well or through the forest, we always go through the word 'well' or the word 'forest', even if we don't express these words or think of any particular lingual reality.171 It must be noted that the act of naming does not follow the discovery of being; hence, it is not an arbitrary act determining interchangeable signs as suggested by French semiotic de Saussure. The original word, which expresses being, is an integral part of the revealment, and preserves being in the open space. Being itself is shaped and revealed in the act of naming, after which being is locked in a lingual semantic relation system with other beings, and if a name is changed into another, then other changes in meaning occur in the semantic network; one change entails other changes. The type of connection between name and being is not that of sign and referent, as the

---

[170] This approach of Heidegger, as presented further on, seems to resemble Bialik's considerably.
[171] Martin Heidegger, "ozu dichter?" (1946), "Why Poets?", in *Off the Beaten Track (Holzewege)*, trans. J. Young & K. Haynes (Cambridge: Cambridge UP, 2002), p. 286.

essence of language is not merely indication.172 Heidegger sees the logos as the origin of the language, enabling words and names to grant a new life to beings, constituting an origin of revealing the truth. The concept 'logos' has multi-meaning, and Heidegger believes that in order to understand the concept usually translated into a word or speech, while perceiving the original meaning of the verb 'posed', the concepts 'to speak' and 'to say' should be understood as 'posed'. Speech means the posing of beings in the open space and turning them into present.

In his essay "An Introduction to Metaphysics"173, Heidegger touches upon the differences between thinking and poetry, however, in "The Essence of Language"174 he deals in detail with the issue. In this essay one sees the way in which Heidegger distances himself from metaphysical language, and describes the way that thought acts through the metaphor of place, introducing the concept of 'neighborhood' ('Gegend'). There is great difficulty in attempting to define the non-metaphorical dimension of its opaque meaning.175 'Neighborhood' is presented as the negation of a method or subject, and is called so, as it liberates that which is given to thinking. Thinking meanders around the paths of the neighborhood. Thinking and poetry are both directed to logos, thus they both dwell in the same neighborhood. Poetry and thinking dwell opposite each other, each desiring the company of the other. This neighboring of poetry and thinking does not appear as a common basis or conceptual framework, but rather as parallel lines that seem to branch out. Neither has priority over the other; they belong to each other while maintaining a distance between themselves, each in its darkness. This distance, however, is closed by a vertical line cutting the two parallels, creating a section, making them closer and binding them - hence the concept indicates common belonging, but also closeness and distance. Poetry and thinking are enigmatic in essence, offering us meaning, enlightenment, but also the possibility to experience through the power of language. In the withdrawal of the world into a darkness sealed to defined determinations, primordial language is the elementary material from which they are composed, and the basis for their closeness.176

Although the poet and the thinker dwell in 'the house of being', the gap between them is as if they were on mountaintops, speaking across an abyss. The difference, which seems to remain unclear from reading Heidegger, lies in the thinker speaking about being, while the poet speaks of the holy. In "A Letter on Humanism"177 it is perhaps hinted at that the difference between thinking and poetry lies in the concealment of being, given to the thinker only

---

[172] See: F. De Saussure, *Writings in General Linguistics* (Oxford: Oxford UP, 2006).
[173] M. Heidegger, *Einführung in die Metaphysik* (1935), trans. G. Fried & R. Polt (New Haven: Yale UP, 2000)).
[174] M. Heidegger, "Dem Wesen der Sprache" (7991), in *Logic as the Question Concerning the Essence of Language*, trans. W. T. Gregory & Y. Unna (New York: SUNY, 2009).
[175] In Hebrew there is a linguistic connection through the common root of 'neighborhood' and 'dwelling'.
[176] (Mansbach, 1998), p. 129.
This issue of thinking and poetry as realized through the gap between them preoccupies Derrida in his discussion of metaphor. He perceives the section between the two as connecting them, but since it belongs to neither, it is not a common property or general concept, nor is it a metaphor. As it is not derived, the section is more basic than thinking and poetry; however, even it is not completely elementary or autonomous - hence it is approximately no-thing.
[177] M. Heidegger, "Brief uber den Humanismus" (7942), in HBW, pp. 213-266.

partially through the language of thinking, and mainly remaining concealed. In connection to the poet, Heidegger does not mention the matter of concealment, entailing perhaps the meaning of 'holiness' as the positive side of being.[178]

The status of poetry is different from that of thinking also in the historical dimension. Heidegger claims that being, as truth-projecting fate, remains clandestine, but the fate of the world announces itself in poetry, prior to becoming embodied in the annals of the entity. Holiness is revealed in the poet's words but not in its transience as history, while it is given to the thinker also as history. As a result of both the poet and the thinker's response to the call of the imbuing being, being becomes words, but its structure as revealed by the thinker is a temporal structure of remembrance. The nature of the past is its distinction between poetry and thinking. In poetry, the past appears as beings through which the poet experienced being, and his action is to name them. The poet sees the elementary action as that of naming a primordial thing, while thinking expresses a historical past in words in order to preserve it through language - the recurring attainment that regenerates it.

Poetry is then expression of the immediate perception of the entity. There is no need for the past, or beings, or human beings. The thinker's perception of being occurs through attention to its calling, by refreshing the meaning of words. The thinker restores the authentic meaning of the words, thereby enabling the logos behind them, the being, to illuminate.

The poet, whose poetry utters holiness, therefore stands in the gap between gods and mortals as a mediating entity - a demigod, exposed to danger and madness, measuring his poetic courage ('Mut') so that he may speak on behalf of his mother (Mutter) - earth.[179] The poet has the courage to live in his times and, with his poetry, mend the rift between the gods and men, thereby granting the mortals their lost 'dwelling'. According to Heidegger, to be a poet in an impoverished world means to join, through singing, the search for the footsteps of the elusive gods. Hence the poet, during the world's night, grants expression to the holy; and thus, for Hölderlin, the world's night is the holy night.

According to Heidegger's method, poetry is a process in which being, as holiness, relays a message to the poet, which he must deliver in words. From the point of view of the holiness, the appeal has the character of delivery containing fate. The holiness is revealed without history, without being, thereby expressing itself as mystery. From the poet's view point, his reaction has the nature of remembrance. In this complex process, holiness is superior to the poet.

Holiness itself is primordial poetry assigning the poet the task of expressing it in words. The poet enables his people to be part of the poetry, thereby living it. When holiness turns to the poet, and the latter responds - he opens up worlds, and history occurs. As Homer's poetry acted upon the Greeks, thus the poet grants a basis for the annals of peoples, preparing the poetic basis for the dwelling of historical people.

Holiness and nature for Hölderlin are regarded by Heidegger as primordial enlightenment, the horizon where nature itself is not being, but all beings are present in it. Nature is an entity as the origin of beings, the 'holy chaos' in

---

[178] (Mansbach, 1998), p. 129-132.
[179] M. Heidegger, *Hölderlins Hymne "Der Ister" (1942)*, trans. W. McNeill & J. Davis (Bloomington: Indiana UP, 1996), p. 128.

the original Greek sense; the gap; the openness of the ancient aperture enveloping all. As a holy chaos, the entity opens the horizon to a historical appearance of beings. Holiness opens the time axis and the space, as a historical context along which beings appear. With the appearance of the holiness, it constitutes a new beginning for another history.[180]

The poet's poetry appears then as poetic delivery of that which was received from the gods. The origin of plenty is the gods, who through the poet's mediation bestow their light. The poet is the one who translates the divine language to the language of men, through the poetic language granting them place. Hence the gift of dwelling is diverted from its ontological context, assuming a character that it is difficult not to call 'onto-theological'.

In his lecture in the winter semester of 1934-35,[181] Heidegger developed the concept of courage ('Mut'), in particular regarding the poet and the thinker. This development, expressed in what turns out to be political, rather than ethical, drew criticism over the years for the transformative reading of Hölderlin's poetry, a way of reading and interpreting that was perceived by critics as representing a proto-fascist dimension in Heidegger's thought.[182]

The purpose of the course as presented by Heidegger was to open up to the effectiveness of poetry - to recreate in our, that is the Germans', Historical Dasein a space and place for that which poetry is. Heidegger's choice of Hölderlin is therefore a historical choice. Hölderlin is the poet of poets and poetry; hence, Hölderlin is the poet of the Germans. Since he is concealed from us, with his writing is difficult and complicated, Hölderlin has not yet become a force in the history of the Germans, and the time has arrived for him to become so. Several years later, in "Hölderlin and the Essence of Poetry",[183] Hölderlin is described as he who poetizes the future of the Germans, poetizing a different history of the return or absence of the gods.

In "Letters on Humanism" as well,[184] one encounters the night of the absence of the gods, or the dawn or their re-appearance, with the closeness to being; and based on this closeness, German privileged rights in history are clarified. Also in his lectures "The End of Philosophy and the Task of Thinking",[185] the task of Hölderlin's poetry echoes: To prepare for the appearance of the gods or the announcement of their concealment, and the past of the Germans as reflecting the future soon to be fulfilled.

---

[180] Mansbach 1998), pp. 729-132.
[181] M. Heidegger, "Hölderlins Hymnen Germanien" und "Der Rhein", Freiburger Vorlesung, Wintersemester (1934/35) , ed. S. Ziegler (Frankfurt a.M.: Vittorio Klostermann, 1980).
[182] (Lacoue-Labarthe, 1999), pp. 85.
[183] M. Heidegger, "Hölderlin und das Wesen der Dichtung" (1936), in *Elucidations of Holderlin's Poetry*, trans. K. Hoeller (New York, Humanity Books 2000).
[184] M. Heidegger, "Brief uber den Humanismus" (1947).
[185] M. Heidegger, "Das Ende der Philosophie und die Aufgabe des Denkens" (1966,) in *HBW*, pp. 422 -449

3.3 Hermeneutical Cartography of Myth

Philippe Lacoue-Labarthe (LL) seeks to show how Heidegger's reading of Hölderlin grants priority to 'myth' as a means to knowledge. This echoes an aesthetic-political romantic passion for the establishing of a new mythology that will also restore the German people to their deserved place in history.[186]

The theological-political is supported by an appeal to myth. It is that which appoints a mission to poetry. The mission is a struggle.[187] If, as Heidegger claims, a struggle is necessary, then there has been a threat, to say nothing of danger. A quality that LL calls 'arche-ethical' is required of poetry that faces danger - a danger, according to Heidegger, that threatens being. Poetry is given responsibility that may be called 'transcendental', as that is the condition for granting history to man.

At the heart of Heidegger's notes on Hölderlin, LL posits the question: Can the Germans enter history and open a new history of becoming Germans - as the Greeks, with unprecedented courage presented by tragedy, became Greeks? The product of this step is the defining of the poet as a hero, in the sense of this concept in "Being and Time",[188] where 'hero' is actually a hero of culture capable of authenticity and of revealing Being, thereby initiating history; a hero who provides his people with a past which they, as a community, may project into the future. When Heidegger claims that historical Dasein must choose their heroes from the tradition, he is actually, at least as depicted by LL, continuing a train of thought of the Nietzschian interpretation of history, and of the ancient Gnostics. The poet appears as much more than a model or example such as found in modern terminology. Departing from his custom, Heidegger adopts the figure of the poet as demigod, mediating between gods and man - in direct connection to Hölderlin's description of him as the one who grasps the signs of the divine in the face of danger, under threat of lightning, to deliver them to man in a valid way. Twenty years later in a lecture in Rome,[189] in this context, Heidegger presented the concept of 'testimony'. In his lecture he claimed that when Hölderlin speaks of language as the "most dangerous of all goods", as such that threatens truth itself, he at the same time also defines it as a gift given to man to testify to what he is. At this point, LL identifies the change that Heidegger generates when theology meets politics.[190]

---

[186] P. Lacoue-Labarthe, *Heidegger and the Politics of Poetry*, trans. J. Fort (Urbana: University of Illinois Press, 2007).
[187] (Lacoue-Labarthe 1999), pp 79-80.
[188] M. Heidegger, Sein und Zeit (1927).
[189] M. Heidegger, "Hölderlin und das Wesen der Dichtung" (1936), *Elucidations of Holderlin's Poetry*, trans. K. Hoeller (New York: Humanity Books, 2000).
[190] (Lacoue-Labarthe, 1999), pp. 79.

For Heidegger and Benjamin, in spite of the differences in the interpretation of truth, poetry is perceived as uttering truth or as speech in the name of truth. If you wish, suggests LL, poetry in the Heideggerian sense is the martyr of truth, thus the poets' fate slips into martyrdom. They are the founders of the prerequisites of poetry - the a-priori. A quasi authority preceding all authority of the poet makes the poet possible. Generally, Labarthe - following Benjamin - describes the dictamen, the synthetic unity of the spiritual and intuitive orders. This unity achieves its particular form in the inner form of the particular work of art. The mythic, he adds, is best understood not as mythological - in the sense of stereotype organization or co-relation of the mythemes of myth - since it is the dictamen, or - the dictamen is existence itself.191

According to LL, Heidegger failed to see the deconstructive extent of Hölderlin's writings, deconstruction that Benjamin identifies and characterizes as what one may call 'divesting the hymn of its authority'. Hölderlin's poems are holy, in Benjamin's opinion, not because they are divine treasures, but in their own right. As they are alive, they are planted beyond any sublimity in the sublime. LL's perception continues this approach of viewing the poems not as mythological expressions, but rather as confirming that which Hölderlin calls 'holy sobriety'.192

Benjamin locates Hölderin's deconstructive element in the principle of 'sobriety', as developed by Hölderin in his remarks to his translation of Sophocles,193 namely - as a guiding principle of modern poetry, as that which dictates the mission. The words 'holy sobriety', writes Benjamin, derive from a promise in which they are planted in Hölderin's spiritual life, allowing and even commanding to be sober.194 According to Benjamin, as emphasized by LL, the poem or hymn has no historical mission or any other, and sobriety fulfills the role as a reminder of the distancing from myth. We know that this is what Benjamin, in his thesis on Jena Romanticism several years later,195 would identify with prose, declaring - while using the speculative concept borrowed from Fichte: "The idea of poetry is prose."196

In Hölderin's poem "Half of Life"197, tension appears between an idyll in the first half of the poem, and what may be termed a 'fall' in the second half. The first stanza describes an idyllic picture of the countryside, the lake and the swans "drunk with kisses" floating on the water. The second stanza breaks the sensual fluid harmony into abysmal despair:

---

[191] Ibid, pp. 83-85.
[192] Heilige Nuchternheit - an expression that is not a contradiction (in other words, a sentence that is always false), but rather a tautology (a sentence that is always true), since that which makes it holy is precisely sobriety.
[193] F. Hölderlin, "Anmerkung zum Oedipus" (1804), in *Essays and Letters on Theory*, ed. and trans. T. Pfau (New York: University of New York Press, 1988), pp.101-109.
[194] BSW - Vol 1, pp.18-36.
[195] W. Benjamin, "Der Begriff der Kunstkritik in der deutschen Romantik" (1920) "The Concept of Criticism in German Romanticism", in BSW (vol. 1, 1996).
[196] Ibid pp. 100-101.
[197] F. Hölderlin, "Halfte des Lebens" (1803-1804) SPF, p. 171.
This is one of German poetry's most well-known poems, translated into Hebrew many times, among others, by Yaacov Fichman, S. Shalom, Leah Goldberg, and Pinchas Sadeh.

With its yellow pears

And wild roses everywhere

The shore hangs into the lake,

O gracious swans,

And drunk with kisses

You dip your heads

In the sobering holy water.

Ah, where will I find

Flowers, come winter,

And where the sunshine

And shade of the earth?

Walls stand cold

And speechless, in the wind

The weather vanes creak.[198]

The key concept for the issue appears at the end of the first stanza - "In the sobering holy water" ("Ins heilignüchterne Wasser"). The idea of sobriety, borrowed from Hölderlin, implanted itself in the early stages of Benjamin's writings. In his discussion on the idea of the 'figure', the central image of his thought, Benjamin defines the proper attitude as that of sobriety.[199] The sobriety discussed here contrasts with the perception of life connected to the cosmic forces of the earth, and the mythic descriptions and imagery expressing a perception of this kind.[200] In "Two Poems by Friedrich Hölderlin", the poet's attitude is depicted as a conflict between sobriety and metaphysical

---

[198] Ibid.
[199] W. Benjamin, "Passagen werk" (1927–40), in *The Arcades Project*, ed. R. Tiedemann (Cambridge: Harvard UP, 1999), pp.871-873.
[200] (Noor, 2009), p. 14.

pathos (Greek) poetry. In "The Origin of German Tragic Drama",[201] Benjamin sees a necessity for critical sobriety confronting the mythical that life seems to evoke.

According to LL one may say, in brief, that sobriety is the courage of poetry, or - the courage of poetry is prose, which to his mind does not exclude versification. This courage of poetry may be understood in two ways, according to LL. It may be a matter of subjective genitive, in other words - that courage is the courage of poetry for itself (in its insistence), and as the revealment of the poetic or the dictamen. Or it may be a matter of objective genitive, so that courage is the courage of poetry in its prophetic-angelic temporality, less than the poem itself and more than what the poem dictates as mission. As opposed to the ethical - the arche-ethical, the concept presented by LL, is ethics that does not know what good is.[202] The arche-ethical's commitment is such that one can barely uphold it. This is the incommensurable responsibility to tear itself away from the mimetic. LL writes that every time philosophy appeals to poetry, it takes responsibility, it is required to respond. Heidegger thinks that courage itself is the courage of history. Benjamin acknowledges the failure of the theological, and directs poetry to prose.

Poetry's courage is therefore the courage to leave the mythological, to extract itself from it, and to deconstruct it. This is the courage to invent and configure the poem as testimony. The future of poetry will actually be in prose, as the true saying of the poem about the poem.

The privileged-rights that Heidegger grants myth originate, according to LL in non-reflective ideology inherited from Romanticism, the configuration of the romantic impulse to create the polis as an enormous work of art, the urge to a magnum opus that finds its philosophical expression in Nietzsche, and which Heidegger, as well as the Nazis, inherited.[203]

Basically, LL's text also opposes Alain Badiou, whose essay "Manifesto for Philosophy" (1989)[204] Lacoue-Labarthe responded to, in texts confronting Heidegger's reading of Hölderlin with Walter Benjamin's reading.

In an essay attempting to make philosophy possible by taking another step toward announcing its end, Badiou expresses his concern over the saturation between philosophy and poetry, proposing a return to removing poetry from philosophy, as proposed by Plato,[205] and unsuturing philosophy from its poetic state (a step in itself totally counter to Heideggerian thought regarding the end of philosophy and the mission of the poets). LL refrains from a comprehensive negation of Badiou's claim, but rather points to a misunderstanding belonging to his entire project, to be found in the fact that the polemic of philosophy and poetry is a polemic constituting the origin of philosophy, so that it is actually not with poetry itself but rather with its ancient source of origin - myth. In other words, while Badiou believes that philosophy in the era of poets, which should be ended, has surrendered - at least from Nietzsche on - and woven itself into poetry, LL suggests that the history of philosophy has woven itself into myth, or to be more precise,

---

[201] W. Benjamín, "Ursprung des deutschen Trauerspiels" (1928).
[202] See: (Lacoue-Labarthe, 1999), pp.90-93, inspired by Jacques Lacan and the ethics of Psychoanalysis.
[203] See: (Lacoue-Labarthe, 2007), p.92.
[204] A. Badiou, "Manifeste pour la philosophie" (1989), in *Manifesto for Philosophy*, ed. N. Madarasz (Albany: New York UP, 1999).
[205] See: Plato, *"The Republic"* ("politeia"), trans. B. Jowett (New York: Cosimo, 2008).

into mytheme,206 and that this weaving entails implications for philosophy, poetry and politics that cannot be ignored. Kant's criticism of metaphysics that repeated Plato's refusal of the mytheme, also presented philosophy's anamnesis, that which was the reactionary basis of Schelling's call for a new mythology - "mythology of reason". According to LL, this romantic aspiration for a new religious mythology led to Heidegger's poetic thought, and inevitably to the Nazi politics of the 1930s.

According to LL, the Kantian criticism paved the way to another channel, one which circumvents the final destination of Romanticism. This is the channel prepared by Hölderlin, which meditates over the difference between the romantic enthusiasm of Greece, and the clear prosaic sobriety suiting the West; a channel that ultimately rejects any mythologization that leads to the project of immanent shaping of a community. In other words: Hölderlin suggests a path that configures the relation between poetry, politics and philosophy in a completely different way. Since Hölderlin's poetry is read by LL as refusing the typographic role with which Heidegger associates it, then Hölderlin - as far as LL is concerned, aspires to de-mythologization of poetry.207

LL finds, in his reading of both Adorno and Benjamin, interpretations working against Heidegger's mythology project. Both characterize a prosaic trend in Hölderlin, namely - a sober style which Heidegger not innocently ignores, according to LL's opinion. This sobriety works against the epistemological role that Heidegger relates to myth, and appears as a failure of poetry to propose a mythological image or type in order for a nation to create its history. Hence, Hölderlin's poetry is described as prosaic, in that way which Heidegger rejects.

Thus Benjamin's analysis is proposed, and his reading - as opposed to Heidegger's. A comparison of their readings, in relation to Hölderlin's perception of the poet's courage, shows that while Heidegger reads Hölderlin as prodding the Germans to bravely enter a new mythology, Benjamin reads him as calling for courage to leave the mythological behind. The courage that Hölderlin presents is the courage to remain sober and reserved in face of the romantic enthusiasm over new mythology. Benjamin, in continuation of this approach, wishes - according to Labarthe - to conduct literalization of the mythologeme, "thereby saving both philosophy and poetry from the epistemological and political threat of the mytheme". Hence, Hölderlin's poetry is described as lacking authority, since it is not the god who dictates poetry but rather his failure.208

If we wish to locate Jean-Luc Nancy's readings of Hölderlin209 within the comprehensive framework of his thought, it is initially best to state that Nancy's discussion is based, first and foremost, on the attempt to reject the submission of art to any type of unequivocal meaning and sense. The 'image', the concept upon which Nancy bases his analysis, and which in his opinion embodies unshackled liberty,210 is the testimony and evidence to the existence

---

[206] See: C .Lévi-Strauss, "La Structure des mythes" (1958), in *Anthropologie Structurale* (Paris: Plon. 1958), pp. 227–255.
[207] (Lacoue-Labarthe, 1999), pp. 74-93.
[208] Ibid.
[209] (Nancy, 1999), pp. 44-73.
[210] J. L Nancy, *The Ground of the Image*, trans. J. Forth (New York: Fordham UP, 2005), pp.1-15.

of complete liberty. In this sense, Nancy's step exceeds terminal positions, such as Derrida's, which bind together the death of god with the end of philosophy and art, as does Jean Baudrillard's highly influential Simulacra model, based on the principle of the non-realization of the images. Contrary to the latter two, Nancy expresses unreserved faith in the everlasting vitality power of the image, and of the 'complete' and open sense uttered through it. This eternal vitality is inherent in the autonomous distinct language of the image, a language that is neither religious, nor philosophical. This is a 'power' that assumes configurations, which are not forms but rather the entering and empowering of energy and violence within themselves, within the image, turning - according to Nancy, to a total, radical intimacy.[211]

Following Heidegger's 'Dichtung', and Hölderlin's 'holy sobriety', Nancy thinks as well that poetry reveals the logic of Ontos of being that the gods left behind in their withdrawal; "Ontology is determined as writing".[212] The poet's mission, described in his essay dealing with Hölderlin, is beyond all - calculation. This concept relates to the action and decision the poet takes before turning to the disposition of the poem, whereby these action and decision inscribe only the consequence.[213] Hölderlin's poetry thus becomes, in his opinion, something other than poetic art, something other than literary and aesthetic theory. Nevertheless, there is also place in this poetry for ars-poetica, the technique of composition, and for the one who is its technician. Poetry is something different from poetry and also different from thought, hence poetry is precisely the double restriction on itself: the poet and his calculation.

Nancy adds that, for Hölderlin, there is no special interest in the poems themselves[214] - the poet seems to have the tendency to abandon them, leave them to themselves and to the particular monotony of their flow, without wishing reconciliation with them. However, in his theoretical mission, or 'theological' as Nancy calls it, Hölderlin makes an effort, pulls, begins again, and largely dries up. Everything pursues a precision that conceals itself as demands are put forth. Sometimes, adds Nancy, one detects in Hölderlin a shortness of breath when he searches for a dialectic and speculative structure, as opposed to his two philosopher friends - Schelling and Hegel - with whom he shared a post-Kantian ideal of 'system'. One sees in Hölderlin a quasi awkwardness and impasse in the philosophical path, especially since he does not pose a solely philosophical question, but rather poses a question regarding the possible existence of a different way to approaching questions in general.

The poet, writes Nancy, must touch something other than synthetic unity. He should touch the absolute point of exactitude, which is more a mission of calculation than construction, production or giving birth. He must touch this point, or settle in it, or place it opposite him. This is a different matter than assembling the elements in articulative

---

[211] See: B.C. Hutchens, *Jean-Luc Nancy and the Future of Philosophy* (Montreal & Kingston: McGill-Queen's UP, 2005). Sparks, Simon, ed. *On Jean-Luc Nancy: The Sense of Philosophy* (London: Routledge, 1997).
[212] J.L. Nancy, *Corpus*, trans. R. A. Rand (New York: Fordham UP, 2008), p. c-17.
[213] This matter brings to mind Heidegger's concept of 'decisive action' ('Handeln') by which man realizes his potential.
[214] (Nancy, 2000), pp. 44-45.

totality. The point eludes assembling. The object of the philosopher is synthesis; the project of the poet is synopsis. The former intends operation, while the latter - apprehension.215

According to Nancy, the Hölderlinian poet is characterized then by the constant precision of the consciousness, through which the poet looks at the 'whole'. The poet has a consciousness that is constant, absolute, perfect, and united, with no residue; it conceals nothing and gives itself completely to the look, which acts not as intention but rather as opening. Obviously, this is not what the philosopher understands as consciousness. The look is directed or turned on ('blick auf') ahead of and outside of the self, it falls on the whole. The totality of this whole, therefore, is touched beyond and outside of any composition or synthesis, in the center, the heart, the connection that is not totalized but is rather the whole. This is, as Nancy calls it: Being complete with the whole that is seen directly and perfectly. This is not the concept, but the figure, and the existence of the whole. The whole reveals itself as the whole. The whole shows itself to the look by a look that is focused precisely to it - for and by the look, which ultimately, is only the whole itself showing itself. The poet is the clearly present whole, he is unquestionable, and the punctual presence of the whole. He is the act that calculates precisely the immediate moment, the transient passing thrust of the presence of the whole; the act that leaves nothing outside, neither the background of the intention nor of the thing itself, but rather the thing itself in the presence of the look, in itself, clarity itself, its precise calculation.

The poet then is not the 'subject' of the representation of the whole, but the place of envisaging in the whole in persona. Hölderlin calls it 'the pure' or 'pure (poetic) individuality'.216 This is pure coincidence of the identical and the different, the human and the divine; coincidence in which the look sees the thing and is concerned about it, only to the extent that it itself becomes. The appearance of the thing is therefore 'exactitude', and is itself pure coincidence. The concepts of 'conciseness' and 'sobriety', central to Hölderlin, do not indicate, according to Nancy's method, anything but this. The matter is less connected to the economics of means, and more to an extreme exactitude of end. We are actually a dialogue; discourse; talking together or with each other ('gesprach'), or better still 'together-talking'. This does not mean that we are in dialogue, but rather that we are our dialogue. We, all of us, the speakers, are defined by the speaking among themselves; we are the 'among ourselves' that is language. And by the same token, language is the 'among ourselves'.217 Calculation, for Nancy, contains consistence of the exact focusing on this being, and nothing else. While the philosopher is free to gloss the 'between', for the poet it is important that the thing is expressed directly outward to the point, in other words, directly to the origin. The poet says 'we', hence speaking for us, in our names, to us and instead of us. 'We', writes Nancy, is what we learn from each other in our discourse itself, every time calculating that which cannot be calculated.

The poetics of calculation, or exactitude, is hence the thought of originary difference of thought itself. It must be understood as the difference itself in primordial thought, as poetry. If thought in general, namely that which

---

[215] Ibid, pp. 46-48.
[216] Ibid, p 46.
[217] (Nancy, 2000), pp. 49-50.

philosophy represents for us, is perceived as ultimate appropriation of the thing; the absorption of the object in the subject, so that the subject itself constitutes the principle of structure of self appropriation of the object. If thought is perceived as raising what is called the 'thing-in- itself' to the status and envisaging of an ideal, also with regard to Hölderlin, then poetics, namely the thought of poetics, or more precisely, the thought about poetic thought, is understood here as other than thought, as non-idealism itself. This is not the poetry that should respond, as with Hegel, to demand - coming into presence is not re-presentation. The movement of the spiritual outward is not its manifesto, but rather, it is its opposing exposition.

Hölderlin is undoubtedly equally involved in the dialectic process of opposites' reconciliation. But nowhere, claims Nancy, is the reconciliation of opposites presented in its proper sense. This leads to complexity, even complication of analysis that Hölderlin attempts to develop, namely: on the procedure of poetic spirit.

According to Nancy, Hölderlin may be heard in the terrifying tone of the Third Reich, but one may also hear the tone of exact and simple measurement, a measurement enabling the tone to be discerned beyond, in non-discernment of manner. This is the question of Germany, claims Nancy; for Hölderlin nothing is given. Even that which he calls 'Germany' is always foreign.[218]

The meaning of the poem unites the extremities by placing, organizing them side by side, bringing them into contact with one another. The contact, says Nancy, is not confusion but the reverse, not a matter of contradiction but of contrariness. Both sides do not exclude each other, and can be false at the same time. One is not negation of the other, nor is the other the manifestation of the one; however, by virtue of their contrast, they touch each other, and the points of contact are the points of the one, as well as the envisaging spectator. The spirit, according to Hölderlin, equalizes all the contrasts, since the poetic meaning disjoins them. In other words: poetic meaning cannot be content of particular meaning. It still needs to distinguish itself from itself. It must be posed and opposed between meaning and the outer impenetrable point - where the content is. In this way, through the poetic cadence, there can be immediate instantaneous understanding, which is also outside understanding. This is not non-understanding, but rather 'love' of the outside that must be touched with 'kairos', by holding and releasing the one. The totality is touched at its point of totality; at its point of unity - 'touched' meaning it is neither penetrated nor embraced or sublimated. To touch does not mean to sublet the difference between the toucher and the touched, but the opposite - to let go of the difference as such in its tension.

'Measurement' is therefore a word and motif in which Hölderlin's thought and poetry intersect. Since this is thought about measurement, it must be poetic. In order to think, it must touch its poetic exterior. Measurement neither restricts nor balances. Hölderlin's measurement is exact since it measures the divergence through which the whole and the unity are possible as whole and as unity. However, the poetics of contact also necessitates a distance, which is the

---

[218] Ibid.

element of touch. The toucher is discerned from the touched - touch is either discreet or it is nothing. One may feel only through the distance of the concurrence. This is not imitation, of the spring, nature, or reality, but rather a touch of the language. Man measures with his foot, while the poet does not maintain this limited measurement of man. The unity is measured in relation to absolute greatness, the place where the existing shows itself and slips at the same time. The poet's speech is truth, not in the sense of whatever he says or claims, but through the measurement, which is a sensitive and exact remnant of the passing of the gods; the passing - which is the gods. The god, therefore, is only the place; the place of departing and returning, of the withdrawing coming that creates the sense. Poetry is the material calculation of the atheist passing. What man measures, writes Nancy, is the incommensurable manifestation of the divine; it is neither sensual manifestation of an object, nor is it intelligible manifestation of an ideal, or self-manifestation of a subject. It is different from all three forms of manifestation, or perhaps all three together.

The heavens are the place of the manifestation, or the manifestation of the place - the divine place, because the divine is the exact manifestation of the place, any place.219 Place is locality; the separation and discretion of the passing, the place where coming to the presence occurs of necessity. If on these conditions there is no 'measure on earth' that is because any measurement is heavenly. The withdrawal of the gods; the passing of the sense, that too is what needs measuring, and against it to measure ourselves. The unity of measurement and its instrument are the poet.

Nancy's discussion on the mission of the poet may be seen as an ontological discussion, connected to the issue of the reality and self-realization of the image. To negate meaning or any role of art, and actually, of the image, which is the primordial entity, Nancy formulates the concepts of his discussion, through that which is defined in logic as 'infinite sentences'. These are negative sentences that construct a complex process of thinking, negating the determination of relation between subject and predicate. In Nancy's discussion, the purpose of the infinite sentences is to negate the determination of any relation between the image and the real object, religious or any other. Tracing this train of thought should yield the insight negating any possibility of seeing in the image a representation of any object.

The total lack of any relation between the image and the 'thing-in-itself', and between the image and object, and indeed, between the image and any representation - is the distinction of the image, and is that which defines it as 'the distinct'. Nancy's discussion is not written as an analytical step, cutting and defining conceptually and unequivocally 'what is an image', or 'what is the distinction of the image'. It is a poetic philosophical discussion, opaque, arbitrary and convoluted. At its base lies the arbitrary and blatant statement claiming to the absolute distinction of the image. Nancy does not explain or prove this statement. His discussion, derived from this prior assumption, is intended to describe this distinction. This is a description that turns the 'distinct-image' not into a concept, but rather into a sensual conscious actuality. The point of departure is arbitrary, also in the sense that it aspires to be a quasi pre-given instruction, unproven - and it determines that the image is sanctified, since both the sanctified and the image represent the distinction from any connection to anything at all. This arbitrary distinction is the embodiment of autonomy and of

---

[219] This matter relates to the concept of 'makom' ('place' in Hebrew), and its status in Jewish tradition as the name of god: "Why shall we call His name place - as He is the place of the world, and not that the world is His place" (Genesis, 68,1).

intimacy. It is the evidence for their existence. Nancy's discussion seeks the nearing of the reader to what he considers a kind of holiness, forever embodying only itself, and realized in the image, in its distinction, which always embodies only itself. This selfness contains 'heavens' within itself, but these are 'the heavens of the artists', and of the image, which are not 'the heavens of religion'.220

The image and the work of art are perceived as liberated, as free. The freedom of the image also includes an ethical possibility, as it directs us to see that which is shackled in the world of phenomena; that which has been deprived of its freedom and absolute selfness. It enables us to notice the other whose privacy, intimacy and truth have been violated and plundered.221

Nancy's discussion, then, raises the question of the connection between the work of art and the ethical deed. The point of departure of this question is found in the theoretical revolt that occurred in the history of art that wished to destroy the institutional and spiritual tyranny of religion. This revolution required conceptualization of a new ethical foundation, autonomous, humanistic, liberated from the hold of theology and bureaucracy. Art - perceived and presented as the embodiment of freedom of the human spirit, was required to serve as a support, and as a new and anti-dogmatic source. The thinkers of enlightenment, in their desire for total rationalization, demanded of ethics as well to become a totally rational area. That demand was turned to art too, through its connection to ethics. Nancy, so it seems, retreated from this approach, which through reduction identifies art with ethics. In his opinion, the image is trapped both by the artist and by the spectator through a conscious and physical uniting step, a creative process of a special kind of mystics - neither Dionysian nor religious. This is mystics in a phenomenological sense, whose meaning is the aspiring to a uniting and plentiful sense of the object of consciousness. This sense is not explicable 'meaning'. Nancy describes this non-conceptual understanding as 'achieving the whole', as the unification with the whole expressed in the image. He employs a way of philosophizing that rejects, then, both the ethical rationalization of art, and Hegel's method which assumes the elimination of the difference in the spirit's dialectic step in history. His discussion on the 'image-distinct' actually claims to an eternal existence of the difference. The image as a work of art expresses, to his mind, autonomous intimacy, which may be 'mixed with truth' and indicate it, but is not identical to it, since art's ontic self-nature is the constant eluding of closed meaning; elusion that contains considerable dangers and ethical threat. By placing the image as a distinct material ever-changing reality, Nancy re-constitutes the reality of 'good' as a principle expressed and conveyed through images, rejecting the principle of 'evil', which motivates the eternal return of the alike. The 'good' is the harmony embodied in the images, harmony described as agreement or an erotic alliance between the alike and the different. The spectator is invited to this intimate harmony of the image, in Nancy's words, to 'enter'. This entrance, it seems to me, enables a special look at the concealed private chamber where the images are

---

[220] See: S. Salhov, "That could not be Chained: Following J.L..Nancy: L'image - le distinct" (Hebrew), *Studio Art Magazine* 118 (February 2001).
[221] Ibid.

thought up and created as a living entity, consoling, whose language is so complex, completely unique, that it cannot be exhausted, only infinitely debated.

In two essays on Hölderlin: "Madness par Excellence"[222] and "The Sacred Speech of Hölderlin",[223] Maurice Blanchot forms the first version of his perception of speech, poetry and writing, a perception later presented extensively in his central work "The Space of Literature",[224] which demonstrates how much it was influenced by the religious and mythical representations in Hölderlin's poetry. Blanchot's critical essays conduct an elusive tension between examination of a particular text, and free reflection on literature. This typical duality appears in his readings of Hölderlin, Mallarmé and Kafka, about whom he wrote, returning again to them. His critical examination dealt with the question about the way literature appears as motivation and theme for the particular writer. Hölderlin is the preferred source for Blanchot, as he states in the opening pages of "The Sacred Speech of Hölderlin". The reason given for this preference is that Hölderlin's poetry wrestles with the very question of the meaning of the existence of the poem.[225]

The reading characterizing Blanchot differs considerably from that accepted in literary criticism, as it does not seek to justify its interpretation through claims and evidence elicited from the text, nor does it examine possible alternative readings or clarify vague portions. In addition, his reading is not precise in its distinction between various poems, and does not relate to notes of others, except for Heidegger. This genre does not seek to contribute knowledge about Hölderlin's poetry or to corroborate a statement through textual facts. Conversely, it is a step motivating the text through its figural and narrative means, while focusing on the basic question, namely: What is the meaning of the fact that the poem exists? This interpretation settles into Hölderlin's poetry, and develops motifs and latent themes.[226]

One such motif is the dramatic figure of expectation recurring in many of his poems. This figure appears as an establishing principle in "The Archipelago"[227], which sings the story of the rise and fall of the ancient Greek civilization. The Greek isles are described as in a state of deterioration, bereft of the praise and honor granted by the temples and songs of the past, and as result, the imminent return is announced, of the spirit of nature and awakening of man's soul, in the image of a riddle-vision largely concentrated on anticipation of festival-day ('Festtag'), indicating the renewed connection between man and divinity. The attitude in the poem is identified as metaphysical insight and mood of expectation, which at the same time also hints to the withdrawal from the existing order of things. In "To the Germans",[228] the poet describes wandering in the country, with the feeling of being present in a workshop of the creative spirit, awareness of something happening, and yet inability to say precisely what, a situation divided between

---

[222] M. Blanchot, "La folie par excellence" (7997), *Critique 45* (February 1951), pp. 99-118. Revised version as preface, in K. Jaspers, *Strindberg and Van Gogh*, trans. O. Grunow & D. Woloshin (Tucson: Arizona UP, 1982).
[223] M. Blanchot, "Hölderlin et la parole sacrée" (1946), in *The Work of Fire (La Part du Feu)*, trans. C.Mandel (Stanford: Stanford UP, 1995), pp. 111-131.
[224] M. Blanchot, "L'Espace litteraire"(1955), trans. A. Smock (Lincoln: Nebraska UP, 1989).
[225] See: M. Hewson, "Two Essays by Blanchot on Hölderlin", *COLLOQUY text theory critique 10* (November 2005).
[226] Ibid.
[227] F. Hölderlin, "Der Archipelagus" (1800-1801) SPF, pp.111-126.
[228] F. Hölderlin "An die Deutschen" (1800). SPF p.15-45

the joy that the sign of change brings, and the conflict with impatience and doubt. The poet looks ahead to the moment when doubt is silenced before the heavenly day (or heavenly light), but remains bereaved in view of the cold winter of his times. He no longer knows or recognizes his contemporaries, nor does he find the community he envisions. For Blanchot this paragraph reveals confirmation of poetic existence, existing of necessity en attente, in constant expectation (attention) to that which is to come. The poet is to exist as attention to himself; as the future of his very existence. He is 'not yet', but he must be 'already' - as he is to be. The 'not yet' structures the essence of the poet's bereavement, his distress and his joy. 'Ich harrte, ich harrte' - this repeated word, according to Blanchot, expresses the suffering and futility of attention, as the word 'ahnen' indicates value and potential. The loneliness of the poet appears as anticipation.

In a representing and direct sense - expectation is projection in the imagination onto a state of affairs that is not yet given, or that is considered possible to come, independently of the imagining subject. Nevertheless, in Blanchot's proposed interpretation of Hölderlin, the projection of the human desire or the wish for a change of its meaning becomes a reaction to something already there, but that has not yet reached clarity; that does not have the necessary strength for existence, and needs the attention of the poet in order to show itself. The true sense is in the chosen relation between the poet and the previous potential power, appearing in Hölderlin as nature, or spirit (Geist), or the holy. Poetry then appears as prophetic mission created not only by its linguistic conventions, but in terms of the gods that grant or refuse to appear. The noumenal presence to which the poet dedicates himself is interpreted through the metaphor of 'the day' (le jour, der tag), which enables Blanchot to present his motif about 'the beginning of light' appearing in several of his texts and in similar senses, evoking a certain kind of Anamnesis, whereby that which is remembered is the point of origin from which everyone goes his way. The remembrance at the beginning, which was forgotten, becomes the basis for expectation directed and operated toward the return in the future, as the dawn of a new era.[229]

The poet's mission then is to awaken the people to the transformation of their time, just as Dionysus awoke his ancient people when he brought the holy wine.[230] The poet is the one who discerns the first signs, and flies like an eagle before the storm to announce the progression of the coming gods. The mission of the poet and the poem is to turn the thing into explicit: to bring it from concealment to light, and to thereby let a new beginning be realized. The first light, describes Blanchot, is the darkest of all; the abyss of the light. This light represents the beginning of the poem, the condition and the chaotic stage of the pale night (helle Nacht) before the morning, when the dwellers of the valley are still in darkness, although the light has begun to shine on the Alpine tops. The poem has its parallel in the bird of storm who knows that the time has come, and calls the day to enforce itself.

In Blanchot's interpretation, poetry is connected to a basic impossibility; to a contradiction pulsating in the heart of poetic existence, and the rhetoric of the essay is characterized by constant production of contradiction. At the end of

---

[229] (Hewson, 2005), p. 229.
[230] F. Hölderlin, "Dichter-beruf" (1800-1801) in SPF, pp.79.

Hermeneutical Cartography of Myth

Blanchot's text, perhaps influenced by Hölderlin's mythical tone, this duality becomes prominent when counter to what was said up to then about poetry as an impossible mission, permission is suddenly granted to the poem to be as an expression of holiness. The poem can now inhabit realization, on condition that one overcomes the poet's existence as a particular individual through his disappearance.[231]

This train of thought, seeming to hint at the drama "The Death of Empedocles"[232] and at Hölderlin's personal life story, is mentioned only in the last paragraph of "The Sacred Speech of Hölderlin"[233] but moves to center stage when Blanchot returns to read Hölderlin in "Madness par Excellence",[234] in a survey of Karl Jaspers' work on the psychology of the poetic work, and the conditions between madness and literature. In the second part of the essay, Blanchot returns to deal with Hölderlin's poetics, through a discussion on "Bread and Wine",[235] which he also identifies as an examination on the nature of poetry, an examination leading from the poet's perception as 'nature' and as 'whole', to a religious and philosophical-historical approach. The historical time of the most modern of Hölderlin's great poems is the time of the gods' absence. The question asked then is: "Who wants poets at all in lean years?"[236], a time when the divinity, announced and celebrated by poetry in the past, has abandoned man's world. The poet bears-suffers the conditions of futility, enforced idleness, nothing to do but wait in his loneliness.[237] Again one sees the poem, in the discussion, as an attempt to deal with the nature of poetry, and again the 'attention' of the poetic condition appears; the concept of 'attention' appears as 'désoeuvrement'.[238] This is the empty time, writes Blanchot, the time of error, when we are aimless, when the certainty of the present and the real here is missing.[239] It is not the case that man can at any time bear the presence of the gods. The misleading night is what assists in going beyond the error. In the negative there is also the sense that indicates the constancy of the relation to truth, and the divine certainty of presence, even when it is absent.[240]

Hence, the work of poetry is done in the endurance and the accomplishment of error, a step proposed in "Bread and Wine" through comparison of the poet to the Dionysian priests moving from their place in the holy night. There is, then, a contradiction between the holy as incommunicable on one hand, and language as constant and defined, on the other. The poet cannot communicate that which is incommunicable, but poetry can be a work of mediation between the divine and human worlds. Mediation symbolizes not only the Promethean step, namely - the betraying of the gods in favor of man, which is valid as a poem, but also - the holy depends on the poet in order to be; to come to itself. The mission of poetry is described as movement from transparency (of the gods residing above the light) to the daylight, or as movement from excess to measure. The fulfillment of the mission demands the sacrifice of worldliness of the poet,

---

[231] (Hewson, 2005), pp. 229-230.
[232] F. Hölderlin, "Der Tod des Empedokles" (1798), trans. D. F. Krell (New York: SUNY, 2008).
[233] (Blanchot, 1946), pp. 111-131.
[234] (Blanchot, 7997).
[235] F.Hölderlin, "Brot und Wein" (1801-1800), in SPF , p. 151.
[236] "Wozu Dichter in dürftiger Zeit?", ibid, stanza 7.
[237] (Hewson, 2005), pp. 291-224.
[238] Ibid, an ambiguous French word connoting a state of idleness or disuse, perhaps most idiomatically translated as ' inertia'.
[239] (Blanchot, 1951), pp. 113.
[240] Ibid, pp. 113-114.

the sacrifice of his particular individual existence. This necessity binds the poet to the sacrifice. The poet sacrifices himself as part of the message.[241]

In his thought about the possible existence of poetry, Blanchot - as does Hölderlin -reaches a perception of poetry as metaphysical activity. Thus his theoretical discourse intertwines with poetics that defines itself in relation to a transcendental point, or a point of authority, and is immersed in heavenly spheres, which only poetry can give meaning and reality. On the other hand, the possibility is preserved too for poetry that is authentic in the dimension it finds itself, and loses itself into the night, into the infinity of the error preceding the primordial announced in the poem. Modern poetry provides criticism with an alternative: It may either remain in the discursive field of research where the question of the origin, or the transcendent, is barricaded and invalid a-priori except for representation of historical experience, or it may persist in the metaphysical field of poetry, interpreted poetically with no reduction to representations. Blanchot, it would seem, has decided to choose the second alternative.[242]

Avital Ronell, in her examination of stupidity, suggests that the poetic act includes self emptying and that the poet "yields entirely, giving in to sheer relatedness".[243] The poet's courage is then expressed in giving up any topological system of security, even of the figurative shield of the "I". This courage consists of taking a step toward pure exposure, toward "pure indifference", which is the untouchable center of all relations. Hence, the poet is not a figure, but rather the principle of a figure, transcendental stupidity located at the life source of the world.[244]

The poets, claims Ronell, know the stupidity, the dimming or weakening that creates the precondition for expression. Perhaps that is why Hölderlin's two poems "Dichtermut" and "Blödigkeit" appear together. The titles of these poems have long been a challenge for translators. Ronell perceives the concept of 'Dichtermut' in its accepted translation of "The Poet's Courage", while - with regard to the translation and interpretation of 'Blödigkeit', she emphasizes the dimension of stupidity inherent in it, a sense that she believes the tradition of translation and philosophical interpretation have sought to understate.

Ronell discerns an enigmatic connection between the poet's courage and the panic-stricken spirit, which is one of the faces of stupidity. In her opinion, a troubling mood pervades the poems, each of them a distorted reflection of the other. As if due to some transcendental commitment, the most meticulous of poets dares to enter the holy domain where language stupidly meets its annulment. Poetic language remains a pure promise, and - as Hölderlin has shown us - it has the power to hear the unsaid; the foreign. When Hölderlin welds "Dichtermut" to "Blodigkeit", awkwardness gives up the heroic-coded mythemes and ultimately discovers the blunted bruised entity of the poet about to carry out the mission assigned him.[245]

---

[241] Ibid, p.116.
[242] (Hewson, 2005), p. 291.
[243] A. Ronell, *Stupidity* (Urbana: Illinois UP, 2002), p. 13.
[244] Ibid, p.14.
[245] Ibid.

Hence, poetic courage according to Ronell is based on the terrible adoption of weakness of the addling brain. The readings and translations, to which Hölderlin's ode "Blödigkeit" gave rise, tended to erase the embarrassing openness with which the poet calls out the name of stupidity, even if it can be restored. This seems to be Hölderlin's way of duplicating Pindaric respect - the meaning the Greeks gave the feeling of respect which overwhelms man - into the Modern era.

According to Walter Benjamin's reading, the troubling moment in the semantic chain is skipped over, so that Benjamin may claim that "Blödigkeit" represents the overcoming of "the poet's courage". Nevertheless, the power of the unread title has a place in Benjamin's interpretation which, according to Ronell, uses extraordinary syntax of subjugation in employing the passive form. This asceticism, this absolute employment of the passive activates the reading that Benjamin and others had avoided, and which may be called 'the disinheritance', which while rewarding and weakening the writer, liberates and trips the knowing subject who comes into contact with the poetic word. The passive voice, as described by Ronell, writes a secret agreement with the title regarding unexplained passivity that it seeks to elude.

We may say with Hölderlin, claims Ronell, that stupidity by nature causes embarrassment. It weakens and deters, while at the same time also liberating. In this respect, she suggests, the poem "Blödigkeit" should not be seen as contrasting to "Dichtermut", but rather as one that clearly emphasizes a reading of poetic courage, perhaps as one who offers another way of calling the holy mission bestowed on the poet.[246]

Hence, Hölderlin - according to Ronell, presents stupidity as a vital poetic sign, basing it on simplicity and weakness, as exemplary self-forgetfulness opening the selfness to another kind of entity. The special reverberation of "Blödigkeit" as something encouraging liberation connects to Rousseau, for whom pareses, and even certain stupidity serve as preconditions to creating connection with the entity; the admired poetic touch, according to Ronell, with corrections and changes that Hölderlin made between the versions. The poem, described as quasi seduction, largely Dichtermut, invites the poetic spirit to dare go out to the time and the world, to let itself remain held in the hands of the god of the heavens, as children held in golden reins. Dealing with the poet's courage, the poem opens with a question mentioning his being part of all life. The later version of "Blödigkeit" opens with the question of the living being known or familiar (bekannt). The initial reading as a question of connection or of closeness and knowledge places the poetic tendency in relation to the living. The poet, or more precisely the poem, is subjugated to passing time. The poet is overcome by the thing that tied his child's soul to reins, bound by golden shackles. The command of restriction of Blödigkeit, as seen by Benjamin and apparently followed by Ronell, becomes the authentic tendency of the poet.

The poet's touch places him in the midst of life, among the living. This placement, however, disrobes the poet, who is left without anything, without a core, with no boundary except for a shapeless entity, totally passive. This kind of self-emptying, according to Benjamin, is the essence of courage, the ability of total surrender. 'Ability', as Ronell

---

[246] Ibid, p.13.

further defines, perhaps continues to maintain an element of cognition. The poet, however, surrenders totally, she emphasizes, giving himself to complete connection. The connection begins and ends in the poet, or better still, in the poem, since by virtue of this extreme tendency to surrender, the poet and poem do not separate again from one another.

The poet (poem) is but the boundary placed to life, pure indifference, the core of all the relations that nothing has touched. The poet, as described by Ronell, is not a figure but rather a principle of figuration. The poet that peeps out from under Blödigkeit is a suspension, caesura;[247] a core that is dead and mute with no center, poetic courage based on taking the first step toward this appearance - a step that is pure exposure.

If the poet is presented as one who was seduced by transience, in that it promised him a passing, then this, among other reasons, is due to the fact that the first withdrawal the poem mentions, while it beseeches, invites, pushes toward life - actually begins without life. The extreme passivity, the threshold of freezing of the senses that characterizes the poetic tendency, places this tendency in dangerous proximity to the emptying side, and even death. This is the reason why the poet is to be awakened and ignited by a promise that is but misleading:

"Therefore, Wander defenseless, Through life and fear nothing" ("Dichtermut"); or: *"So then, my genius, just step up boldly into life without care!"* ("Blödigkeit").[248]

The poetic spirit is invited to come to life with no protection or concern, naked, to the sound of war-beating drums, or following a command that comes from another place of selfness. In the second version, the torn poet himself turns to the spirit or genius existing in Blödigkeit. The poet dares to proceed without protection, courageous, states Ronell, as "The Idiot Boy" by William Wordsworth. It is there, while he is inexplicably immune and protected, that the greatest danger lurks.

The gesture of crossing the dangerous area and taking the risk does not indicate, to Ronell's method, a morpheme of a purposeful action hero, ready for his mission, but rather an impoverished entity delaying through panic or indifference (we never know which of the two), an entity that from the beginning is awe-stricken, not really present, not really there.

---

[247] A term originating from music - a pause in the continuum, sharp break, after which there is a continuation. In music, it refers to the silence between the sounds which is part of the melody: a pause, or natural break that is part of the flow of the music.
[248] F. Hölderlin, *Odes and Elegies: Bilingual German-English*, ed. and trans. N. Hoff (Middletown: Wesleyan UP, 2008).

3.4 "Who Needs Poets in Lean Years?"

The map of the interpretational discourse of Hölderlin's poetry, shown by this chapter's discussion, proposes then two main interpretational trends, each presenting a different response regarding the possible mission of the poet in a world in crisis, bereft of divinity. From the various readings and view points, it turns out that the question of the paradoxical existence of myth, in an era that does not recognize its transcendental origin, is a central motif of the controversy of the interpretational arena. The mapping of the outlines of the controversy shows a hermeneutical cartography organized between two polar positions or opposing interpretational trends, which may be called 're-mythologization' on the one hand, and 'de-mythologization', on the other.

The 're-mythologization' pole is indicated in Heidegger's reading, which presents Hölderlin's poetry as the embodiment of the ideal of poetry, bearing a constituting quality, as it opens an aperture to the appearance of being. The poet appears as one who exists within the rift of the concealed face of the gods; one who still converses with them and announces their absence/return. The poet then is a 'demigod', preserving the divine fire for man, and the one who delivers to him the onto-theological plenty, thereby granting him a place in the world. This approach sides with myth, seeing in it an essential element of meaning and history. In this context, the poet is perceived as a hero of his culture, who also prods his people as a prophet, to courageously enter a new mythology.

As opposed to this trend, and as its dialectic contrast, the second interpretational direction of 'de-mythologization' is presented by Benjamin and his followers. This approach, in the spirit of Lacoue-Labarthe reading Benjamin on his reading of Hölderlin - the favored approach in current literary research, and supported by the readings of Jean-Luc Nancy and Avital Ronell, emphasizes the poet's status as a failing prophet, and his mission - as the abandonment of myth, and generally, any 'mission'. The courage that Hölderlin presents, according to this interpretation, is the courage to be sober in face of romantic enthusiasm over a new mythology. Hölderlin's poetry is perceived as expressing the divesting of the poem of its mythical authority. In its absence, the poet's state is described as that of non-mission and non-action; a state of attention and infinite openness, a position of 'stupidity' and of total surrender to relations. Hence, and following Benjamin, poetry will also be that which disintegrates itself in its movement toward prose.

The image of the poet, the nature of his mission and his fate turn out to be, in this chapter, a response that Hölderlin's poetry presents in face of the crisis that gave rise to it, and which it identified early on. However, it seems that each of the two poles, which established possible interpretational alternatives to the perception of the poet's image, is problematic in itself, and insufficient.

On the one hand - there is the re-mythologization interpretation, presented here by Heidegger, which sees the poet as a prophet who preserves and revives, with his language, the people's contact with its withdrawing origin. The poet's fate is that of a martyr: Exposed to the danger of the divine plenty, the poet restores his people to history, until he is overwhelmed, stricken by madness. The weakness of this approach is in its actually embodying (as described by Benjamin) a 'romantic' yearning to the 'absolute', and as such entails the choice dangers of myth - its subjugating power; its latent survivability (also in seemingly secular institutions of society); and its non-arbitrary historical tendency (as described by Lacoue-Labarthe) to become realized as 'political theology'.

On the other hand - the de-mythologization approach, represented by Benjamin and supported, as mentioned, by the readings of Adorno, Nancy and Ronell, declares itself as the position of 'sobriety', in face of myth.

This sobriety is stretched into an effort of purification from myth, disintegration of the hymn, and liberation of poetry from its shackles and messages, in favor of attention and complete openness. This approach actually internalizes Benjamin's perception of his contemporary reality (as Benjamin also interpreted Hölderlin's approach to his times), as the being of 'fall' to a damaged reality where language, already lacking the mythic dimension, is in exile from the world. It seems that the weakness of this approach is in its tendency to quickly transform into a state of melancholy (a matter not at all foreign to Benjamin), as a pathological reaction to loss, appearing as a principled refusal of any alternate object. This approach of 'sobriety' entails the empowerment of passivity which neutralizes possibilities of action, and leaves unanswered the question of the transition from it to politics of justice. Hence, while it wishes to be free of myth (and it is not clear that this is at all possible), it turns out that the same known Cartesian meditation is reverberating, which in its striving to the reasoned element of consciousness, seeks to purify and shed itself of any prejudice. Thus it seems that the de-mythologization approach is in danger of falling into the temptation of an 'absolute' of another kind.

In view of the cartography of the interpretational discourse of Hölderlin's poetry, organized in a dichotomy between supporters of myth and its opponents, it seems that the discussion at this stage requires two directions of examination. One direction touches upon the concept of 'myth' itself, which needs to be deepened, placing the interpretational-dialectic controversy in relation to it in a historical context. The second deals with the examination of the place and status of 'myth' in Bialik's poetry.

These things never happened, but always are.

(Sallustius: On the Gods and the World)[249]

Behind speculation, and beneath gnosis and anti-gnosis constructions, we find myth.

(Paul Ricoeur, Symbolism of Evil)[250]

4. On Myth and Paradox

Myth (from Greek 'muthos') is a folk story. Inherent in the meaning of the original word is the dimension of speech, the oral dimension. The most general definition accepted in research sees myth as a holy story about the gods, expressing that which the abstract word (logos) cannot,[251] speech sanctified by history, and whose sanctity influences life; or as defined by Plato: Myth is the story of the divine occurrence in the tangible reality.[252] The Greek myths describe the relations of the gods among themselves, and between themselves and men. The heroes of the myths of ancient world, whether gods in human attire, or men in gods', also represent human traits, such as revenge, love, hate. Contrary to mythology, accepted by its believers as a real story, modern myth is perceived not as part of reality but as its own consciousness in the eyes of its creators. From Homer to contemporary interpreters of myth, a dialectic reversal has taken place in the meaning of the word 'myth', from 'real story' to 'fable story'. In Homer's days, myth was a factual state and its meaning was the telling of truth, but in the Modern era (and some say that actually already back in Greece)[253] myth has become a beneficial fiction, and a functional story with a historical core. The concept of 'myth', of which we shall make use, deals with myth itself as revealed in literature, in other words - in the original meaning of the word: A story of the gods and their traits. This essay examines the expansive aspect of the concept of 'myth', common in the social sciences and also including ideas, ideologies, and other psychological structures. However, the focus of the discussion is 'myth', specifically in terms of that which cannot be reduced to general concepts.[254]

---

[249] See: G. Murray, *Five Stages of Greek Religion* (London: Courier Dover Publications 1935).
[250] P. Ricoeur, *Symbolism of Evil*, trans. E. Buchanan (Boston: Beacon Press, 1986), p. 9.
[251] See: "Myth", in M. Eliade ed., *Encyclopedia of Religion* (New York: Macmillan, 1987).
[252] See: Plato, *The Republic (politeia),* trans. B. Jowett (New York: Cosimo, 2008) pp. 359-360, where Plato describes myth as non-reasoned and false.
[253] See: P. Veyne, *Did the Greeks Believe in their Myths,* trans. P. Wissing (Chicago: Chicago UP, 1983).
[254] Y. Libes, "De Natura Dei", in *Studies in Jewish Myth and Jewish Messianism* (1993) 1-64, 151-169.

Dialectics of Myth

4.1 Dialectics of Myth

A discussion on the issue of myth and historical memory may relate to the entire succession of sources of human culture, from their first documentation up to present-day literature. However, this discussion - with all its assumptions, definitions and questions it raises - is in itself modern, and manifests the crisis of religious consciousness, stemming from processes of secularization and the application of research methods of modern science to history and religion.

'Myth' and 'history', claims Eliezer Schweid,[255] are both terms that have been redefined and received their current sense in the context of philosophical and scientific effort to locate and describe immanent powers shaping the history of a people, and creating religion as one of its culture's components. And indeed, from within these methodological efforts, a large problem has arisen, which philosophy of modern religion has had to face again and again, from the era of Enlightenment to our times: The problem of the authenticity of belief and religious world view which understands itself as a historical cultural work, and interprets the religious message it receives from its historical sources in terms of myth and mythology - problematic, since this kind of understanding of religion collides with traditional religious consciousness, to which modern religious consciousness relates as its source. It is clear that the distinction separating modern critical historiography and the traditional historical story raises the question about the original qualities of the old historical memory. On the one hand, it is not possible to accept it as historical memory in the critical scientific sense, since it was selective and 'biased' in principle, and underwent an ongoing process of interpretational 're-adaptation', perhaps even visionary, while delivering from generation to generation. On the other hand, it was not possible to refute its classification as authentic historical memory, according to the way in which it was perceived when written and delivered. The writers' and deliverers' intention was to render faithful documentation of facts, events, deeds, experiences, and thoughts as they were. And indeed, one cannot deny the fact that, as far as the ancient witnesses and documenters were concerned, the religious meaning of these memories was conditioned upon their acceptance as real history, that is - a succession of true facts that were documented and delivered in complete adherence to the way they occurred.[256]

Pico della Mirandola claimed that religious or philosophical development does not necessarily entail alienation to the basic character of mythical thought, and that myth and religion are connected. As to the chapters of prophecy, perceived as a later and more 'developed' stage than the Torah ones, there is no meaning without the mythic experience. The great spiritual creators, the prophets who prophesized out of supreme religious inspiration, diverged - in his opinion - from divine language, since they had to speak the human language of miracle, experience and myth. Greek philosophy, as well, of the late Hellenistic period maintained religious and mythical elements. Hence, for

---

[255] (Schweid, 1996), pp. 41-72.
[256] Ibid.

example, a central concept in Stoic philosophy is that of 'pronoia', divine observance, which leads the world toward its purpose. Even according to this thought, man - as a creature of reason with critical consciousness, must act for the Divine, since living with the gods means acting with them.[257]

As a reversal of the above approaches containing myth as an inseparable component of their thought, other approaches appeared - with the development of the Enlightenment thinking - seeking to refute myth and explain it as an appendage of contemplation, culture and religion. According to Eliezer Schweid,[258] Baruch Spinoza's thought well-represents that which may be called a process of 'de-mythologization'. Spinoza presents the beliefs and opinions of the sources in their literal simplicity, but while describing them annotates them ironically, presenting them as figments of enthused and ignorant imagination, involved as well in the positive moral passion of the prophets. To his perception, although there is true historical information in religious sources, it is ridden with enthusiastic misunderstandings and fables, some of which may have had, or still have, certain social benefit, while some are very harmful. For Spinoza, the indication of the mythological character (and in his language: the prophetic visionary) of the message of the Holy Scriptures is in itself a refutation of the religious beliefs included in it. Spinoza was not interested that all his readers understand that; for the simple man, he thought, the visionary message of the prophets is a support of absolute authority for valid moral commands, and as they are beneficial for social existence, they are better accepted as truth.[259] In other words: Insofar as religious 'myth' is functional and positive, its contention of truth must be given protection of silence. One may even claim that it presents the multitudes with vital truth, which they would not heed if not for the religious fable, since without piety in the fundamentalist sense, they would not feel total obligation to maintain the moral commands and political order. The educated, on the other hand, will easily understand that between 'belief' in its religious sense and 'knowledge' in its reasoned scientific sense, there is - in Spinoza's opinion - a contradiction that cannot be bridged. Hence, it is clear that in his consistent battle for the freedom of thought of philosophers, he is actually battling for refutation of belief in the Holy Scriptures, and the undermining of their status as such. His ultimate mission then was rationalist secularization, which may be interpreted as de-mythologization of culture.

This rational approach gradually developed in its philosophical attire, in the dialectic Idealism of German philosophy, and Schweid describes how together with reasoned radicalism - intended inter alia for cleansing religion of all its irrational residue, and maintaining it "within the boundaries of reason alone" as Kant's famous sentence says - Idealism developed dialectic thinking, which requires deep historical perspective understanding of the spiritual phenomena it is battling, including mythology and mystics. The historical dialectic understanding of religion was therefore a sophisticated means to fight against the irrational element in it, seemingly from within it and in the name of its truth. However, in retrospect, it was also an overcoming of the alienated and externalized single-dimensionality of the anti-religious rationalism of Spinoza or Voltaire. The scholar of Enlightenment was obliged to penetrate the depths of religious imagination and emotion, their code signs, understand them empathically better than their 'spontaneous'

---

[257] B. Malinowski, *Myth in Primitive Psychology* (London: Norton, 1926), p. 216.
[258] E. Schweid, "Myth and Judaism in Kaufmann, Buber and Baeck", *Eshel Beer Sheva* vol. 4 (BG University, 1995), pp. 342-365.
[259] , J. Israel, *The Radical Enlightenment: Philosophy and the Making of Modernity 1650-1750* (Oxford: Oxford UP, 2001), pp.258-274.

creators had, thus discovering the 'pre-reasoned' kernel of truth inherent in mythology.[260] Idealism was prepared to recognize that historically-speaking, that is - in terms of the inner laws of the development of human thinking, mythology is a necessary stage on the path to attaining pure truth. For the scholars of Enlightenment, the ability to understand mystics and mythology from within was a sophisticated battle tool for de-mythologization and de-mystification; however, the task was perceived now not as demolition or total refutation of the refuted spiritual trends (as understood by Spinoza), but rather, according to Hegel's version, as raising these trends from within, by exposing their reasoned kernel of truth, removing the negative and misleading 'wraps', and developing the kernel of truth to a higher level of understanding. Thus an opening was conceived for a new understanding, completely different from Spinoza's, of the phenomena of myth. That which Spinoza perceived as a work combining hallucination and ignorance, was now perceived as primal symbolic manifestation of intuitive reasoned recognition of truth.[261]

According to dialectic philosophy, myth then is a pre-philosophical form of thinking compatible with the historical development of culture in its first stages. In this way, myth is perceived as that which, in its time, had fulfilled a positive role. Moreover, every man seems to repeat - in his process of spiritual development from childhood to maturity - all the stages of development of his culture, reaching its highest level only in his spiritual maturity. This means that these innocent myths, as they are, also have an actual educational role, namely: At a certain stage of development of culture, and at a certain stage of every human's development, myth - in its direct and innocent understanding -fulfills a positive and vital role; and with the dialectic tools, myth is perceived as the role of creative imagination anchored in a kind of intuitive understanding, and by way of empathic experiencing. Although myth has no reflection, the philosophical kernel of truth is already in it. In this context, Schweid notes that the discerning methodical use of the concepts of 'myth' and 'mythology' in modern historical and philosophical-religious research thought appeared as the product of reflexive-dialectic examination, and it is possible to say that the concept of 'myth' is needed by this examination as its methodical requirement, and has embodied it. Hence, the term 'myth' was defined in this thought as visionary imaginary embodiment, or as metaphorical, poetic or narrative imagery, 'pre-reason', of truth. This truth will reach its full development and utmost clarity as an 'ideal', with its 'sublimation' to the level of consciousness in which man's reason discovers itself as the true source of all the contents that the sensory imagination perceives as external beings.[262]

Partial legitimization of myth was then the first step necessary for achieving the desired de-mythologization. That however opened the way for further development toward positive understanding of myth, even to certain re-mythologization of religion, if only for defining it as religion of reason. In quite an ironically dialectic way, this development was already encompassed in the process of thinking that used dialectics for gradual de-mythologization, which does not destroy the historical succession of the consciousness. To achieve its purpose, the historicist research guided by dialectic philosophy needed to reflect traditional memory within a formalized and solidified historical story. This was done, as Schweid described, through projection of the Idealist epistemology, which rigorously discerns

---

[260])Schweid, 1995) p. 942.
[261] Ibid, p.349.
[262] Ibid, p. 350.

between the various stages of development of thought from sensory to reason, onto a description of the structure of history.

According to this approach, the history of every people is an organic deterministic process dictated by the development of the human consciousness. Each period is a quasi chapter or stage in the process, with a predestined purpose: To bring about development and full revealment of defined spiritual cultural content. This pattern was forced upon historigraphical data by dialectic historiosophy. Although it was exposed to critical philological tools, it also underwent a process of interpretational literary adaptation, which actually poured the content of traditional religious myth into the jar of philosophy. According to this philosophical theory - the history of all peoples has a cyclical structure parallel to the cycle of organic life in nature: childhood, adolescence, old age. Each people complete its culture gradually, from its material foundations to the fullness of its spiritual achievements in religion, art, science, and philosophy. This occurs throughout one life cycle, whose pinnacle is political independence, after which the people disintegrate and disappear, leaving behind their heritage for a younger people following.[263] All this seems to lead to exposing the developmental-purposeful structure of history, bringing the de-mythologization process to its perfection and peak. However, a historical perspective view, from the distance of one generation alone, will suffice to show that what seems innocently like history is nothing but philosophical myth, in other words - the embodiment of a philosophical ideal as a tangible story. It is clear that this kind of critical discovery, when perceived and internalized, gives a push to a new and more sophisticated interpretation of the concept of 'myth', and to presenting the question of the place of myth in religion and culture in a much more complex way.

The next stage in the process that darts between establishing the place of myth and its rejection, that is - between de-mythologization and re-mythologization, was - as Schweid described it - a reflexive attempt to rehabilitate myth in the spirit of pure reason, in other words: To bring the process of de-mythologization of tradition to its pinnacle by reasoned re-mythologization, which is well-aware of the meaning of its deed. In general philosophy, this reversal achieved great influential expression in the second theory of Friedrich Wilhelm Schelling.[264]

Schelling sought to rectify the distortion created by philosophy's presumptuous attempt to inherit religion, supposedly by sublimating its visionary contents to the level of reason. Although religion has an intellectual dimension unifying it within a comprehensive world view, and this dimension, in Schelling's opinion, is represented by philosophy - religion itself is a personal social process of life of its own fullness, which no conceptual philosophical system can take over. Moreover, no conceptual philosophical system can guide the processes of creation of symbols and of rites that are so central to religion, as they directly express the supreme processes of life of man, and are taken directly from contents of religious experiencing. Philosophy may interpret these symbols, thereby fulfilling a vital role, but again and again: The interpretation of a symbol cannot come instead of it or fulfill its role.[265] This perception of Schelling, that for various reasons achieved little recognition in his time, seems to shed a new light upon myth. Revealment of the self-content of religion leads to identifying religion with myth, whereby its story and its

---

[263] See: F. C. Beiser, German Idealism. The Struggle against Subjectivism, 1781-1801 (Cambridge: Harvard UP, 2002).
[264] (Schweid, 1995), pp. 351-354.
[265] Ibid, p.354.

Dialectics of Myth

substantiation by symbols of rite are the experiencing of it. It seems then that the truth of myth is not merely of an ideal that it 'represents' at the pre-philosophical level, although it is possible to find in it this dimension as well. Rather, the center of myth appears as the experiencing itself. In other words: Subjective internalization and entry into an objective reality denominator, whole or partial, which man discovers through unmediated experiencing of his direct life surroundings - natural, human, and social. Myth then appears as a special type of comprehensive life experiencing. It constitutes a discovery, a determination that fully substantiates the claims of the prophets that they have achieved direct divine revelation, and that they are capable of bestowing it upon those who follow them. In other words, as such - the creation of myth is described as a spiritual event parceled and delivered in its authentic story. Again: As such it is worthy of being the object of philosophical study, and may be, and is, worthy of guiding philosophical study, however, philosophical study cannot take its place.

In the second half of the nineteenth century, the historians took the central place belonging until then to the philosophers as those who determined the intellectual agenda. This trend is characterized by Schweid in the aspiration to objectivity, the challenge of divesting the facts of their interpretational attire, and the presumption to understand things as they were. Nietzsche's thought appears as a revolt against this presumption, and his aim was to destroy belief in the historical past as conveying any exclusive truth, as serving a general ideal or being a universal key. For him, although the past carries many truths serving various interests, men must look at history according to the guiding aim in their lives, instead of seeing it as a reasoned oracle, objective compass or moral lighthouse. Chaos contains interpretations as numerous as the subjects composing it, and each subject structures reality in a perspective manner, hence - every existence is in essence interpretational. History is exchanged by Nietzsche with a collective memory of many details, struggling over its constant shape. The universal striving of truth or reason to reach an 'objective' reality 'in itself', is replaced by perspective and mythic constructions of reality, or to be precise - realities.

If truth is the object of history, and reason is the object of philosophy, then myth, according to Nietzsche, is the object of culture.

"Yet without myth all culture loses its healthy and natural creative power: only a horizon surrounded by myths can unify an entire cultural movement."[266]

Historical events lacking significance for life do not interest Nietzsche, and in his opinion there is no value in preserving them in the collective consciousness. To corroborate his claim he presents Goethe's motto:

"Moreover I hate everything that merely instructs me without increasing or directly quickening my activity."[267]

Thus, history itself, as a chronological collection of facts, is not important. Myth is important, as a cultural mold of basic events and ways of existence, creating patterns in which past and present move. Claude Lévi-Strauss

---

[266] F. Nietzsche, "Die Geburt der Tragödie aus dem Geiste der Musik" (1872), *The Birth of Tragedy from the Spirit of Music*, trans. Douglas Smith (Oxford University Press, 2008).
[267] See: F. Nietzsche, "Vom Nutzen und Nachtheil der Historie für das Leben" (1874), "On the Use and Abuse of History for Life" (1874), in *Unfashionable Observations: The Works of F. Nietzsche*, trans. R. T. Gray (Stanford: Stanford University Press, 1995).

speaks about mythological use in history,[268] noting that a good mythological explanation must be a global explanation for many defined phenomena. This kind of explanation cannot currently be valid, since mythological thought has shattered into several sciences.

Contrary to the presumption of history to reflect objective truth, myth - as described by David Ohana and Robert S. Wistrich,[269] represents a way of interpretation, an angle of vision that has inner cohesion and spiritual topography, emphasizing or concealing that which it deems worthy of emphasizing or concealing. Myth also has a liminal dimension; it describes a certain state of affairs becoming another state; in other words: The way in which the temporary fixates into eternal; the arbitrary soars to the significant; the accidental shapes a norm; the tribal constitutes the social; and the social constitutes the national. Myth grants the event, man, or institution meaning beyond their time and place. Myth is a permanent formative element of culture, society, and nation. It is created by culture, and at the same time also creates it. Hence, beyond the question of the existence or non-existence of myths in cultures, or the question of their meaning, content and the role they fulfill in society and in politics - it is important to identify who the creators are of myths of culture, politics or communication. The question of identification presupposes that myths are created by certain people, and in our times - culture critics, artists, journalists, politicians, etc. But is this so? And perhaps Claude Lévi-Strauss' assumption is right that we do not think or create myths, but rather that myths think themselves through us?[270] This assumption of Lévi-Strauss, that myths are structural constructions existing and standing forever, was influenced, as was all of French Structuralism, by Martin Heidegger's theory, and its sources are deep in German thought of the nineteenth century; men are not sovereign in their thought, but rather language is that which thinks and speaks by creating a-personal and a-historical forms. The forms govern with the aid of symbols and metaphors, and organize the socio-economic reality. At the turn of the century, in the years 1880-1930, central intellectuals in Europe, as Schweid notes, questioned the progressive and reasoned interpretation of the course of history.[271] To their perception, the world had lost its sense of direction, and men began to search for a new world view that would restore equilibrium to things. Lévi-Strauss formulated this mythic passion claiming that the need for a comprehensive explanation is a basic need of human nature. Schweid continues this approach, stating that we shall never be released from the need for mythology, and that the crisis of Western civilization can be largely expressed in the fact that we are not capable of collectively accepting a comprehensive explanation such as that provided by mythology to mankind for so long a time. In his opinion, mythic is then that which is meaningful.[272]

Erich Fromm describes myth as an imaginary story similar to a dream, and occurring in space and time, expressing through symbols philosophical and religious ideas touching upon the essence of human existence and the important and central psychological experiences.[273] Carl Gustav Jung described myths as permanent structures constituting part of the sub-conscious common to the entire human race.[274] Ernest Cassirer described man's life as

---

[268] C. Lévi-Strauss, *Structural Anthropology*, trans. C. Jacobson (New York: Basic Books, 1963).
[269] (Ohana and Wistrich, 1996), pp. 11-37.
[270] C. Lévi-Strauss, *Myth and Meaning* (New York: Schocken Books, 1978), p.3.
[271] (Schweid, 1996), pp. 68-72.
[272] Ibid.
[273] E. Fromm, *The Forgotten Language (1951)*, (Austin: Holt, Rinehart & Winston, 1976).
[274] C. G. Jung, *Psychiatric Studies 1902–1905*, vol. 1 (London: Routledge, 1953).

diverging from mere natural existence, and as existing too in the dimension of symbols woven into human experience, as a net of signs guiding us in our world. As man cannot face reality unmediated, he seemingly shields himself with forms of language, art imagery, religious rites, or symbols of myth, which interpret and mediate the things themselves which we cannot know.[275] Man, as 'homo symbolicus', makes use of myths in order to construct his reality. The world is perceived as characterized by chaos, and the symbols that man creates for himself enable him to experience chaos as cosmos, as meaningful. In all of these modern approaches there is evidence of the impression left by Kant's claim that we shall never know the thing-in-itself, and that our knowledge depends on structures of consciousness.

Sociologists Émile Durkheim and Georges Sorel, each according to his method, define the essence of myth, but make opposite use of the role they ascribe it. In Durkheim's opinion, society cannot remain stable without a high degree of social solidarity, which depends on the strength of the prevailing social myths. The role of myths then is to unite society; hence, they are a necessary condition for social stability.[276] Sorel, however, claims the opposite. He thinks that the role of myths is not to stabilize but rather to provide inspiration for action, to urge on, spur, induce, and serve as a tool for social mobilization.[277] According to Durkheim, the present seeks to be consolidated, and therefore shapes myths that are capable of maintaining the existing order. On the other hand, according to Sorel, the present seeks revolution - hence it shapes myths that are capable of destroying and renewing.

Influenced by the thought of Henri Bergson, Sorel developed the concept of 'political myth', as a replacement of religious myth in the non-religious society. In his opinion, myth is a political belief whose truth is not measured by the evidence of its past existence or the probability of its future realization, but rather by its influence on men's deeds. The 'American dream', for instance, according to which anybody can get rich in the United States, is a myth. Whether it is correct sociologically or statistically, it influences the behavior of millions of people, and in this sense it is true. Sorel wished to advance revolutionary myths, and first and foremost, what was called 'the general strike', his perception which developed in the left-wing of modern political theory, but quickly became a tool of the fascist agenda for advancing nationalist, racist and anti-Semitic myths.[278]

The dismal acknowledgement that reason and its distinct creation, science, had not yielded the desired results, had not provided man with answers to burning questions preoccupying him, but instead had abandoned him to a world of fake progress and bitter disappointment - lays as well at the basis of Max Horkheimer and Theodor Adorno's work, both prominent representatives of the Frankfurt School. However, Horkheimer and Adorno went further than Sorel, who blamed modernity for impotence. They claimed that it is a matter of actual deceit. In their joint essay "Dialectic of Enlightenment",[279] the two presented the story of reason as an ongoing struggle for ruling, which began back in ancient times. Man's supposed release from the yoke of ancient myth actually laid the foundation for a new

---

[275] E. Cassirer, *An Essay on Man: An Introduction to a Philosophy of Human Culture* (New Haven: Yale University Press, 1944).
[276] E. Durkheim, *The Division of Labor in Society*, trans. L. A. Coser (New York: Free Press, 1997), pp. 39, 60, 108.
[277] G. Sorel, *Reflections on Violence* (1908), trans. T. E. Hulme & J. Roth, (New York: Collier, 1950), pp.26-56.
[278] (Ohana and Wistrich, 1996), pp. 24.
[279] T. W. Adorno and M. Horkheimer, "Dialektik der Aufklärung" (7942), *Dialectic of Enlightenment*, trans. E. Jephcott (Stanford: Stanford UP, 2002).

mythology. Instead of critical and reflexive thinking, instead of nourishing 'essential' rationality, modernity has subjugated the masses to the greedy and empty rule of instrumental rationality.

According to Adorno and Horkheimer, both myth and epos, in spite of their differences, bear influence upon society and reality. This claim is not compatible with Marx's approach, whereby the relations of production are the motivating power of history, and also shape the super-structure, namely - philosophy, literature and culture in general, including myth and epos. The approach of Adorno and Horkheimer then is a development and refining of the radical materialism of Marx's school, which claims that being shapes the consciousness - whereas they emphasize that one must take into account the influence of the consciousness on being, and their reciprocity. They maintain that the technological process - into which the subject grew stronger after having been banished from the consciousness, free of the multiple meanings of mythical thinking, as it is free of any kind of meaning - turned reason into myth, in other words, into a mere pawn for the all-encompassing economic system. This claim is based on the motivation to erect, on the ruins of myth, 'essential' rationality that manifests the release from the mythic hold; however, the very criticism of the place to which enlightenment fell, namely - resubmission to myth, and this time the submission of reason; and acknowledging the reciprocal influence of consciousness and being - raises the question: Is this kind of release from myth at all possible?

In the introduction to the book "Mythologies", one may identify the essence of Roland Barthes' research aim: "Unrelenting identification and denunciation of the processes of mythologization that lead us in vain in many different fields, even here and today."[280] Hence, while identifying the tendencies of folk discourse on one hand, and formal discourse on the other, to turn social historical reality - saturated with desires, interests and power relations between individuals and groups - into a collection of entities anchored in nature, Barthes harnessed himself, through his essays in the 1950s in France, to a process of de-mythologization of culture.

Myth, to Barthes' method, is speech! Any speech. Myth is a communication system, a message. Myth is a way of imbuing meaning, it is shape. Everything may then become myth. Every object in the world may go from a state of closed existence, mute - to an oral state, speech that is open to appropriation by society. Myth may be shaped in various ways and representations: written discourse, but also photography, film, newspaper article, sports - all of these may serve as the basis of mythic speech if the laws of the mythic system, which is actually a semiotic system, are preserved. Research of myths, according to Barthes' method, should focus on two aspects: the semiotic and the ideological, which are inseparable. The methodological course was based on the method of Ferdinand de Saussure for deciphering language, while expanding and improving upon the method of his mentor, for semiotic analysis of imagery, and interacting with the method of American researcher Charles Peirce. Barthes presents, for example, a problem existing in photography,[281] explaining that it has a system of analogue and non-decodable signifiers; a denotative system of signs that indicates the world as their signified and which is responsible for the creation of a system of connotative referents, based on the meanings evoked in the spectator as he is exposed to the sequence of

---

[280] R. Barthes, *Mythologies* (Paris: Editions de Seuil, 1957), trans. A. Lavers (London: Paladin, 1972), p. 8.
[281] R. Barthes, *Image, Music, Text* "The Photographic Message", ed. and trans: Stephen Heath (New York: Hill, 1977), 15-31.

denotative signs. The leaning of a connotative system of signifieds on signifiers that are a denotative system of signs, that is - of natural spontaneous appearance, creates, in his opinion, naturalization of the connotative message, which leads to the spectator's illusion that meaning stems from the world. Barthes ascribed this semiotic step to myths, so that myth is ideological naturalization, or naturalization of connotations expressing ideology.[282]

Already in Barthes' time, and gradually gathering force, the electronic communication media were established as one of the dominant factors in shaping the consciousness of modern man, and now appear as the arena of the construction of myths. Electronic communications also serves as a medium for transmitting mythic and historical meanings, while - itself - gradually creating mythic images duplicated in public and political discourse. Marshall McLuhan described communications as modern mythology, through which we are starting to rebuild the ancient feelings from which we were detached, and starting to live myth again.[283] Contrary to Mesopotamian and Greek mythology, modern communications mythology recreates itself constantly, being self-aware, and without metaphysical presumption. Its intensity and hurriedness empty it of presuming a meaningful statement; communications myths are short of breath. And yet - communications returns us to the mythological, as it prefers the multiple and perspective to the search for the one truth, sanctifying relativism of value, and replacing the worthy with the existing, reality with experiencing, and ideology - with myth. Communications as mythology, claim Ohana and Wistrich, is meant to remove any vestige of value from that which exists. Some of myth's traits may be projected onto communications: It is archaic (in the Greek sense, that is - it creates archetypes and grants them an irrational basis); it does not explain but rather corroborates facts. And if we continue the line of thought of Lévi-Strauss, who contends that myth is a structure of action and not a structure for action, then communications myth is not a structure for ideological or moral action, but rather a structure unto itself. Communications for communications. This apparently is what McLuhan meant in his well-known assumption that "The medium is the message". Communications substitutes criticism with experience, ethics with aesthetics, general with private, objective with perspective, truth with culture, and historical consciousness with myth.[284]

---

[282] Barthes, analyzes as we know, by way of example of myth, a photograph on the cover of a French magazine, in which a black soldier salutes the French flag. On one hand, the denotative photo, due to its signs (salute gesture, uniform, flag as the symbol of France, soldier's skin color) indicates an event in the world, so that the concealed text of the photo would be: "Here we see an event in which a black soldier salutes the French flag". However, in the mind of the French spectator who is culture-aware, and who encounters the same denotative system of signs, the ideological connotations will surface, such as: "The people of the Third World loyally accept French imperialism". The problem: This connotative system seems to have grown naturally from leaning on the denotative system, therefore what occurs here is a "naturalization" of imperialist ideology.
[283] M. Mcluhan, "Myth and Mass Media", in *Daedalus*, vol. 88, No. 2, *Myth and Mythmaking* (spring, 1959), pp. 339-348.
[284] (Ohana and Wistrich, 1996), pp. 21-29.

4.2 Small Genealogy of (Jewish) Historical Memory

In the small (partial and limited) history presented so far, one may notice a necessary distinction - three dimensions of dialectics combined and characterizing the historical transformation of the meaning of the concept 'myth'. The first of them deals with the tension between perception of the concept as bearing truth, and seeing it as fable. The second dimension leans on the first, and deals with affirming or denying the place of myth in contemporary culture, in other words, between de-mythologization on the one hand, and re-mythologization of culture, on the other. The third deals with expanding the perception of the concept of 'myth', and its divergence beyond its religious framework, so that it includes ideas that work albeit in the constituting and motivating format of religious myth, but also in a variety of other arenas of social being, as a system of discipline and power. It is in this dimension that dialectics pulsates, in itself derived from the first dimension, between concealment of myth to its revealment as such.

At this stage, after having surveyed (within the limitations imposed by the extent of this essay) the transformation of the concept in Western history, it seems necessary to conduct a parallel study of the transformation of 'myth' in Jewish tradition and historiography. Apart from the need to dwell on the matter in order to examine Bialik's poetry through it, it seems that dialectics, or to be more precise, the multiple-dialectics of myth as appearing in Jewish traditions, may sharpen the perception of the movement of the concept, by presenting addition tension - between particular and universal.

The word 'myth' or 'mythology' is lacking in canonic pre-modern Jewish literature.[285] We shall then refer to the concept 'historical memory', appearing in the Bible as 'Toldot' (the annals), as representing the 'Jewish myth' and preserving the original sense of the concept, as a story about the god (and his people).

One cannot ignore the fact that, in spite of the selective, partial and splintered telling of the traditional historical story, a cohesive image of a whole and significant sequence was formed in the memory and consciousness of Jews educated on the accumulative traditional literature, so that the present of each generation is connected with the comprehensive memories of the past, directing a view to the future, and expectations of it. How then is it possible to evaluate the weight of 'myth' or traditional memory, as a factor shaping history through the consciousness of those operating in it? How does 'myth' act in preserving the continuity of historical consciousness?

In his essay "Myth and Historical Memory in Modern Jewish Thought", Eliezer Schweid seeks to trace the change that took place in the historical consciousness of the Jewish people during the period of Enlightenment.[286] It is accepted in historical research and in the philosophy of modern Jewish religion that the Jewish people were - from the

---

[285] It should be noted that Greek mythology as formulated by Homer receives complex relation in the literature of the Sages (See: Jerusalem Talmud, Sanhedrin, chap. 10), a matter in itself worthy of examining elsewhere.
[286] (Schweid, 1996), pp. 41-72.

start, because of the unique characteristics of the religion that constituted and unified it - a people with distinct historical consciousness. The historical memory, both the constituting and establishing, as well as the accumulative, and that described as a way rising to its purpose, is a main component in the religious-Jewish world view. It is a source both for the developing religious thought, and for the religious way of life, its continuity and opening to renewing memories. Hence, it is accepted and agreed upon in historical research and the philosophy of modern Jewish religion that one cannot understand the Jewish religion, or reduce the essence unique to it and unifying it, according to dogmatic elements - not even according to the 'Halacha' laws, but only based on the fullness of its annals: Judaism is the history of the people of Israel documented in its literature. However, together with the determining of these routine agreements, the tension rose from the critical methodology of modern historical research, expressed in the question regarding the reliability of the knowledge. This question is sharpened in view of the fact that from the destruction of the Second Temple and up to the period of Enlightenment, there was almost no creation - in this culture characterized by remembering and historical consciousness - of any significant historiographic literature. How then was the historical consciousness of this people formed and preserved?

The literary historical research and the historiographic research of "Hachmat Yisrael" (Wissenschaft des Judentums) of the early nineteenth century, as Schweid describes it, looked for answers to these questions, by delving into the historical information that could be gleaned from the historiography of nations near which or within which Jews resided;[287] from the meager chronicles, sparse and few occasionally written and for various purposes; from references of Jewish theologians to questions of the status of Jews within the nations, especially during the period of exile; or from different literary sources, mainly of Halacha, not originally intended as historiography but containing in retrospect much historical information. However, claims Schweid, it is clear that one is speaking of a modern work, using its resources not as it was, and thus attempting not only to knowingly restore to the Jews their forgotten historical memory, but also to shape its concept of history, and interpret accordingly the ancient historiographic literature that survived in the Biblical literature and the external or Deuterocanonical literature of the period of the Second Temple. Instead of historiography documenting the events within the selective religious interpretational framework of the idea of the covenant between the people of Israel and god, and instead of the 'ritualistic' memory consolidated through Bible studies; the 'Siddur' of prayers; notes of generations of the oral Bible interpretation tradition; the theological and ethical literature studies, which interpreted the meaning of the state of exile and the messianic destiny of Judaism; and also several chronicles connected to situations of 'Kiddush Hashem' ("sanctification of the name") - instead of all of these, "Hachmat Yisrael" shaped the modern critical historical memory aspiring to perceive and understand history "from within itself" as a sequence of events, processes and works interconnected by causal and circumstantial connections immanent in memory itself. There is no need to state that this was a revolutionary change of far-reaching implications. It required considerable extension of the historical fields of interest (especially the social, economic, political and cultural fields of activity), an approach characterized by maximal fullness of details, but also an extreme change in relation to historical time dimensions. Memories of the past were

---

[287] Ibid, p.44.

interpreted in the context unique to them, well-discerned from the present that was distancing from them; and - with the claiming of causal and contextual meaning influencing the present, they lost their status as authority.

The activity in the present and the image of the future were thus released from the direct and formative presence of past memories, which tradition granted a status of beyond time. Actually, they pushed the past, precisely discerned from the present, to its past, thereby opening the possibility of substituting the dominance of religion with the idea of development and progress.[288]

In his essay, Schweid presents the work and constituting historiosophy of Enlightenment scholar Rabbi Nachman Kohen Krochmal - who developed a critical research methodology meant to extract, from the evidence of the sources, the authentic historical 'kernel', and develop modern critical historical memory from within the traditional story. Krochmal's intention was to propose a quasi modern link of tradition, while reversing its tools, judgments, and evaluations. This step cannot be done in a convincing way in terms of the tradition and modern research, without attributing authentic historical value also to the non-historical 'attire' of the traditional story, since even if this 'attire' does not bear witness to the events documented in it, it does testify to the way of thinking and the form of orientation in time characteristic of the testifiers, and explaining their thought and the culture of their time. This is also the manner in which the anachronistic interpretational 'attire' of the story is perceived, after being critically discerned, not only as a source of important authentic historical information for the period in which it was created, but also as a factor of authority, shaping their consciousness, action, and the actual reality of life of those who remember.[289] Schweid then defines Krochmal's critical and historiosophic research work as exposing the mythological characteristics of the traditional historic story; hence it is also a deliberate act of 'de-mythologization'. However, as he notes, one must not ignore the ironic moment manifest in this work, since the criticism of Enlightenment, intended to eliminate the element of myth and reveal history in its anachronistic attire, itself leans on an a-priori developmental assumption which is, in itself, but myth of the Enlightenment period. The history of modern Jewish historiography appears then in retrospect as a continuous process, in which every researcher of a new generation has attempted to expose the "prejudice" of his predecessors and - amidst re-examination of known facts and discovery of additional ones - to shape an image of historical truth, according to the prejudice suitable to his times, and which is destined to be removed as "historical myth" by those to follow him.[290] Despite these attempts throughout history to offer an interpretational alternative to tradition, its primary presence as a formative factor of historical memory was not eliminated.

And it seems that the very "anachronistic" role of tradition is that which acted as the main realistic historical factor uniting the consciousness of the people, at least in the past. It is clear then that with the total abandoning of the historical traditional image, the history of the Jewish people will lose the cohesion that makes it the guiding memory of a nation. Hence, it is possible, beyond all attempts of de-mythologization of Jewish history, to see the recurring action of traditional myth, even if it is lessening.

---

[288] Ibid, p. 45.
[289] Ibid, pp. 46-49.
[290] Ibid, pp. 44.

Small Geneaology of (Jewish) Historical Memory

The direct theoretical study of the types of myth, and its place in the religious world view and in the religious way of life of the Jewish people, appeared in the broader context of research and study which sought to extract from the traditional sources a world view and way of life compatible with the 'consciousness of culture' of the new times. The perceptions of cognitive truth and universal moral values, as well as the social and political aspirations of researchers and thinkers who identified with modernity, generated a critical approach to tradition as such, and explicitly raised the demand for de-mythologization, or de-mythologization of religion. This matter is illustrated radically, according to Schweid, in Spinoza's "Tractatus Theologico-Politicus" (1677).

Modern Jewish thinkers that came after Spinoza, aspiring to withhold religion and not refute the message of the Holy Scriptures, inherited his critical rationalist approach, but went back to search for it within the Holy Scriptures themselves. For them, claims Schweid, the demand for de-mythologization pertains to the Holy Scriptures themselves by virtue of the truth inherent in them. Furthermore, de-mythologization is perceived by them as the main message of the sources. Judaism, so they claimed, is inherently a 'mind religion' or 'religion of reason', with no mythology and no myth. Conversely, mythology and myth are the essential characteristics of idolatry, while Jewish monotheism, defined by these thinkers as 'ethical monotheism' is the victory of reason over mythology. Hence, in its uncompromising battle against idolatry, Jewish monotheism first fought against the remnants of idolatry mythology within Jewish folk belief, and then against the mythology of idolatry religions that faced it, including the mythology that Christianity inherited from idolatry. This approach, claims Schweid, actually became a sanctified convention of Jewish religious modernist thought, of the Enlightenment.[291] The research of "Hachmat Yisrael" scholars, he emphasizes, did not ignore the existence of mythological elements in the Biblical sources, nor the "penetration" of such elements into the legends of the Sages, the Deuterocanonical literature, and especially the apocryptic books, and Kabbalistic theology of the Middle Ages. However, in research of Jewish thought in the nineteenth century, the mythological characteristics were mainly described as external influence, distinctly idolatry, which characterized 'folk religion', while the authentic leaders of the religion of historical Judaism - the prophets, the great thinkers of the 'Halacha', and the philosophers - fought against these trends, according to the modern thinkers. The distress of exile, which sank the multitudes of Jews into poverty and deterioration, is the reason for an increasing influence of "dark" mysticism over the Jewish people in the last generations before Enlightenment. These distortions then need to be removed, with a return to the original faith of the prophets. This is the religious role of Enlightenment: To fight against mythology, and grant ethical monotheism its final victory over idolatry.

In this context, claims Schweid, the story of the annals of the Jewish people as the battle of uniquely reasoned faith against mythological idolatry is a big myth of modernist Judaism, from the end of the eighteenth century until the beginning of the twentieth century.[292] According to his approach, the Enlightened rationalist perception should be understood in a double historical context: First, the terrifying sounds of Sabbateanism, whose Frankist residues demonstrated their danger as an actual threat to the spiritual and moral immunity of Jewish society; in the eyes of the

---

[291] Ibid, p. 45.
[292] Ibid, p. 46.

Enlightenment scholars, Kabbalistic mythology was a spiritual "virus" that caught the Jewish people up in messianic hallucinations. Secondly, the Enlightenment movement had to struggle against the strong opposition of the rabbinical and Hasidic leadership, who still ruled over the people with full authority. The Hasidic movement, adhering to mysticism, was the strongest inner religious factor that rose against the Enlightenment. In this double context, it is no wonder that even moderate Enlightenment scholars such as Krochmal described Kabbalah, and especially 'practical Kabbalah' as a most dangerous spiritual and moral pathology, which has to be vehemently battled. The de-mythologization and de-mystification of Judaism were then perceived as a vital rescue mission for saving the spirit of the people.

Krochmal, who openly opposed the dangers of Kabbalist Sabbateanism and Hasidism, was an idealistic and dialectic philosopher of Jewish thought, who sought to expose the kernel of truth that existed, in his opinion, in Kabbalah at its initial stage of development, and not only in it, but even in idolatry mythology. Moreover, he was ready to acknowledge that historically, in other words - in terms of the inner laws of the development of human thinking, these mythological factors are a necessary stage on the way to reaching the truth.

According to Schweid, Krochmal knew how to distinguish between the positive and authentic revealments of myth, and the negative and pathological ones.[293] Partial legitimization of prophetic and Kabbalist myth for him was the first necessary step toward achieving de-mythologization. In his opinion, the Jewish people, as opposed to the rest of the nations that rise and disappear as part of the life cycle, is not transient, will not pass from the world in one life cycle, and has a unique destiny: To unite all of the achievements of human culture within the ideal of comprehensive unity that is special to his religion. Since the destiny of the Jewish people cannot be achieved in one life cycle, it is revived after completing every cycle of cultural creation, beginning anew in a more highly developed cultural surrounding than their previous one. Thus, the Chosen People have passed through all the great civilizations that rendered an essential contribution to the development of human culture - absorbing the positive, and eliminating the negative, uniting it all in their own culture. According to Krochmal, they underwent three historical life cycles. With the onset of Emancipation they are again at the beginning of a new life cycle, the fourth and last, that will raise the totalities of culture accumulated in their historical memory to the highest universal level - the level of reason, or pure spiritual level. Thus will the Jewish people actually unite human history, and fulfill their mission as the chosen people.[294] For Krochmal, this perception, which is but the mirror-image of the Hegelian perception of history, reflects the regulation of history, that is - its ideal absolute actuality. Hence, the exposure of the developmental purposeful structure of history brings the de-mythologization process of traditional historical memory to its perfection and its pinnacle.

If Krochmal's theory enables us to see a process of re-mythologization conducted innocently and unintentionally, then the next stage is a reflexive attempt to restore myth in the spirit of pure reason, through reasoned re-

---

[293] Ibid, p. 47.
[294] Ibid, p.44.

mythologization. In general philosophy this reversal is expressed in the second theory of Friedrich Schelling[295] and in philosophy of the Jewish religion - in the theory of Samuel Hirsch, who may be considered a student of Schelling, but also an original philosopher, who adapted his studies from his teacher to his own heritage. In his expansive methodical book "Die Religionphilosophie der Juden" (1842) Hirsch sought to rectify the distortion created by the presumptuous attempt of philosophy to replace religion. To his perception, religion itself is a personal social process of life with a fullness that cannot be substituted by a conceptual philosophical system.

Is it possible, in view of this perception of the role of myth in religion, to posit the rationalist assumption that the ethical monotheism of Judaism is anti-mythological, and that the Holy Scriptures reflect an ongoing process of de-mythologization? Hirsch's answer was dialectic: No, and yet - yes. The 'no' refers to a simple fact that the previous idealistic interpretation preferred to ignore: except for those remnants of idolatry mythology - Canaanite, Egyptian, Babylonian, Persian, Greek, and Roman - found in the Bible, in the external literature and in parts of the Sages legends, and against which great religious teachers of Judaism fought - there are also distinct revealments of myth, all signs of which show that they were self-creation and not penetration of outside influence, and which are essential to the Jewish religion to the extent that their removal would empty Judaism of all content. The myths in question are of course the story of the creation, especially the creation of man and the story of the Garden of Eden, the story of the flood, the tower of Babylon, the forefathers, the story of Joseph, the move to Egypt, the slavery in Egypt, the exodus of Egypt and all its miracles, the opening of the sea, and the Mount Sinai event. All of these, claims Hirsch, join into a myth whose creation we follow, as well as its perpetuation by delivery from generation to generation. It seems then that not only is there myth in Judaism, but that myth is essential for Judaism, as it is essential for every other religion. Nevertheless, there is a process of de-mythologization in the Holy Scriptures of Judaism, which really is a religion of reason, and thereby distinguished from idolatry, which is not.[296] De-mythologization then is connected to the rejection of a certain type of myth - pagan mythology. This is rejected in favor of authentic reasoned myth of Judaism. Hirsch's main discovery is that this is not a confrontation between mythological religion and anti-mythological religion, but rather between two types of myth. Pagan myth, claims Hirch, takes its materials from nature. It reflects the laws of nature and thus turns nature into a level of life including and encompassing man. The result: Imposing a natural, causal, deterministic cycle of life over the spiritual and moral life of man. In idolatry myth there is "blind" fate that rules over the life of the individual, of society and of the state. It cannot be avoided. This means that in pagan mythology, man appears as having used his freedom of choice to give it up, and submit to the deterministic cycle of nature. This is the sin of idolatry, and of course the anti-reason element in it - anti-reason in the sense of refusing the moral imperative of reason, which is identical to freedom of the spirit. Jewish myth, on the other hand, is described by Hirsch as taking its materials from history, and manifesting the spiritual dimension, supra-nature, the dimension of moral freedom. Judaism is a historical religion in essence, and it is this fact that manifests its reasonedness. However, it is not historiography that embodies this fact initially, but rather historical myth, which then repeatedly instructs the writing of historiography.

---

[295] Previously elaborated on.
[296] (Schweid, 1996), pp. 49-54.

Small Geneaology of (Jewish) Historical Memory

The next stage in the Hirsch's study is to clarify the relation between historical myth and historiography. This relation is shown, in his opinion, in the Bible itself, by gradual transference: The myth of Creation posited supra-metaphysical assumptions, within the framework of which is expressed the moral relation between god and the world and man, and the moral dilemmas of human existence appear - between freedom of the spirit and predetermination of nature. Then the historical elements penetrate gradually. When we progress with the reading of the Torah stories and go from them to the books of the first prophets, the charge of realistic historical memory increases; first it receives mythic shape, and is actually delivered as pre-history memory. Finally, in the books of the first prophets a distinct historiography is reached. The story of history in the Holy Scriptures then has history and 'ontology', but it is from its beginning an inseparable part of history itself, even that listed as a scientific discipline.

Historiography, which faithfully reflects a certain choice of events as they occurred, is definitely necessary for the Jewish religion. As far as it is concerned, in Hirsch's opinion, there is supreme religious meaning to the fact that the events occurred one way and not another. However, this historiography as well, when it reaches the time that its tools grow more sophisticated, still remains bound to the ancient myth that had guided it. Even according to historical scientific data, myth is a historical factor of enormous realistic power. As long as the Jewish people remain faithful to the Bible and its historical destiny, it continues, and will continue, the patterns of structure revealed in historical myths of Genesis and Exodus. In this spirit, Hirsch claimed that the very fact of the Jewish people's existence and their history among the nations is testimony to the wonder of revelation and the wonder of providence. The Jewish people are a miracle of revelation of the freedom of the spirit in the struggle against nature. They testify to the truth of their historical myth by virtue of their actual historical presence. In other words: During the de-mythologization conducted both by noting the mythic quality of the foundation stories of the Holy Scriptures, and by preparing the obligatory transfer from historical myth to scientific historiography, Hirsch knowingly created a process of re-mythologization. His book expresses both of these processes: On the one hand, it reflects extensively and in detail the historiographic research of the history of the Jewish people, from the forefathers up to modern times; on the other, he knowingly adopts the structure of the myth of Genesis and Exodus, and shapes the realistic history of the Jewish people. If this history has meaning - then ancient historical myth is that which shapes it.

Similarly to the later ideas of Schelling, so too Samuel Hirsch's thought did not take hold or influence many of his contemporaries. Only in the first half of the twentieth century did the readiness ripen to absorb, develop and apply it. Schweid claims that three central processes contributed to this readiness:

1. The consolidation of the scientific discipline of researching Jewish mysticism, the methodical accumulation of knowledge regarding the history of mysticism, and the connection between it and the phenomenon of Jewish and pagan myth.

2. The development of comparative research of religion on one hand, and the increase of the sense of emptiness caused by the philosophical religion substitutes, which placed religion 'solely within the boundaries of reason' on the other. These two developments, which consolidated each other, together brought about renewed revealment of the irrational or the supra-rational elements essential to religion as such.

3. The elaborate creation of modern myths: On the one hand, at the ideological level, as a quasi religion substitute for leading the masses, and on the other, at the poetic literary level, specifically to express experiences of heart-break at the personal level.[297]

The development in the field of scientific research of the history of Jewish mysticism is first and foremost connected to the scientific endeavor of Gershom Scholem, anchored in the criticism of the philosophical-religious research work of "Hachmat Yisrael" in the nineteenth century, as well as the disappointment with the religion substitutes of philosophical idealism. Thus began a re-evaluation toward the latest original mystic movement of 'Hasidic Judaism', against which all the first leaders of Enlightenment had risen. Following the re-evaluation of the folk vitality, creativity and profound experiencing of Hasidic Judaism, the research level began to criticize the attitude of "Hachmat Yisrael" toward the phenomenon of mysticism, and of Kabbalah in general, since extensive Jewish literature had been pushed aside, dismissed as marginal, and denounced as idolatry influence that had penetrated Jewish thought from outside sources. In his research endeavor, then, Scholem sought to refute these claims as superficial rationalist prejudice, and to prove the opposite: There exists Jewish mysticism, and it is far from being marginal. Indeed, one may say that from the period of the Second Temple (Scholem agrees that in the Bible there is no mysticism) it had become more central, and in the last few generations before Enlightenment it had swept the whole of the Jewish people in its impact. Since it had been assimilated and become so central, it was clear that it could not be described as merely another penetration of external influence, although there had been external influence upon Jewish mysticism, as there had been such on Halachah and philosophical thought. According to Scholem, basically, each religion has its own mysticism, and the Jewish religion has mysticism of distinct Jewish characteristics.[298] Scholem's research endeavor was meant not only to prove these critical claims, but also to discover their historical weight by exposing the various trends of Jewish mysticism. Thus he sought to show that this mysticism, upon its creation, became a central factor rejuvenating Judaism after crises it had undergone. Schweid emphasizes that, as far as Scholem was concerned, by any definition of mysticism - myth constitutes a necessary foundation. This means that rediscovery of the centrality of mysticism in Judaism is necessarily rediscovery of the centrality of myth therein. One may then describe Scholem's research endeavor as re-mythologization of the concept of 'Judaism' in research relating to the past. However, it is easy to see the implications for his times of this type of historical claim. Scholem ascribed importance to Sabbateanism and to Hasidic Judaism, considering these two movements to be reactions that contained early understanding of the crisis of modern times, and that by virtue of this fact they had formative influence as well upon the movements that represented modernity itself: Enlightenment and Zionism.[299]

In Scholem's opinion, Sabbateanism - as the example that the advocates of Enlightenment waved against the advocates of mysticism, was actually a point of departure of Enlightenment itself, the point from which began the bursting outside the walls of the ghetto, to beyond the restrictions of the Halachah. Scholem further claimed that only the power of a mystic movement could rejuvenate the vitality of Judaism from within the crisis of modernity - which,

---

[297] Ibid, p. 50-51.
[298] G. Scholem, *Major Trends in Jewish Mysticism*)1941(, (New York: Schocken, 1995), p.490.
[299] (Schweid, 1996), pp. 52-53.

in his opinion, was the greatest and deepest crisis Judaism had ever known. As a man of science researching the past, he did not wish to speculate on the characteristics of future mysticism; however, it seems that this had indeed guided his motivation to research the mystic heritage, and pass on the knowledge of it to future generations, preparing and delivering it as the potential of renewing creation. Schweid then describes Scholem's research as expressing a consolidated trend of re-mythologization of Judaism, opposing the trend of de-mythologization that had characterized the nineteenth century. Scholem's criticism of idealist philosophy and the substitutes of religion offered in the nineteenth century projected as well on his approach to the Jewish rationalism of the Middle Ages, and Jewish philosophy of the twentieth century - including religious Existentialism of philosophers such as Martin Buber, Franz Rosenzweig and Abraham Joshua Heschel, although they related positively and with identification to mysticism and myth in Judaism. In Scholem's opinion, these too were unauthentic attempts, especially since they presented myth by way of an experiencing, whose only validity is subjective - thus placing it as a basis for faith and a religious way of life that diverge in essence from orthodox fundamentalism. Basically, it seems that, in Scholem's opinion, only fundamentalism, which perceives the myth of the commandments as objective and absolute historical truth, can establish authentic religiousness. With this claim, Scholem pointed to a problem in the perception of myth in theories of modern religion philosophers. However, these existentialist philosophers, as described by Schweid, were the ones, each in his own way, who restored myth to the center of a religious world view, and the center of actual experiencing.[300]

As a reaction to the revealment, by comparative phenomenological research of religions, of the irrational element essential to religion on one hand,[301] and to dissatisfaction with the intellectual substitutes that Idealist philosophy proposed to the perception of personal and supra-universe divinity of the Bible on the other, there grew at the turn of the twentieth century, as described by Schweid, a movement of returning to the Jewish sources, deriving from enormous religious thirst that originated in the sense of excessive distancing and emptying of authentic Jewish contents. Although it was not a widespread movement, qualifies Schweid, it was represented by several highly influential personalities, including central Jewish philosophers of religion of the first half of the twentieth century: Hermann Cohen, Martin Buber, Franz Rosenzweig, Leo Baeck, Gershom Scholem, and Leo Strauss. The thought of these scholars presents, in various ways, the same aspiration to return to the sources, namely, to the Holy Scriptures, and to re-discover through them authentic Jewish religious experiencing, which is - to the best of their knowledge - experiencing the presence of a vibrant god, a personal god who commands and judges, guides, redeems, and hears prayer. Not an abstract philosophical ideal.

Naturally, at the center of the religious thought of these thinkers is the question of the relation to myth in the Bible, in the legends of the Sages, the Siddur of prayers, and in religious contemplation, especially the Kabbalah. The question asked is: What is the truth embodied in historical myth, which renews, changes, reverses and varies, while

---

[300] E. Schweid, "Myth and Judaism in Kaufmann, Buber and Baeck")Hebrew), *Eshel Beer Sheva* vol. 4. (BG University, 1995), pp. 342-365.
[301] See: The research and philosophical-religious works of William James, Rudolf Otto, Friedrich Schleiermacher, and also to a certain extent, sociological research of religion, especially the works of Émile Durkheim and Max Weber.

maintaining the continuity of its historical pattern, and the continuity of its main contents and symbols? What in it enriches the world view and creative work of the Jew educated in modern secular humanistic culture?

However, claims Schweid,[302] one must consider the fact that not in all cases - and perhaps it is better to say: not in most of them - does the question arise directly about the stories of the sources and their content in myth. This fact is important to our matter since even refraining from use of the concept - which was already accepted and had even become trite in the discourse of research of religions and the philosophy of religions in the twentieth century - reveals a particular view of its meaning and validity. And indeed, in examining the way in which the question arose, even for those researchers and philosophers of religion who needed the concept of 'myth' and contributed as well to its clarification, it seems that their main actual religious question does not touch directly upon myth itself, but rather upon the status of the literature that delivers the religious heritage in all of its ways: the commands, laws, and judgments, prophecies and reprimands, beliefs and opinions and words of morality, the historical and supra-historical books, which all together constitute the totality of contents of the religious literature in which the Jewish people anchored their delivered heritage. The question to be asked is actually: What is the truth to which this literature testifies as Jewish national religious literature? In other words: What is the origin of its authority, or what is the source of its power to influence, educate, shape a world view and way of life of a nation and its individuals for generations?

At the basis of the questions regarding the character of the Holy Scriptures lays the question of myth, claims Schweid.[303] However, the question of myth may be circumvented without ignoring the question of the authority and the formative influence of the sources, as long as the subject is debated within the context of literary historical research, and using philological tools, in the framework of a humanistic approach to Judaism as a national culture, as literature in itself, or as communication between generations. This perception may include myth, but in itself, supposedly, is not myth. Its presence as a continuous institutional process of writing and disseminating, teaching and reading, interpreting and rewriting, is a historical fact in which to anchor its cultural value and educational authority; its ways of creation, establishment, and influence upon people for generations - which are certainly not myth. These may be given a scientifically researched explanation, and may even justify by it the need for these very sources, as an affiliating and enriching factor in the educational process. If these sources are treated from the beginning as cultural religious heritage of a people, or if they are confronted in order to examine which of their contents still enrich thought, stir up emotion, stimulate the creative imagination, and even generate religious experience - then the question of myth will not seem necessary, and in any case it will not initially be deemed central. Reference to particular chapters in the literature of the sources will, however, raise the question - as a private focused matter, and hence, as a secondary issue in terms of the weight of the sources.[304]

---

[302] (Schweid, 1996), pp. 55-57.
[303] Ibid.
[304] Ibid, p. 54.

Myths as a Form of Literature

4.3 Myth as a Form of Literature

From the point of view of humanism filled with religiosity, it is then possible to explain the phenomenon of myth quite easily, with the use of various types of 'licentia poetica', or in other words: lyrical poetry and epic poetry, fiction, wise literature, etc., all included in 'belles lettres' - the classics. They are sufficient to explain and justify the moral and aesthetic inspiration, and even the religious inspiration rendered by the sources. Religious literature is considered the original creation of the geniuses of faith and religion: the prophets, writers, sages, and Kabbalists. It is a sufficient explanation for the status of their works as national literature, and their power of influence which is delivered from generation to generation.

At the basis of the thought of writers and Jewish philosophers of religion in the twentieth century, from the beginning, there was reference to the sources as to a given fact whose very presence shapes and unifies the history of the religious culture of the Jewish people. Indeed, there is room to claim that the question of the relation to myth hovers in the background, even when given the humanistic research answer before the question was asked; and it seems, thinks Schweid, that this may have been done to prevent raising it. Acceptance of this literature as a source of national culture, and especially acceptance of the religious component in it as a message of actual meaning - were they really "self-evident", as implied by the way in which they were presented? Was not the very presentation of this literature as authoritative literature, or classic national literature, actually anchored in myth (not yet identified as such) that took shape in the process of delivery, spouting from this literature itself, or from the reflective consciousness of the writers and interpreters? Was the image that this literature imagined itself to its readers and pupils, and through which it became influential, not in itself myth? It seems that it was not possible not to ask these questions in the context of the development of modern (philological, historical) Biblical criticism, since Biblical criticism was in a collision course with the myth of the status of the Holy Scriptures. That is why the orthodoxy objected so vehemently to Biblical criticism, and it is also the reason why liberal and non-orthodox religious trends have accepted it with reservation.

Biblical criticism, by applying its research methods based on assumptions contrary to traditional interpretation, led, according to Schweid's approach, to the dismantling of the central myth that had united the Jewish people and their religion beyond all controversy - the myth of the 'Torah'. Schweid refers not to the books themselves, but to their manner of presence in the people, and their symbolic essence as a vibrant spiritual entity connecting the Jewish people with god, since the Torah "from Sinai" or "from heaven" is perceived both as a constant revelation of god's will in itself, and in the eternal soul of the people. In this sense the Torah itself is myth. Indeed, it would have been possible to cope with the problem that Biblical criticism raised toward the shape of traditional perception of the Torah as a formative factor in the being of the Jewish people, without defining it as myth. Schweid claims that most researchers and philosophers of the Jewish religion preferred this way, basing themselves on scientific theory, and on philosophical theory that was consolidated as the tradition of "Hachmat Yisrael" in the previous century, namely - the humanistic theory of 'national literature'.[305]

According to the humanistic understanding of the essence of 'national literature', and the cultural established process that formed it, 'national literature' is the comprehensive work created by the nation. However, not every literary work is included in it, but only those perceived, by a concealed principle, as representing the national essence, since the statement that one is speaking of the totality that "the people created" relates, again according to some hidden principle, to the people themselves as a comprehensive entity capable of directly expressing itself. Schweid claims then that in a perspective view, it is easy to note the fact that Biblical criticism, presented as completely scientific, had actually swallowed whole the traditional Torah myth, without an external sign of it. Nevertheless, there is a clear sign hinting to it, and that is the idea advocated by the school of Idealist philosophy: 'the national spirit', whose existence was certainly based on the element of self reflection of reason.

Every nation has its 'national spirit' unique to it, revealed in its culture, and so too the Jewish people, according to Krochmal's theory. This basic assumption is repeated, according to Schweid, with only minor changes in the philosophical religious thought of the nineteenth century, and the beginning of the twentieth century, as well as his secular perception in which the Jewish people are unique as a 'spiritual nation'. When one persists with the concept of 'national spirit', pondering over its precise meaning, the circular argument becomes clear: It is clear that the 'national spirit' is identified with the power of creation revealed in the culture of the nation, in its developing totality, and especially in literary works. There is no other indication of the experiential existence of the 'national spirit' except for the literature in which it resides. The literary creators are private people; however, they are perceived, according to this philosophical approach, as vehicles conveying the inspiration they had received from the presence of the national whole, as a unifying ideal, whose content is the national historical memory. The use of national language - in itself must be seen as a primary revealment of a collective soul, inspiring the power of creation of the individual. Secondly, the literary creators draw the contents from the previous literary totality, which appears as a formative heritage; and finally - they experience, as individuals, the experiences of the nation, and express the spiritual process of life of their national collective. This is ultimately the test, as well, for determining their status: If they succeed in creating a work that the nation will accept as a faithful expression of its spirit and will continue to be educated on for generations, then it is shifted from their private domain, and enters the collective memory of the nation, sanctified as an authentic expression of the 'spirit of the nation'. By the way, in this context, the status is also created of the 'national writer' and 'national poet', which are analogous to the status of the 'prophets', 'writers' and 'sages' in traditional literature.[306]

Although Idealist philosophy of the nineteenth century was based on scientific analysis of the connection between the work of the individual and national language and literature as an accumulative totality, it became clear that subsequently a quasi dialogue was conducted to reach a meaningful ontological symbolic determination, uniquely

---

[305] Ibid, p.55.
[306] Ibid, p. 56.

granting the 'national spirit' the entity status of a reasoned eternal ideal, uniting within it the totality of historical memory of the nation, and perhaps even being the origin of this memory. Of course, no empirical scientific research can corroborate the ontological status of the spirit; hence it will ultimately anchor in the consciousness of reason itself. It seems that there is "predetermined" compatibility between this reflective consciousness of the reason and the religious reflective consciousness of the creators of the 'national literature' of the Jewish people, who considered their work divine revelation, or inspiration of the 'holy spirit'. Thus, it was evidently probable that the theory of the 'national spirit' be accepted by the scholars of Jewish religious studies who had left tradition behind. In other words, it is possible to say that the inner correlation between religious myth and philosophical myth enabled the latter to "translate" into the former, without either one identifying itself to the other as myth.[307] Nevertheless, it should be emphasized that also researchers, thinkers, and Jewish philosophers of the twentieth century who moved away from Idealist philosophy and even rejected it vehemently, needed that category of 'national literature' that represents the spirit of the nation as a metaphysical entity imbuing authority and holiness - among them being Ahad Ha'am[308] and Bialik.

How then can one justify the concept of 'national spirit' as a scientific concept beyond Idealism? Several of the thinkers mentioned above assumed it simply as a matter of empirical evidence: Whoever reads the sources empathically will identify the national spirit in language, style and the layer of historical memories. There were, however, a few attempts at humanistic secular explanation, albeit saturated with religious fervor, such as Ahad Ha'am's psycho-biological one, anchored in the theory of 'the object of national existence' and the 'national I'. According to this theory, the historical memory that is delivered to individuals precedes personal memory, similarly to the succession of generations that preceded them prior to their existence. They are but individuals that represent their people, as in nature the individuals represent their kind; or the psycho-sociological explanation (close to that of Émile Durkheim) of M. J. Berdyczewski, based on the development of a quasi collective 'super I', supported by the fact that society, ontologically, is more than the sum total of the individuals comprising it; or the existentialist explanation of A. D. Gordon, which distinguishes between external 'consciousness', and internalized 'experience', anchoring the individual in the being of the universe through the links of connection of family and nation; and the explanation of Yehezkel Kaufmann, actually based on syncretistic combination of recognizing the independence of the human intellect as a free power that creates ideals, and recognizing the historical factors (economic, social and political) that cause certain ideas to be perceived as more functional than others, thereby becoming a factor unifying a nation over generations.[309]

According to Schweid's version, all of these attempts together show that we have before of us a contemplative step parallel to that of Idealist philosophy of the preceding century, aimed at explaining and justifying the traditional perception of the status of the Biblical sources on a new conceptual basis. Later on, of course, all the theological questions will be raised concerning the religious message of the sources: faith in god, creation, revelation, providence,

---

[307] Ibid, p. 57.
[308] Pen-name of Asher-Zvi Ginsberg.
[309] See: (Schweid, 1996), p. 91.

miracle, etc. These will require of each researcher or philosopher to answer according to his method, thus examining the degree of compatibility between understanding these concepts of religion, and its theology. However, in this connection too the concept of 'myth' does not seem central, and could be circumvented easily, and even rejected, presenting the whole variety of sources under the general title of "religious literature".

One may then claim that all the above explanations are actually different ways of explaining the creation and contents of myth as a special literary genre. In this context, it seems that even refraining from deliberate use of the concept 'myth' constitutes an interpretational relation to the phenomenon it represents. Schweid emphasizes that we should not blur the meaning of this deliberate refrainment. It expresses a perception that refuses to accept several theological connotations which might be implied in the concept 'myth', regarding the authenticity of the religious experience, and the historiness of events constituted in religion. The concept of 'myth', at least in common folk sense, has the connotation of fable, or of subjective bending, so that religion relying on it as a historical event may lose the validity of objective truth. Moreover, occasionally, refrainment from using the concept 'myth' expresses an affiliation to the rationalist Idealist claim of the nineteenth century that there is no myth in Judaism, since myth, as a story of the gods and their relation to men is a distinct idolatry phenomenon, and Judaism fought against it through religious literature of a totally different kind - literature representing an essentially different relation both to the concept of 'divinity' and to the concept of 'nature'. Myth, claim the twentieth century followers of nineteenth century thought, tells of the lives of gods in nature, with 'epiphany' being central to it, whereas there is no epiphany in the Holy Scriptures of the Jewish people. They describe only the nature that god had created, only the creation, only the acts of god and his words, and never god himself. Hence, even if the historical events in the Bible are raised at their peak to poetic visionary heights - it is not myth, but rather historical poetry.

If there is no epiphany, claim the philosophers of religion and researchers such as Hermann Cohen and Yehezkel Kaufmann, there is no myth. The religious literature of the Jewish people then constitutes a special category, essential to monotheism not only in terms of its objects and its religious thought content, but also in its quality, forms, expressions, and the validity of truth to which it testifies. Schweid emphasizes that those same twentieth century Jewish researchers and philosophers of religion who still needed the concept of 'myth', did not refute the validity of these claims. Hence, they too spoke of a special kind of myth. But why, he asks, did they still need the concept? Schweid pinpoints the answer for this in the 'existential' emotional characteristics, supra-ethical and supra-reason of religion, which they sought to rejuvenate in their thought. We have before us researchers and philosophers of religion who aspired to rehabilitate the religious experience of the sources in its primordial power, using the modern scientific and philosophical tools at their disposal. They needed, of course, a modern interpretation, yet aspired to reach through it not only the sense and meaning of the event itself, but the core of the experience, which is always unique and absolute: The presence of god is perceived not only by man's mind, but with his entire personality. In other words - the very ones who wished to rehabilitate the ecstatic religious event to which the sources testify, and to enable it to "speak" directly to the present and from within it, needed the concept that could fail them in the fictional connotation it includes. These thinkers, who themselves felt a religious mission and power of religious creation, could not ignore the difference between national literature in its classic sense, and unique essence embodied in the Holy Scriptures.

Myths as a Form of Literature

Although without divine epiphany, when god speaks directly to man, or through the power of the creation, man's entire personality is stamped by the overwhelming presence. Man, says Schweid, then lives god's fervor, his love to him and his demands of him. This means that we have before us a different myth, and yet a myth. These thinkers could not ignore the mythic meaning of the concept 'national spirit', which is equivalent in philosophy to the theological 'remaining of the soul'. And if they had confirmed the truth of their way, they should have called it by its name - 'myth'; that is - literature which is not only "documentation" of an event, but is the event itself, the speech that is heard anew every time it is listened to.[310]

The most distinct, developed and influential expression of a perception such as this in Jewish thought in modern times is to be found, according to Schweid, in the theories of philosophy of religion of Martin Buber and Franz Rosenzweig on one hand, and Leo Baeck on the other. Buber and Rosenzweig's common basis, as described by Schweid, is the opinion that myth in actuality embodies an event that brings together the human "I" of the individuals, or the "we" of the group, with the eternal divine "Thou". They insist that literary documentation is not a reflection or later memory of the event of revelation in which god and man were present and spoke, but rather it is the event itself; the spoken and speaking speech; the encounter with god, which is entirely visual literal emotional content. Thus, they insist upon the unique characteristic of the Biblical text, which does not tell about the past, but rather presents it always anew from within the present, repeatedly telling it as an event occurring at the time of the telling itself, and thereby capable of illuminating every "now" with its special context and details.[311] In Martin Buber's theory, the discussion on the issue of myth is concentrated on the direct actual historical interpretation of the Biblical text, and particularly the methodical assumptions directed toward rectifying the philological historical approaches of Biblical criticism. From the point of view of existentialist religious philosophy, Buber thinks that one should distinguish between the historiographic literature of the books of Samuel and Kings, taken as objective scientific historiography, depicted in tight prose, delivered in writing, and from the point of view external to the events - and historical legend or myth, which is delivered orally, in poetic language, and not about the event but rather from within it. Schweid emphasizes that all of these characteristics are of principled importance to Buber: The subjective vs. objective position; poetic enthused language vs. understated prose; oral delivery (the teller and listeners identifying with the event) vs. written delivery; and the testimony from the "now" of the dramatic happening vs. the testimony from a remote present from which one observes that which had occurred and is done.

According to Buber,[312] these characteristics were preserved in the mythic historical Biblical text even when the stories were expanded during their oral delivery from generation to generation, and when written as well. We still have before us the text created for oral delivery, during dramatic experiencing, introducing us into the events, identifying us and creating an organic continuum also expressed in the continuation of changes that entered the text at the time of repeated telling. Thus we have not only a documented event, but also its continuous history. The conclusions entailed

---

[310] Ibid, p. 59.
[311] (Schweid, 1995), pp. 47-49.
[312] See: M. Buber, *The Kingship of God* (Jerusalem: Bialik Institute, 2000); *Moses* (New York: Humanity 1998); *Te'udah Ve-yi'ud* (Jerusalem: Bialik Institute, 1984).

from these assumptions regarding the historical authenticity of myth, and the religious truth delivered in it, according to Schweid, are far-reaching, since even if we cannot perceive the course of events itself, we may still learn a great deal from the text about the way in which it was perceived by the people present at that event. We can learn about the encounter of this people with a great historical event happening, the legend-creating enthusiasm with which the people absorbed the enormous events and delivered them to a creative memory; an encounter of a people with events so powerful that they could not but be attributed to the deeds of heavenly powers, which - according to Buber, is true historical powerfulness. In his view, the role of interpreting the legends through criticism of the tradition brings us closer to that very encounter, in relation to which we must give up the separation of "objective reality" from within the legend. The historical kernel of the legend, in his opinion, cannot be acquired by removing the element of enthusiasm from it, and one cannot purify and extract history from within the historical miracle. Concerning historical stories such as Mount Sinai, claims Buber, it would not be right to speak about 'historization of myth'; it would seem that they should be called 'mythization of history', if one only maintains the assumption that myth does not mean here - as opposed to the common concept in the history of religion - more than the story of the enthused about that which happened to him. And it is doubtful whether the story of some unenthused chronicle-teller would better suit the truth. "There is no understanding of scientific history other than the rational understanding", writes Buber, but it must begin with "The large reason overcoming the smaller one."[313]

Contrary to Buber's focus on the issue of the relation between myth and history, Franz Rosenzweig focused on the background of the concept he coined 'the new thinking'.

Regarding the problem of myth as reliable religious language,[314] Rosenzweig defined his existentialist lingual method as "reliable science", thereby - from the beginning - removing that problem of relation between religious truth and scientific truth that Buber wished to solve in his way. Rosenzweig's basic claim is that thinking is an ongoing dialogue that man conducts with his surroundings. The universe speaks to man in its way, as a message of sensory information which it transmits to man, who receives and replies, so that a dialogue is created.

Human society and human beings speak to each other; god and man too communicate. As mentioned, each dialogue has its own language. However, the understanding that thinking is basically speech turns the question of the truth of knowledge into the question of reliability of language, or reliability of languages. And this is created, according to Rosenzweig, spontaneously while speaking. To conduct a dialogue means to create belief among the speakers. This is a basic position without which there is no human existence. In Rosenzweig's opinion, the foundation is in the basic pattern of speech inherent in man's soul. This does not primarily refer to actual language, which is of agreement, but rather to the primordial ability which is revealed through it. The ability to speak, as an inherent trait of man, according to Rosenzweig, is pre-language - an abstract pattern of language identifying with the human in man's soul. It is implanted in the soul, and cannot have any source but the primary source which the Bible teaches, namely: God created it in man, and that is the meaning of the creation of man - "In the image of god." God created man in

---

[313] M. Buber, *Moses: The Revelation and the Covenant* (New York: Humanity 1998), pp. 14-16.
See also: (Schweid, 1996), p. 60.
[314] F. Rosenzweig, "Der Stern Der Erlosung" (1921), *The Star of Redemption,* trans. B.E. Galli (Madison: Wisconsin UP, 2005).

speech; he implanted speech in him, so that speech is also the immediate revelation of god in man. According to Rosenzweig, these are the basic assumptions of every science. These assumptions are interpreted by him in various ways regarding each field of reference of man. Each field has a language specific to the different kind of discourse, both in terms of the absorbed information and the answer given. Our matter is especially concerned with the discourse between god and man, in other words - religious language: What makes it unique? What may it convey between god and man? We must bear in mind that according to Rosenzweig - god created man by his speaking to him; that is, by implanting in him the ability to speak in the form of an ancient pattern of language, subsequently actualized by agreement-bound, acquired language.

The obvious conclusion then is that the discourse between god and man is conducted in that ancient lingual pattern. This is the pattern which grants language its reliability; it creates from, and in, it the pre-disposition of man to believe. In this discourse with god, the ancient pattern of language is directly revealed, from amidst the agreement-bound language, accentuating the existential characteristics of language - those characteristics which enable language to represent reality through all of its formal, sensory and mimetic qualities. Thus the agreement-bound language "translates" the ancient pattern of language, which - in turn - "translates" the divine speech that created it, and together with it - also the reality it represents. Moreover, by sublimation of divine speech, human speech - rising to the elevated level of expressing belief through myth, prayer and ritual - is also able to "create" actual reality between man and man, and between god and man. The belief-bound speech creates those alliance connections and encounters of love that overcome death, bringing redemption to man and to the world. The truth of myth, as the truth of the prophetic vision, or the truth of prayer and ritual, is then the truth of the encounter created through the structural existential qualities of language. Rosenzweig too warns his readers that the encounter taking place between god and man is the redeeming speech of love, not divine epiphany, nor mystical unification. Myth, or prophetic vision, delivers the ecstasy of the entire personality in the presence of divine speech. These are actual events that occurred between god and the world, and god and man, as man received them, inspired by the encounter. Rosenzweig, as well, distinguishes between Biblical myth and idolatry myth, including epiphany. Idolatry myth appears as expressing an ancient stage in the religious development of man, in which he is still captive to the predetermination of nature, and god has not yet revealed himself to him. Conversely, monotheistic myth of the Bible is the story of revelation that released man from the predetermination of nature - opening him to a free, redeemed and redeeming relation - to god, to society, and to the universe.

Leo Baeck's theory of the essence of myth is much simpler, and strongly connected to the issue of his relation to Jewish mysticism.[315] Baeck's thought, as described by Schweid, underwent gradual change. At the beginning of his way, as a distinct student of Hermann Cohen, he refuted both mysticism and myth, and denied their existence in original Judaism. Later he recognized the fact that there is mysticism in the religious literature of the Jewish people, and mysticism of distinct Jewish characteristics fulfilling a vital role in the religion. Finally, he tended to attribute to mysticism a central role, preferable to philosophy. According to Baeck, mysticism is a unique and supreme product of

---

[315] L. Baeck, *Wege im Judentum* (Berlin: Schocken, 1933), pp.90-103.

a natural ability found in every child, and preserved in adults as the 'genius' of poets and artists; in other words: the power of creative imagination. This is a human talent which Baeck perceives similarly to Yehuda Halevi in explaining the matter of prophecy. The creative imagination, he thinks, is a kind of openness to inspiration absorbed from hidden supreme spiritual spheres, from divinity itself. This means that creative imagination cannot be seen as the mere talent to process sensory impressions according to a formal aesthetic or intellectual idea. It is the talent to connect to the hidden domain and experience the divine presence, receive its messages, and then render expression of this experiencing in a symbolic way, indicating - through the expressible - that which is not. For this purpose, Baeck added a distinction that he considered essential, between art for the sake of art, serving the aesthetic matter and hence designing a fictional reality, and art that uses the aesthetic tool to express a reality beyond man. The first type of art is more prevalent, and in his eyes is the most negative, especially when it assumes a romantic mood that takes man out of actual reality to the sphere of fake sublimation, during which it releases man from moral responsibility and 'mitzvah' (religious commands). Having characterized Christianity as a "romantic religion", Baeck thus characterizes its art and myth as well. Without saying it explicitly, he repeats the traditional Jewish polemic determination that Christianity is idolatry. Conversely, art of the second kind is authentic religious art, of which Aristotle said in "Poetica" that it is more philosophical, that is - closer to the truth, "than history". In his last writings, Baeck often quoted this Aristotelian phrase, parallel to his growing tendency to quote Biblical poetry or to express himself with his own poetic prose imbued with pathos, especially when he wished to give his readers and listeners a sense of the image and the comprehensive meaning of Jewish history. The power of creative imagination in his original authentic action is then the talent of the soul absorbing mystical inspiration and enabling-constituting an encounter with god; and the art created to express the mystical inspiration and deliver its messages is authentic religious art. The Jewish people saw themselves as a nation whose beginning is anchored in the Creation itself, a unique nation that god leads with revealed and concealed miracles. Undoubtedly, these stories are myth and not history, says Baeck. Although myth does not describe the events as they took place, it perceives their true meaning from the divine eternal perspective. There are moments in which the divine eternity pervades time; in these moments myth and history conjoin, and furthermore - in these moments history assumes the image of myth.[316]

The philosophers of religion who pointed to the central presence of myth in Judaism characterized it mainly as historical myth. They rejected the view, which they considered superficial, that myth is but fictional creation embodying at the very most "subjective truth", and saw it as the manifestation of actual events; that which occurred at the level perceived in historiographic scientific description, they complement by indicating the event that occurred at the spiritual level above it - the very level from which alone may historical meaning be perceived, and its purpose observed. Similarly, adds Schweid, these philosophers of religion, who expounded the necessity of myth in religion in general, and in Judaism in particular, did not make do with the role of apologizing and interpreting, but rather assumed the role of delivering myth, with full awareness of its creative continuous character. Buber, Rosenzweig and Baeck conducted the role of 're-mythologization' of Judaism - as researchers of the past; as its justifiers and interpreters for purposes of the present; and as re-shapers of their times - in the spirit of poetic and narrative art, and the power of

---

[316] (Schweid, 1996), p. 62-63.

creative imagination, each in his own way and personal style. In their attempts to recreate Jewish myth and continue it into their times, Buber, Rosenzweig and Baeck are not alone. According to Schweid's approach, they illustrate a contemplative and literary phenomenon that is typical both in the field of religious and national thought, and in the field of fictional writing and poetry. Alongside these three philosophers of religion mentioned above Schweid enumerates a list of such thinkers.[317] All of them restore the myth of 'eternal people' by religious creation - either by contemplative tools or by poetic legends. However, to Schweid's method, it was the new Hebrew literature that particularly excelled at it, defining itself as "the literature of the revival generation".[318]

---

[317] Ibid.
[318] The Period of Revival in Hebrew literature: a prevalent name for the 60 years from the end of Enlightenment at the end of the 19th century ("May Laws" in 1881) until the UN resolution of division of the Land of Israel. Characterizing the period: the Zionist influence upon the European Jews, revival of the Hebrew language and competition with Yiddish, and establishing the Hebrew literary community in the Land of Israel. Mendele Mocher Sforim, Bialik, Tchernichovsky, Berdyczewski, Brenner, Gnessin, and Hazaz are identified as writers of the period.

4.4 Bialik and the Gap between Past and Future

This metaphoric transformation of religious contents, with their full emotional power, into national social contents is at the foundation of the great myths of Hebrew and Yiddish poetry and fiction in the first half of the twentieth century. The most prominent example, both in terms of creative power and width and depth of influence, is the myth created in the poetry of H.N. Bialik, through the blending of personal biographical materials with traditional, Biblical, legend, and Kabbalistic ones.

The myth of childhood appears in the poems "Zohar" (1901); "The Pond" (1908); "The Talmud Student" (1898); "At the House of Study's Threshold" (1894). The myth of exile appears in "The Fire Scroll" (1909) and "in the City of Slaughter" (1903); and the myth of the Zionist revival - in "The Dead of the Desert" (1902).

The rare blending of traditional myth materials through the prism of personal experiencing, perceived from it and in it as 'typological', and in this sense as prophetic - places Bialik's entire extensive works, and especially its parts of myth, within the broad context of the traditional literature, as its dialectic continuation. However, the uniqueness of this continuation, from the point of its content and form, is manifest in a crisis of faith, or a crisis of traditional myth, as part of its own narrative continuity. Study of Bialik's mythic work reveals that it is still aware of itself as religious poetry coping with the traumatic event of the crisis of faith; hence, it is not about metaphorical use of myth, but rather about authentic myth.

According to Schweid's approach, live myth should not be identified with its literary manifestation as a studied text, but rather with its formative presence in the consciousness of a public that is unified by it into acting and striving together toward one common goal.[319] And indeed, if we examine the works of myth of the literature of the Revival generation from this point of view, we find that this is literature which succeeded in creating the operation of myth in the consciousness of an entire layer of the nation. Furthermore, there was continuity of this process of reconstituting the national myth in new Hebrew literature, at least for three generations. Actually, claims Schweid, most of the prominently influential works (of Berdyczewski, Brenner, Agnon and Hazaz) reflected the new national myth, or assumed it as an internalized foundation, occasionally with direct identification, or with an ironic one, and sometimes out of refutational identification, expressing a profound spiritual rift. In all of these ways, the writers of this generation perceived the 'comprehensive being' of their period through some hue of national myth, thus delivering the myth, modulating and continuing it. Although their own works cannot be defined as works of myth, it seems that the presence of poetry striving toward expression and direct formation of the essence of myth was a continuous constant phenomenon as well.[320]

---

[319] (Schweid, 1996), p. 65-66.
[320] See in this context, in particular, the poetry of Uri Zvi Grinberg, David Shimoni, Yitzhak Lamdan, Shin Shalom and Natan Alterman.

Parallel processes in the field of research of the sciences of Judaism, philosophy of Judaism, and literary creativity indicate a process of re-mythologization as a complex process, basically ambiguous, and thereby imbued with paradoxality and irony, both deliberate and non-deliberate. Despite the essential differences between the view advocating de-mythologization in the nineteenth century, and the one advocating re-mythologization in the first half of the twentieth century, the two approaches maintain a developmental dialectic continuum between them, rather than mutual exclusion; at the revealed theoretical level one sees that the advocates of re-mythologization accepted the bulk of their predecessors' claim about the essential difference between the perception of life expressed in idolatry mythology, and the perception of life of monotheism; and between the type of religious literature of idolatry, and the type of religious literature of monotheism. Therefore, one can go back and discover the original myth of Judaism only by distinguishing between various types of myth, whose difference is essential not only from the aspect of narrative contemplative content, but also in terms of the quality of the myth itself. Actually, it was deemed necessary to redefine the phenomenon of myth within the monotheistic context, and one easily sees that this redefinition introduced - as internalized conscious tension - reservations regarding the qualities of idolatry mythology, which is reservation about the danger inherent in mythic perception itself; hence, the sharp distinction, which is the need to bridge between the inner truth of myth, and the objective truth of history. Similarly, at the concealed level, it seems that researchers and philosophers of religion, during the process of re-mythologization, revealed the foundation of concealed myth as philosophical ideal in the thought of their predecessors, who had refuted myth. Indeed, for them the revealing of this paradox was the strongest evidence of the claim of the necessity of myth as the basis of any religion and any comprehensive world view. This, however, did not stop them from connecting, in their way and openly, to the myth concealed from their predecessors, and from exposing its dialectic connections with traditional religious myth. Determining the dialectic continuum between the course of de-mythologization and the course of re-mythologization will assist us in discerning additional ambiguity and irony manifest there. The course of thought which acknowledges the necessity of myth and its vitality in the existence of authentic religiousness, goes together with acknowledging the crisis of the intellectual and emotional ability of modern people to accept traditional religious myth - with the conviction of the world view it draws, and the orientation it determines. Thus, the intellectual and emotional ability of modern people decreases in innocently needing myth as myth - even when they want it.[321]

It seems then that the crisis expressed openly by various forms of leaving the traditional pattern of religion - whether in the direction of modern religiousness or in the direction of wavering, heresy, or total indifference to religion - was also expressed by new definitions given to myth, and in contents and forms of myth renewed in the literature of the revival generation. The consciousness of the crisis of faith entered myth as a central event of dramatic 'fall' into the abyss of disappointment and despair. Moreover, the story of the 'fall' is myth's way of generating the transformation of the power of traditional religious experience into national experience. These then are the means with which myth was legitimized, and its credibility restored in modern consciousness; or in other words, traditional myth received a limited "life extension" as revolutionary nation myth. Although the very phenomenon is not new of

---

[321] (Schweid, 1996), p. 66.

attempting to overcome the crisis of religious consciousness by continuing myth through it - as an event joining the previous story, and going back to interpret it - it does embody within itself the vitality of myth, or the vitality of religion that can rejuvenate from within the great crises of its primary sources.

The research of Gershom Sholem in the history of Jewish mysticism presents several turning points in the perception of myth, of which the later and most documented is the creation of the myth of 'reduction' and of 'fall' in the Kabbalah of the Ari.[322] However, the Ari's Kabbalah, even in its most extreme transformation in Sabbateanism, which introduced heresy itself into the myth of faith, still does not speak of the transformation of the power of religious experience into the power of national experience, that is - in the course of knowingly distancing from religiousness itself. Myth that rejuvenates beyond the boundary line marked retroactively by orthodoxy is myth that withstands a difficult test both of authenticity and of legitimacy - two sides of the same problem (and the reason why Sholem found fault in nearly all modern attempts to renew Judaism beyond the orthodox patterns). Is this not the reason why ultimately, even in the period of re-mythologization, the most efficient myths in terms of their social and national role were those defined only retrospectively and retroactively? In other words: Those created by structural, intellectual, emotional and imagery depth projections of rationalist ideologies, which in the name of science continued to struggle against the old myths? Is this not the reason why myths created as well in literature and influential as such, reflected ideologies such as these, deliberately or unintentionally? In any case, it is quite clear that in the first half of the twentieth century, the universal influence of ideologies was prevalent, in Europe in general, and among the Jewish people in particular. However, the determination that re-mythologization became widespread under the influence of ideologies that did not initially introduce themselves as myth, will seem to us sufficiently convincing only if we acknowledge that their power of influence was not limited to the partially scientific findings and selective rationalist analyses that they called to their help, but rather to the representation of the cohesive comprehensive picture of reality, granting definite orientation and strong motivation to action, originating in the supra-organizing pattern. In other words: the success of modern ideology was dependent on its ability to shape, from a well-defined point of view, prominent historical memories and immediate personal experiences of masses of people, and through them to create in the masses a sense of orientation, within a dramatic narrative event in which they are called to take an active part, and convey it to the goal - the great vision, which is clearly seen on the near historical horizon. Thus they managed to generate, at least for a short period, emotional motivation that was seemingly religious. These discussed myths must not be identified with the ideologies themselves, but only together with the emotional and visionary effect that these ideologies created in the consciousness of the masses. This, states Schweid, is of course the reason why as long as the ideologies were effective they were not acknowledged as myths, but only became identified with them retrospectively. Hence, it is possible to say that the phenomenon of re-mythologization may be seen not only as a dialectic reversal of the process of de-mythologization, but as its actual continuation, or as a counter move - which is a stage in the process of gradual decrease of the plenty. If we consider the states of mind prevalent in Jewish thought in the second half of the century, we see that the myths created in the literature of the revival generation lost their impact as myths; and it

---

[322] The developments of Kabbalah associated with Isaac (ben Solomon) Luria Ashkenazi (app. 1534-1572).

seems that they could not pass on to a second generation of creators and readers that same power of emotion and of traditional religious thought, whose transformation into national emotion and thought had generated them. Since they did not deliver their sources in the way that their creators had received them in the formative biographical stage that shaped their traditional religious education, they too did not pass on to the next generation through myths, but only through poetry of aesthetic or historical value. It turns out, however, that those ideologies as well that had generated myth in the consciousness of their advocates did not attain a longer period of grace. The second generation - whether it saw them in their relative success at achieving their goals or in their failure - lost interest in them. One way or another, they ceased to be the generation's determiners of orientation in historical situations that had totally changed. They were hence exposed and identified as myths whose time had passed, and their very identification as myths was sufficient to dismiss or "shatter" them. It seems then, adds Schweid, that the second half of the twentieth century may be again noted as a period of de-mythologization, of course without losing the good lesson of the two previous periods, since from now on, the fact of the myth's presence and centrality will no longer be denied, at least in traditional religious Jewish thought.

4.5 De Natura Dei

The act of symbolization - as presented by Ohana and Wistrich,[323] influences and shapes reality and actuality through its creation with symbols and myths. Symbolization is perception of a thing through another thing, an action of deciphering through shaping. Language, science, religion, art and myth in the history of man became sign systems interpreting and shaping the world for the individuals, as for communities that share a sign system. However, collective symbols enable common world views, comprehensive images, and collective myths. This common placing of myth and science side by side as sign systems differing in their language, and offering different explanations for being, does not blur the distinction between the status of the symbol in myth, and that of the symbol in science - since while science acknowledges its symbolic characteristic, myth has no consciousness of symbolism; or in other words: the mythic position does not perceive itself as symbolic.

The narrative characteristic distinguishes myth from idea. Holiness enveloping the events distinguishes myth from legends or from folklore; irrelevance of corroboration or refutation distinguishes myth from history; drama and personification distinguish myth from ideology. Sociological and anthropological research indicate the action of myth as constituting solidarity, identity, and structure of thought, whose main role is to reconciliate contradictions between people, and some see its main role not in symbolic representation or explaining power, but rather in granting legitimization to the present.

As for the distinction between myth, which is non-reasoned, and ideology which is reasoned, this distinction, claim Ohana and Wistrich, is a misconception: Myth is not necessarily non-reasoned, there is reasoned myth and non-reasoned myth. Myth and ideology, they believe, are neutral concepts that may be charged with various contents.[324]

It is possible that the mistake of those who see myth as non-reasoned derives from myth usually appealing to the aesthetic dimension, with expressions in metaphoric, symbolic and visual language. One must remember, however, that this is the appealing language of myth, not its content, reasoned or not. Myth hints at the unity of man and his world, hence, in its appeal, it personally binds the consciousness of its beholder with the mythic object. Or, in other words, if in the eyes of the myth builders or in the eyes of their followers, ideology is intended for the educated, and is too abstract or theoretical, political or ethnic, thereby alienated - then myth speaks the language of the ordinary people; that is - myth is more "humane" than ideology or utopia. Functionality as the prime character of myth distinguishes it from legend, but the question of which functionality remains open.

---

[323] (Ohana and Wistrich, 1996), p.11.
[324] Ibid, p. 19.

Myth is not a story drawn from artistic imagination or theoretical explanation, but rather it appears as a reality according to which one lives. The question of myth's credibility is not relevant, since pondering the "factuality" of political myths is similar to pondering the truth of objects; myth is beyond refutation or proof, and all that is left is to examine its degree of effectiveness in granting inspiration, intensifying emotions, and directing people to actions. Intellectual attempts to explain myth as allegorical expression of contemplative or moral truth have ignored mythical experience, hence are condemned in advance to failure; theories about myth are problematic, as myth essentially is not theoretical; however, behind myth hide images and symbols, and the role of critical thought is to reveal the political or social meanings behind the construction of myth.

Myth then appears as perspective truth; as another way of interpreting. The historian, according to Ohana and Wistrich, examines society diachronically; the sociologist analyzes synchronically, at a given point in time; whereas the researcher of myth oversees the axis of depth: The axis of dreams, yearning and memories.[325]

Myth is a way of thinking, an ideal story through which society tells about itself - where it came from and where it is going. Historical and sociological research, claim Ohana and Wistrich, should not deny myth a-priori with iconoclastic passion, by undermining it retroactively, but rather should examine it - ask critical questions, strive to reveal its inner logic, understand its secret of vitality, and try to find the place of myth in constructing reality.

There is a dialectic relation between myth and historical present, claims Schweid,[326] whereby each one creates the other in its image; or in other words, myth is the creation of the past in order to shape the present.

The mythic event is perceived as a repeated precedent in the course of the flow of time, and it shapes it, giving it form. The story of Exodus is considered a central mythic event in Judaism, and it is introduced in the Bible not to teach history in the "historiological" sense of Thomas Mann, or in the sense of the stories in Kings, which are simple historiography with no mobilizing meaning and lesson to learn. The story of Exodus teaches us that in every generation man must see himself as if he had experienced the historical event; in every generation man shapes the mythic event of Exodus from his view of the historical present he is in. The Friday night Kiddush is the weekly ritualization of this mythic event, by saying "In memory of the Exodus from Egypt". Myths, beyond being occasionally rationalizations justifying a certain status quo, at the same time fulfill many roles, not all negative. They can indeed provide legitimacy for existing social and political customs, for a ruling elite or social group, but myth also constitutes a motivating factor and strengthens toward commitment or identification with a sublime goal, as has happened over the last two hundred years. Most of the myths are narratives seeking to anchor the present in the past. As a particular kind of narrative, myths are symbolic statements or a frame of reference, granting meaning to the past, and as such - they are not necessarily false examples or test cases of pseudo-history. Their true meaning is inherent in their ability to tell us about the ways in which a nation, or social group or system of individuals wish to organize their unique collective memory, and establish their distinct identity. The process of analysis and deconstruction of myth

---

[325] Ibid.
[326] (Schweid, 1996), pp. 68-70.

enriches in its revealment of the deep and unconscious social needs, and in its locating the symbolic order of political structure or the past of a community.

It seems that a difficulty arises here in denying the fact that myths rejuvenate, and will rejuvenate, due to what seems to be theoretical and historical necessity, namely, that meaningful perception of reality, capable of granting people general orientation and marshalling their necessary energies for a purposeful enterprise of historical extent, is not possible without myth. Myth is "the meaningful", at least due to the fact that approaches seeking to divest themselves of it find themselves, perhaps even of necessity, appealing to that which diverges from the meaning (and as may be assumed, will transform into new meanings).

The crisis of the withdrawal of the gods or the 'hidden face' of the god, which Bialik and Hölderlin experienced, each in his own way, is superimposed on the basic crisis of the culture and politics of our times, which may be seen, on the one hand, as connected to the difficulty in collectively attaining a comprehensive and extensive explanation such as myth had provided humanity for such a long time; and on the other hand, as a dialectic pole of this view, with the increase of fundamentalist myths in an interpretational mimetic version, insular and enforcing. The (theological-political) dangers manifest in myths on one hand, and that which seems to be the necessity of its presence - as the condition for cultural rejuvenation - on the other, raise questions about the very possibility of the delivery of a constituting idea over the course of time; or in the words of Hannah Arendt: How is it possible to deliver to the future the experience, concepts and culture of the tradition of the past, without dragging in all the accompanying problems?[327] This, according to Arendt, would be a political question, and this matter returns the course of study of this essay to the issue of the status-role of myth in the poetry of Bialik.

---

[327] H. Arendt, Between Past and Future: Six Exercises in Political Thought (New York: Viking, 1961), p. 17.

... between one concealment to the next, the abyss flickers.
(C.N. Bialik, Revealment and Concealment in Language)[328]

5. The Myth Carriers

A joint analysis of Bialik's poems "Zohar"[329] (1901) and "Shirati"[330] (1900), which were originally two parts of a long lyrical poem (divided by the poet), shows Bialik's poetic origin as stemming from what may be called a 'threshold experience', residing in the gap or rift between 'twin worlds'. On the one hand, there is the old and crumbling world that bears a forgotten truth, while on the other - a new, shining and promising one which also misleads, floating in the air. Bialik's dialectic poetics is revealed from within the crisis of traditional language, with the aid of research works by Ziva Shamir[331] and Eliezer Schweid,[332] as poetics of sobriety, according to which the old may not be cast away in the Nietzschian sense, but rather - the new should be rebuilt from the mixture of new with old. Thus Bialik indicates the direction and way to a quasi new solution, which is also the transformation of an old idea: 'tikkun', for which he presents a 'new poetry' in the form of personal and collective myth, blending within it and weaving together varied layers of mythic materials from the past, re-activated in order to take place as an 'event' in the present.

---

[328] C. N. Bialik, "Revealment and Concealment in Language" (Hebrew), in Literature (Tel Aviv: Dvir, 1977), pp. 24-31.
[329] C.N. Bialik, "Zohar" (1900), BYP.
[330] C.N. Bialik, "Shirati" (1900), BYP.
[331] See: Z. Shamir, "To Compile Sparkles amidst the Broken Vessels", in *Sadan, Studies in Hebrew Literature*, vol. 4, ed. A. Holtzman (Tel Aviv: Tel Aviv UP, 2000), pp. 75-113.
[332] (Schweid, 1998), pp. 104-143.

5.1 Bialik's Meta-Poesis

Do you know where I got my song?

In my father's house a lonely singer lived,

modest, unobtrusive, diffident,

a dweller in dark holes and murky grooves.

He knew one melody, familiar, fixed.

And when my heart grew dumb, and my tongue clove

to the roof of my mouth in silent misery

and stifled weeping welled up in my throat at

that tune re-echoed through my empty soul -

the chirp of cricket - bard of poverty.

My father's want profaned the Sabbath feast.

His table carried neither wine nor bread;

a few thin ragged candles stuck in earth

Were all that took the place of his pawned lamps;

and seven children hungry, half-asleep,

intoned a welcome to the Sabbath angel.

My mother listened downcast to the song.

My father, shamed, disheartened, cut black bread

and tails of salt fish with a damaged knife.

We chewed our salt and sour fare: all's one,

both tepid, and as tasteless as the tears

of deprivation and of wretchedness.

We raised our voices to our father's songs

with rumbling bellies and with hollow hearts,

and the cricket joined the dismal chorus then,

singing from his crevice in the dark.[333]

"Shirati" (1900)[334] was a long lyrical poem divided by Bialik in order to fit printing in Ahad Ha'am's newspaper "Hashiloach". The first part is short and full of meaning - "Shirati" (comprising a third of the full poem), and the second is "Zohar", long and relatively sparse; on the one hand, a dark and sad poem, and on the other - a poem of light and joy. The division of the poem into two parts, claims Shamir, blurred the historiographic ideas from the fields of poetics and politics, which had formed the basis of the complete poem that had contained conceptual continuity and a tight structure.[335] In all publications of his writings the two poems appear consecutively; and in the collections of Bialik's poetry two pictures appear one after the other, as described by Shamir, of two opposites. The first is a dismal chamber picture in the center of which is a dark room, from which the monotonous sound of playing is heard, and the second - an illuminated negative full of singing and ecstatic dances in a golden-green field. The first is Father's home, in the multiple sense of the word, inside the crumbling Jewish ruins, the depressing poverty-stricken interior, whereas the second is in idyllic nature full of boundless joy (at least seemingly). One being takes place in a dark winter night and dusky dawn, while the second is in the morning, and a summery noon washed with light and glow. One is in the somber image of the miserable father who has exhausted his energies, a widowed mother struggling with her bitter fate, and the orphaned brothers huddling tightly together, teeth clicking with cold and fear. The other is in the exuberant company of seductive and mysterious friends bursting into the child's life, and then disappearing in the same way. Here - hunger and torture of body and soul, and there - intoxication and pleasures of body and soul. In this one - a group picture erasing the uniqueness of the individual, swallowing him into the general (the narrator-poet as one of seven orphans), and in that one - a broad and shining picture of togetherness emphasizing the 'I' and intensifying it. This one is accompanied by the hollow sound of the cricket hiding in the crevices of the house, and that one - by the delightful sounds of the cricket hopping amongst the grass blades of the meadow. This one is in no-exit stagnation, in a reality bound with shackles that have long lost their content and language, and that one exceeds all boundaries in a frenzied movement of explosion, licentiousness, and daring breaking of conventions. The first describes the death of the father-god in the midst of the Sabbath violently desecrated, and the second - the festive glistening weekdays which the orphan absorbs as "free and happy", left to himself, abandoning the shadows of the

---

[333] C. N. Bialik, "Shirati" (1900) (My Song), in *Selected Poems, (Bilingual)*, trans. R. Nevo (Jerusalem: Dvir and Jerusalem Post, 1981).
[334] C. N. Bialik, "Shirati" (1900) - BYP.
[335] (Shamir, 2000), pp. 76.

room for the fields where he can grow alone as a wild weed, unattended. All of this, as described by Shamir, is ambiguous, a text rich with various possibilities of reading and interpreting.[336]

Over the years the literary interpretation dealt more with "Shirati" and less with "Zohar". "Shirati" is laden with meanings and symbols, with countless reverberations from generations of Hebrew and Western literature; hence, it challenges the interpreter endlessly. Conversely, "Zohar" is more denotative and less elusive, punctuated with arbitrary (seemingly at least) details of reality, and does not posit that same boundless joy. Shamir claims that we do not encounter here a simple and simplistic binary division. "Shirati" presents both the advantages and disadvantages of the classic and classicist world, both protective and choking in its multiple interpersonal traditions, whereas "Zohar" presents the advantages and disadvantages of the romantic symbolist world that breaks rules and frameworks, with numerous individual enjoyments, both attracting and threatening, which it offers the young adventurous people who are willing to dare try it out. At the center of "Zohar" is the story of the child making love with the light airy breezes, and in large portions of it there is no multiplicity of dialogues with collective treasures of the past that characterize "Shirati". However, it is the very breezes - earlier discussed and the pivot of the personal and unique experiences of the child in nature - with which Bialik paradoxically formulated such an overwhelming multiplicity and infinity of dialogues with cultural treasures of East and West, until the interpreter is rendered unable to exhaust the abundance of possible readings.[337] The complete poem was divided into a tertiary structure, that is - three chapters, each opening with an elevating question, and the first two are in the style of the wisdom chapters of Job, a question with a low ironic reply of a folk humor nature, sharply contrasting with the classic character of the implied text and the divine context from which the mold of the question is taken: The form of conjugating the verb in the first and third question - "Do you know?" (appearing twice in the Book of Job, when pondering the secrets of the Creation and cosmic order). The first chapter, opening with "Do you know where I got my song?" tells about the origin of the poet's poetry, continuing with the description of his family whose father was suddenly taken, leaving the cricket's song reverberating in the dismal home. The second chapter, on the source of his sighing: "Do you know where my sigh comes from?" continues to describe the widowed mother who passed her grief onto the poet. The third chapter opens with the question about his dreams and continues with a description of the orphaned child left to himself in nature. The last, in contrast to the preceding ones, is not anchored in classic and neo-classic origins, as it is basically new ("And the sources of my childhood dreams, do you now?"), serving as a quasi prologue for a distinct romantic description in whose center is the excursion into nature, the return to the childhood memories and being swept into the realms of imagination. Bialik left the first two questions in the text, while deleting the third when he divided the entire poem into two independent ones.[338]

Upon awakening, the poet discovers - to his sorrow and joy - that "the song of the Zohar has become forever silent, but its sounds still echo deep in the poet's heart." Here the narrator-poet, employing contemplative abstract language, re-discusses the issue of the origins of his poetry, and reaches a conclusion that includes a quasi return (with

---

[336] Ibid, p. 76.
[337] Ibid, p. 77.
[338] Ibid, p. 77-79.

changes)[339] to the point of departure, and to the opening question of "Do you know where I got my song?". Ultimately, he is surprised to discover that the origin of his poetry is not only in the experiencing of poverty and pain at home, but also in that of the natural joy, which is both demonic and divine, attracting him - the individual and the people - beyond the walls. Here Shamir expresses her perception regarding Bialik's multi-layered and multi-meaning method, and reads an ars-poetica conclusion in the poem: Only from the synthesis of poverty and riches, pain and joy, shadows and glow, materialism and idealism, reality and imagination, Hebraic asceticism and Hellenistic Dionysianism, collective fate and personal choice - may new worthy poetry grow in the Modern era.[340]

Allusions to the stories of Samson (and Zedakiah) and Moses (and Isaiah) at the end of the poem ("My eyes were blinded and my lips burned") presents the personal myth blending the soldier hero and the hero of spirit, the political leader (judge, king) and the spiritual one (prophet), the beginning of the mission and its tragic ending with the awakening from the childhood dreams to the blinding light of a realistic sobering truth. According to Shamir, through the inter-textual language, two stories blend here of the mission, one from its end, and the other from its beginning: the story of the blinded Samson, and the story of Moses, who according to the legend became hard of speaking after his mouth was burnt by an ember - a mixture that in itself is of Hebraism and Hellenism within the boundaries of the Bible. The character of Samson, describes Shamir, is the most Hellenistic in the Bible (remarkable in physical courage and in appearance - his long hair), and he also bound his fate to that of a woman of the Philistines, who originated in the Greek islands. Moses, on the other hand, is the most Hebraist: the epitome of all prophets, a principled man of extremes, and one who mediated and brought his people and humanity the faith of uniqueness.[341] Through the three-stage dialectics Shamir shows that the new poetry, as too the new national history, are located in the tension between the discomfort from home and the seductive dreams around the corner; on the one hand, the death of the father and the mother-nation's failure to sustain her children, and on the other - the dedication of the eldest son to his poetic mission. In addition, the chapter of being swept after the dream of the imps appears as that which was needed for the individual and the people to awaken from their easy and non-committing world of childhood dreams, to the gray and committed responsibility of adult life. The dreams do not speak in vain - however, the blinding of the eyes and burning of the mouth, in other words - the sobriety from seductions entering from outside of the world of tradition, without giving up on the inspiration they may later evoke - is a necessary stage in preparing the individual and the generation for their new poetry and new Torah.

Hence, Bialik's 'awakening' may be seen as parallel to the Hölderlinian 'sobriety', but is also somewhat different: The 'sobriety' appearing in Hölderlin, blending with 'holiness', is an adjective that functions as a mechanism of judgment, in the gap, in the distance between the divine plenty and the human abyss; it seems to be acknowledgement of the inability, in spite of expectations and yearning, to bridge the distance and blend with the whole. Conversely, Bialik's 'awakening' has a double appearance: On the one hand, awakening from the sleeping freezing tradition in its dark room to the promises of the glistening new world outside, while on the other - sobering

---

[339] Reminiscent, in this context, of Hölderlin's "eccentric path".
[340] (Shamir, 2000), p. 80.
[341] Ibid.

from the promises of the new world that are undoubtedly destined to fail. It is possible that this accentuates the difference in the times of the poets, regarding the historical development of modernity, whereby Hölderlin was early to identify and express the crisis of modernity, and Bialik - who had grown up into it, already describes its double course, bearing (on the eve of the first World War) both the crisis of the promises of the era and its failed hopes. The 'fall' is noted as a central idea in the poetry of both, and this too is differentiated, so that in Bialik there is a trend of melancholic opening and optimistic ending, which is quite the opposite of the repeated trend in Hölderlin's poetry (see for example "Hyperion", 1799; "Schicksalslied", 1803-1804; and "Halfte des Lebens"), characterized by a 'fall' from heaven unto an abyss.

How did the readers of "Hashiloach" understand the poem, asks Shamir, and how was it received in those few years of optimism beginning with the first Zionist congress and ending with the crisis of Uganda and Theodor Herzl's death? [342] As a mythic a-mimetic poem telling a story whose rules and symbols were known to all, or a concrete mimetic one telling an authentic life story, hidden from the eye? A melancholy poem or a clever satire? To Shamir's perception, all the elements are blended together, their compound creating a new synthesis which is both one and the other, and neither of each; and since this is a compound, as opposed to a mixture, the separation of the elements is an elusive interpretational task.[343] Bialik succeeded, according to Shamir, in creating a sense of unity of contrasts: Desecrated holiness and sanctified secularity; joyful poverty and icy, desolate riches; a personal confession which reveals nothing - idiosyncratic, intimate and, at the same time, a typical story of a national collective fate turning into personal and heart-rending. Any reader could apparently choose the side closest to him and see in it the whole.

This mystic mimetic life story and the concrete dimension, according to Shamir, is no more than an outer layer covering depths of historiography and contemplation. Bialik did not use first person singular as a stylistic variation, but rather supplied personal elements, quasi autobiographical, and a quasi particular reality, with a convincingly personal and emotional sense. He deliberately distorted the authentic biographical data to create a personal and collective myth. Up until then, no poem had existed in Hebrew poetry so convincing in its personal approach - an approach that apparently misled Joseph Klausner into considering it a merely autobiographical poem.[344]

Bialik, as described by Shamir, created in his poetry a monologuist image, symbolizing the exiled Jew - orphaned from father, the son of a depleted mother - who returns to his childhood, to the morning of his life, during which he also tells his story - the story of his anointment to poet-prophet, an anointment originating in the national and personal need and ability that had ripened. However, this story of personal destiny should be understood as a single circle, important though it may be in the series of concentric ones embracing the story of the nation in the past and the present, and the story of the entire human culture. The poet perceived the appearance of the chosen individual in the trend of literature and history as one detail in a series of historical, cultural, social, national and universal processes, whose time to ripen had come. For this purpose, he seemingly gathered all the stories of anointment from the Hebrew and Greek classics, blending them while creating a personal and collective biographical myth. Thus, the cricket's

---

[342] Herzl (1860-1904) was a Jewish Austro-Hungarian journalist and father of modern political Zionism.
[343] (Shamir, 2000), pp. 80-81.
[344] Joseph Klausner (1874-1958), one of the founders of Hebrew literature research.

revealment to the child, as it chirps in the wall, is a distorted configuration of the revealment to Moses of god hiding in the rock. Thus, eating the bread baked from the dough into which the mother's tear falls appears as a low and folk configuration of Ezekiel eating the lament-written scroll in his anointment to prophet. Not only stories of the Hebrew classics were blended in by Bialik, emphasizes Shamir, since Fishel Lahover had already expounded the similarity between "Shirati" and the story of Pindar, the greatest of Greek lyricists, in whose childhood a bee had dropped honey onto his lips while he was sleeping on Mount Helicon (the Mountain of the Muses).[345] Thus Bialik saw himself, and his poetry, as one who in his childhood ate tearful bread mixed with the sighs of the widowed mother. Blindness comes at the end of Samson but also of Oedipus in Sophocles' play. Bialik, then, created a myth describing an end and a threshold, the chapter of exile and the chapter of redemption, the dying and the revival that was necessary for him and for each of his generation's chosen, in order to be anointed to prophecy and leadership. In the terms of Nietzsche, who at that time was the oracle of the young Westernizing people surrounding Herzl, this myth is an interesting encounter between Hebraism and Hellenism, from which a deep collective truth rises; the story of a poor abandoned nation, and the story of its orphaned son, left to himself, awakening from the nightmares of exile to a clear morning with the flavor of an exciting adventure.[346]

As a response to the question of the origin of the poetry, "Do you know where I got my song?" Shamir characterizes four sources, from which - to her perception - Bialik and his generation drew their poetry. Two are classic, two are modern, two Hebraist and two Hellenistic:

1. From the Hebrew Biblical classics, where the poetry was that of poets located in the Temple, or the poetry of prophets who wished to celebrate the defeat of the enemy after battles;

2. From the Greek classics, which elevated poetry to the peaks of the Olympus, producing the Homerian epos;

3. From the modern transformation of Greek culture; from German classic-romantic German poetry, inspired by the Greek classics;

4. From the modern transformation of Biblical poetry, from the "Tiferet" poetry (=poetry of glory) of the Enlightenment, inspired both by the Bible, and by German classic-romantic poetry.

To Shamir's perception,[347] it was only natural that in tracing the sources of his poetry, Bialik would draw on all four sources, and their reflection one in another as in a mirrored maze. After having blended, in the first part of the poem, a series of symbolic descriptions from the national myth (the destruction of the personal and national home; the description of the father as a Cohen (=priest) near the table-desecrated alter; the description of the mother as a vendor in the market of life, and the seven orphans as candles squashed in clay), the second part comes with the description of

---

[345] F. Lahover, *Bialik, His Life and Works* (Hebrew) (Tel Aviv: Dvir, 1956), pp. 321-322.
[346] (Shamir, 2000), p. 84.
[347] Ibid.

the imps - the breezes of morning and west. These are tiny creatures embodying the ancient Greek culture and the romantic West, the modern transformation of the beauty- and hero-seeking Hellenism, bursting into the Jewish room. Bialik actually turns the 'zafir' of Shaul Tchernichovsky[348] (the light western wind of the Greek mythology, often appearing in Humanistic poetry and in its classic-romantic transformations) into the Hebrew 'zafrir', which is one of the morning imps, according to the Kabbalists. In this way, claims Shamir, Bialik hinted to his readers: May Tchernichovsky go to the Greeks and their mythological creatures; I'll go to their parallels in the Jewish sources.

Hence, Bialik used the description of the child as a fable for every young person leaving the room-Heder, in the poem "Zohar", to Nature in all of its meanings, language and concepts - converting the non-Jewish Nature into Jewish. In the concept of 'zafririm' as well, Bialik - as mentioned - re-activates the old concealed concept of Kabbalist demonology (zafririn), and restores it to the life cycle of modern Hebrew literature as a renewed personal concept.

Bialik blended many meanings into the concept. Their essence remains in the realm of deep mystery, since the concept of 'wind' for Bialik is not only of air blowing around, and frequently it has demonic meanings in his works (ghosts); hence, the 'zafririm' are also morning imps, and not just pleasant breezes. Due to their literal resemblance to 'tzafir', the 'zafririm' also look like goats, as the tiny restrained transformation of the licentious satyrs of Greek mythology, such as Nietzsche had glorified in "The Birth of Tragedy";[349] and as Shamir mentions, also the goat, 'tsafir', in Daniel's vision, which is but a fable for the kingdom of Greece.

The imps seduce the child to a series of rascally acts: The concept, which began as a dialogue with the Bible and Greek mythology - mediated by Percy Bysshe Shelley, the British romantic poet, whose famous work "Ode to the West Wind" (1820) has left considerable traces in "Zohar"[350], and by the "Greek" Tchernichovsky, who translated much of Western literature - was turned by Bialik into a personal, enigmatic, and inexhaustible symbol. The divine idolatry imps, angelic and demonic, are also connected, according to Shamir, to the morning of the life of the nation, and of the whole of humanity, with the beginning of a new century. From this delightful and torturous assimilation in the depths of the sparkling sea, he manages to emerge intact, thanks to the painful awakening, blinded eyes and burning lips. At this stage, the time is ripe to fulfill the mission properly. Now, claims Shamir, Bialik knows the right synthesis between internal and external, between reality and imagination, between responsibility and being swept along, between maturity and pranks of childhood and adolescence, and between intoxication and sobriety.

It seems that in all of Bialik's work, adds Shamir, there is not one simple description that does not trail behind it a train of symbolic, abstract, national and universal ideas. Thus too, the imps of light are not only a personal childhood vision, but also the unique embodiment of a new and spell-bounding Nietzschian phenomenon that burst into the national reality from the modern transformation of Greek culture, and the worshiping of beauty and the natural passions of German Romanticism. The realistic fullness of the romantic picture is what occasionally blurs the elements

---

[348] Shaul Tchernichovsky (1875-1943), identified with the poetry of nature, highly influenced by the ancient Greek culture.
[349] F. Nietzsche, *The Birth of Tragedy from the Spirit of Music* (1872), trans. Douglas Smith (Oxford University Press, 2008).
[350] (Shamir, 2000), p. 86.

of order and planning, and diminishes the contemplative trend. The feast of the poor described in the opening of "Shirati" is as the last supper in a ruined temple with a sour slice (dipping in vinegar, not in wine), the color of the blood of suffering. Then the father disappears, and the son is left with the mother and the Holy Ghost, and with the sigh that became inspiration and poetry. As in the Christian story, the poem is full of transfiguration. The sigh and the tear are swallowed into the dough that the orphaned son chews, thereby turning them, by virtue of his talent, into poetry. The focusing on the Sabbath and Passover table as reality, as a symbol and as a central myth of the Jewish fate and the general human fate, Bialik learned, claims Shamir, from J. L. Gordon[351] and presented it in its full version, combining Judaism and Christianity, in "The Trumpet Was Ashamed".[352] on the one hand hints that "We have one father", by way of mocking the anti-Semites who do not acknowledge the hidden common root of Judaism and Christianity, while on the other - hinting that anti-Semitism has deep roots going back to the crucifixion, and that the beautiful humanistic slogans of the Enlightenment movement could not eradicate them. In his Yiddish poem "The Last Thing",[353] Bialik describes a prophet wounded and bleeding, similar to Jeremiah, to Jesus, to a prophet bringing forth a new Torah, a new Testament - but whose people bully him, as in the case of the image of the Christian messiah. Shamir claims that Bialik blends all of this in his work into a declaration of the destruction of an era and the building of a new one.

In "Shirati", Shamir describes how Bialik - as in many other of his works - took quasi miniature proverbs and extended them, breathing life into them, until they became a personal, credible, and convincing story, whose collective and a-mimetic character was almost completely blurred. This appropriation of proverbs and turning them into part of his private life story has granted his poetry a collective and symbolic dimension beyond the literal, so that the life story becomes a chronicle whose course is known in advance. The description of the seven hungry orphans, singing together the Sabbath song-prayers, evokes the proverbs about the many children of the beggar: "At the beggar's, the children grow up densely" (in Yiddish there is a play on words, so that 'densely' and 'poet' share the same sounds). This proverb served Mendele Mocher Sforim in "The Vale of Tears": "Nothing can be as poetic as much as poverty".[354] According to this tragic-comic proverb, only poverty nourishes poetry, with all of its ramifications (poesie, poetry sung as Sabbath song-prayers).[355] This connection between Mendele's "The Vale of Tears" and Bialik's "Shirati" is explained by their both being products of the turn of the 20th century, between two stages in the life of the nation, between the walls of the room and the outdoor nature. One may assume that if Ahad Ha'am had not identified the poem's connection to national and general contemplation, it is doubtful whether he would have published it in his ideological journal, which steered away from the lyrical and heart-pouring glorification of nature and the beauty of love, such as found in the poetry of nations. Contrary to biographical interpreters who latch onto the personal components of the poem, while somewhat denying its collective ones, Shamir claims that at the center of the work

---

[351] Judah Leib Gordon (7191 -7192) was a Hebrew poet of the Jewish Enlightenment.
[352] C. N.Bialik, "Hahatsotserah Nitbayshah" (1915), BYP.
[353] C. N.Bialik, "Das letzte wart" (Yiddish), "The Last Thing" in *Bialik's Yiddish poems*, trans. A. Zeitlin (Tel Aviv: Dvir, 1956), pp.27-35.
[354] Mendele Mocher Sforim is the pen name of Sholem Yankev Abramovich (1836-1917), one of the most prominent Yiddish and Hebrew writers of the Modern era.
See: "Be'emek Habacha" (1897-8) "The Vale of Tears", in *Kol Kkitvei Mendele Mōcher Sforim* (Hebrew), (Tel Aviv: Dvir, 1958), book 7, chapter I.

[355] (Shamir, 2000), p. 97.

there is actually synthesis between the personal and the national story, which probably has no equivalent in world literature. To her approach, this is a mock heroic epos, whose young hero undergoes difficult experiences and temptations, but cannot carry out real acts of heroism, only pranks and rascally deeds of a young scholar who has left the religious studies, and which are but an anti-heroic Jewish substitute for the external deeds of the real Hellenistic epos. This is personal lyricism with no real individual "I", and which constitutes a mixture of personal and impersonal statements, whose purpose is profound and abstract, as well as tangible, contemplative and emotional. This is a tragedy, which - contrary to all the classic conventions - opens at the death scene, and concludes with an unraveled opaque ending that is not an actual one, and even has, unexpectedly, elements of folk humor and comic relief moments; and at the same time it is poetry of passion, joining the tradition of carpe diem, but without actual bodily lust, but rather - it is entirely real or imagined Dionysian love-making with the imps, with the breezes, at dawn, at sunrise.[356]

In a lecture on the poetry of Judah Halevi,[357] Bialik refuted the possibility of distinguishing in it between internal and external, and between content and form. This claim, according to Shamir, holds true for Bialik's poetry itself. The innovation in "Shirati" is in the image of the young child as a symbol and as reality. The child awakens to a world washed in light, an unbridled world of imagination and legend, and from which he then awakens to a world of dreary compelling Halachah, a world of maturity and responsibility. Although Bialik had already made use of a childlike narrator in his poem "Zafririm" (1899), the character here is more complex - it is the character of a child who is both a Jewish home-sitting student and a reckless hedonist Greek youth; a child who knows how to change melancholy into joy, and poverty into riches; a child who is no longer one, but who cherishes the childhood experiences in his heart, together with eyes open from day-dreaming to the dismal sober reality.

Indeed, the poet is part child recollecting the yesteryears, and part old man longing for his childhood. Bialik, in his essay "Shirateinu Hatse'ira" (our young poetry) - similarly to Ahad Ha'am - mocked the young writers, lovers of Nietzsche, comparing them to a servant who had served her lady, and upon returning to her father's dismal tent sees everything as flawed.[358] The imagery of a young Nietzschian as a poor man craving a palace he does not have, created the description, in "Zohar", of crystal palaces and glass mansions floating in the air; palaces that are an imaginary transfiguration of useless and worthless glass baubles, rolling around outside amongst cobwebs and rusty junk. The poet knows very well that the palaces are an imaginary transient construct, both a moment before he is swept away to realms of the imagination and a moment after awakening from the fantastic vision. It is hinted here that the vacuous declarations of the young, the imps and the fancy towers they build in the air, are but a dream. Behind the impressive façade of crystal palaces are hidden those old rusty broken objects that they bring from home. Bialik shows the foreign, fantastical and nightmarish reality entailed in the Nietzschian idea of changing all values, and he advocates, at the end of the poem, a sobering wide-eyed synthesis between new and old, between Hebraism and Hellenism. Sobriety, in Bialik's version, appears here as oriented in two directions: On the one hand, sobriety from the slumbering

---

[356] Ibid, pp. 95-96.
[357] C. N. Bialik, "On Judah Halevi" (1912), in *Things by Heart* (Hebrew), (Tel Aviv: Dvir, 1935), part 2 p. 166.
[358] C. N. Bialik, "Shirateinu Hatse'ira" 1907 (Hebrew), BYP.

tradition and its failures, and on the other - sobriety from the dreams of freedom and the illusion of liberation. Hence, his poetic movement creates the intermediate space between the possibilities.

Shamir recommends that we do not forget, or let be forgotten, the shadows of the room, nor the wondrous blinding light that imbued the individual and the nation for a few sweet fleeting moments of dream; and that only from the blending of two contrasting components - the body of the world and the light of the world - can a new being of Hebrewness and humanness grow (in the terms of Ahad Ha'am - the being of "man in his tent"); and only from the successful blending of the materialist element with the idealist one, the static element at home with the dynamic one outside - may rejuvenation be created.

Ahad Ha'am advised the Jew to receive into his midst only those foreign elements which he can digest, and which are necessary for strengthening his diminishing contents. Conversely, the Westernizing young demanded to put the personal "I" at the center, and do away with the narrow national dimension, in their opinion impinging upon the universality of the renewing Hebrew culture. Bialik, as was his way, stood in the middle - between conflicting and contrasting trends that fed the national thought of his generation. It seems that Bialik tended toward Ahad Ha'am's approach of careful evolution, but was also attracted to the light, beauty and eroticism demanded by the Nietzschian wing. The poem "Zohar" is washed with gold: The color of the Nietzschian über-man; the lions' manes are golden; and it is hinted that if the poet weren't bound to the tradition of father's home, he would be swept after the temptations of the imps, and drown in a glistening sea, completely assimilating into it.

In view of the Nietzschian assumption that the world of books has corrupted the urges and repressed man's ability to enjoy the beauty of nature, Bialik shows pure nature in terms of the world of books (using ambiguous combinations, such as "Be-ovi ha-korah" - into the thick of things; or "Shem ha-Mephorash") with the irony of a religious student who has left his studies, and sees an actual tree as the Tree of Knowledge. When a young Jew is attracted to nature and to Western culture, it is implied here, he still remains shackled to the tent flaps, trailing behind him a train of associations from the world of books.[359]

Contrasting with Nietzsche's perception that to build one temple, another must be destroyed, Bialik described Jewish dilapidated ruins, while in the second part - crystal palaces that are but an illusion and pipe-dream. The ruins are full of broken old ware and glass fragments, so that behind the wall the child builds in his imagination towers in the air, a temple with no substance. In other words: Do not cast away the old as junk, but rather build the new with a mixture of the old. In contrast to a binary approach of 'either/or' (Berdyczewski's "to be or to cease"; the nation must decide if it faces West or East), Bialik presents a dialectic one (both one and the other) which gives rise to a new synthesis blending East and West, inward and outward, old age and adolescence.

---

[359] (Shamir, 2000), p.102.

5.2 Crisis and Language

The prominent fact, according to Schweid,[360] regarding Bialik's poetry and that of other poets of the 'Revival generation' is that one is speaking of a deliberate revolution against traditional continuity; first, by adapting modern language and modern stylistic forms, and secondly - by connecting directly to the style of the Biblical sources of the written prophets (the latter prophets). It is possible, in this poetry, to also locate linguistic material representing the "middle" traditional layers, such as the legends of the Sages, poetry of the middle ages, philosophy, Kabbalah, and generations of ethic literature; however, the very mixture of these stylistic layers and their blending together, with a quasi Biblical style of prophecy, presents a distinct character of the new style, relating to tradition by free will, in accordance with modern poetics, and without accepting the norms of traditional styles as dictates. From the point of view of the style of speech itself - sounding the voice through the qualities of language - Revival poetry in general seems to aspire to a direct encounter between styles and structures of modern poetry, and the way of sounding the prophetic voice.

It is easy to see, claims Schweid, that deliberate detachment from the continuity of the later literary tradition, and with it a direct appeal to the primary source, is a way of coping with the deep rift in the connection of the new-generation Jew to the traditional established religiousness, whose literary language expression and patterns were its Bible-based core. The voice that had arrived for generations through the pipeline of the oral tradition of Torah, the legends and Halachah, contemplative literature, poetry, Kabalah, and ethics was mute to the new generation. As far as they were concerned, the conveying pipes had clogged up, and their faith was shaken. Whoever rose then, in this generation, to have his voice heard, felt he must appeal directly to the primary source that had constituted prophecy prior to its becoming part of the establishment, and reconstruct it in the agonizing reality of his times.[361]

The shaking of faith in tradition, as a result of the encounter with the secularized modern world, is connected with the shaking of faith in its language, which religion needed to bring out the interior, selfness, soul and spirit of life, and hence - its ability to express and deliver experiences that hold meaning and determine orientation beyond the mundane. In the sense of the man who feels the "call" to sound out deliberate truth in public, and to operate a commanding authority, this is a crisis of faith in the sole "tool" at his disposal that would assuredly support him, his truths, and his ability to deliver it in a way that would enable others to discover it in their conscience, as he had.

---

[360] (Schweid, 1998), pp. 109-143.
[361] Ibid.

Crisis and Language

The connection between the crisis of faith in religion and its institution, and the crisis of faith in language, as described by Schweid, is general, and relates to the space of cultural creation. Religion was the authority that vouched for the credibility of language communicating and unifying society around its values, beliefs, and moral and spiritual goals. Since unifying and shared faith was shaken, language was also included, and its credibility shaken as a means of spiritual communication. Things are no longer unified, and language itself has ceased to be one and the same for whoever needs it, and each one understands it differently in his way. A crisis of faith in language is similar to losing a way of life. It evokes the sense of existential need to overcome the crisis, and to find the unifying and directing truth again, delivering it to each and every individual, and to all together. From within the crisis, then, the yearning is born for a revelation that will reconstitute the language which can deliver its truth, as in previous times. However, how is such rejuvenation possible? This is a vicious circle: Language is born from existing language and delivered from one generation to the next. And if this language has lost its credibility, what will come to its aid? The only possibility is to break through the language into the language that had preceded it, had enabled it, and which is still there at its roots.[362]

The question of the credibility of language is discussed in Bialik's theoretical-poetic essay "Revealment and Concealment in Language",[363] which presents his perception of language by differentiating between poetry and prose. The central image in this context appears toward the end of the article, and describes the prose writers as walking on a frozen river as if they were walking on solid ground, with no fear of danger. They create an impression of orderly and permanent language, although the water beneath them is turbulent and tempestuous. In contrast, the poetry writers are described as walking on a frozen river with broken ice floes, so that they must hop from floe to floe, above the turbulent abyss. We usually think, claims Bialik, that language reveals that which is hidden in the heart of the speaker, but Bialik hints that the opposite is true, and that language - as it reveals, it also conceals; and further on it will be shown that it conceals even more than it reveals. Moreover, it seems that this is the purpose for which it was created: In order to reveal it must conceal, and its revealments too are a clever form of concealment. It turns out that just as people have the need to disclose the secrets of their heart, and the secrets of their encounters with their surroundings, they also have the need to keep them hidden, and not only from others, but especially from themselves. The secrets of the soul and the universe are an indecipherable mystery, and ungovernable. Their revealments as they are constitute a threat to the safety of existence on the one hand, and to the safety of self-identity, on the other. The desire to reveal is basically a desire to dissolve the moment of fear and puzzlement in order to overcome it. However, one overcomes the abysmal threat by its restriction, namely, by pushing it back to its darkness: To peek into the abyss in order to conceal it, supposedly by means of its appearance.

---

[362] Ibid, p. 112.
[363] C. N. Bialik, "Gilui ve-Kisui Balashon" (1917) (Hebrew), in *Literature* (Tel Aviv: Dvir, 1977).
The principle of Bialik's approach in his essay - that language is a form of concealing and hiding of the entity, and at the same time, the only way of the entity to be revealed - is a basic position in two cultural extremes which Bialik's world appears to connect: Jewish mysticism on the one hand, and Heidegger's theory on the other. In this essay time and again the similarity arises between Heidegger's thought and that of Bialik, perhaps requiring methodical examination elsewhere. Bialik certainly did not manage to be exposed to the essays that are the peak of Heidegger's writing, but the discussion and distinctions between essence and language seem to represent the spirit of the times.
See: (Inbari, 2002), pp. 56-86.

Crisis and Language

Schweid's methodical discussion of the article proposes a distinction between two types of expression: On the one hand, the type relating to the dimension of the uniqueness of experiencing inner and external life; and on the other, the type relating to the routine daily expression that repeats itself in the self-evident path of the permanent needs of our life. The first type of speech is primordial: Embodied in it is the secret of the creation of language from the sensory, emotional and intellectual experiences themselves. Speech of the second type is secondary: It is reused for characteristic and permanent phenomena in a reality in which we aspire to function, not to encounter it for the first time. Hence, we make do with their identification on the basis of similarity, and ignore the element of uniqueness that we will never understand, unless from within it, but not on the basis of comparison.

Bialik's contention is that speech of the second type, defined in linguistic discourse as denotative utterance, is secondary speech that conceals the selfness of the things. It denotes them to enable us their identification, and to use them as we need. In that process, we are spared the need to relate to them themselves (and to ourselves through them) in their uniqueness of being as they are. For the sake of safe functioning in daily life, it is both convenient and desirable for us precisely in this way, since only with this type of speech may the illusion be created of full safety in our existence, and their existence in our determinations, together with their permanence. This is why language in its denotative function seems sufficient and credible, and lives up to our expectations. However, claims Bialik, this is not the case when one desires to express human existential experiences in the universe. These are experiences that poetry (and religion) is meant to express. Here we aspire to express ourselves in connection to the selfness of the universe surrounding us. Hence, denotation identified by indicating and comparing repeated phenomena through agreed signs is not only insufficient, but also seems a priori disappointing. Thus, according to Bialik, a crisis of faith in language is created. The ready words of daily life appear as empty envelopes, whose content - which they supposedly identify by indicating - is not in them at all. They cannot, then, create contact with the essence or with the selfness of things we wish to express; therefore, we feel that our speech is mute or that the senses and the things surrounding us are but superficial senses - the sight of shadows and the sounds reverberating off things whose essence is concealed from us, without our being able to relate to it. Their actuality has been emptied, and they have disappeared around us. This is the feeling of chaos in all its horror.

As to the issue of the difference between poetry and prose, and in connection to the spreading of the hymn into prose, as noted by Benjamin and his students, we should emphasize that the division of clear roles according to Bialik's perception - between prose and poetry - is formulated at the end of the essay. He says there that prose is characterized by literal language, whose owners rely on the permanent in language, the accepted version, while poetry aspires to express the transient moment never to be repeated, of the unique soul and selfness of the things as received at a given moment in the soul of their beholder; hence, it eludes the permanent in language, and causes "unceasing movement" in the meanings of words.[364] Prose and poetry are therefore two genres, each with a totally different aesthetic purpose and system of means, as are tragedy and comedy in Arisoteles' poetic theory.

---

[364] C. N. Bialik, "Gilui ve-Kisui Balashon" (1917) (Hebrew), in *Literature* (Tel Aviv: Dvir, 1977), pp. 30-31.

How then, asks Schweid, is poetry possible that aspires to express the feelings themselves, the attempts and experiences themselves, in view of the world itself? How can we express the things and our self-relation to them, and not only indicate them or speak about them? This question is equivalent to the question: How is language created from the beginning, and how have humans come to connecting a certain word with a certain phenomenon, so that the word becomes evident in its expression to the other person who - together with us - faces the same phenomenon?

Denotation, as mentioned, is language that has already been created and acquired, and which we relate to as given, together with the things it denotes by agreement. However, when we wish to express our connection to the selfness of things, we have to face not only the enigma of their being, but also the enigma of the creation of the words meant to express them. It is possible that if we solve this mystery, we will find the secret connection between the things and the words that express them, and we shall restore to ourselves the ability to talk and communicate with reality.

How then is an expressing and communicating word created for the first time? Bialik suggests that each word at its onset is mimetic memory of the encounter between the soul of man and the phenomenon in the universe surrounding it. Man responds to the phenomena that impress him by imitating physically, and especially with his voice, the prominent sensory impressions (the qualities) that the phenomenon had stamped in his soul, thereby reconstructing the external phenomenon for himself, within himself, then externalizing the reconstruction expressing his impression outwardly. This is mimetic internalization. Man, as it were, enters the same phenomenon he presents to himself and to the other person experiencing with him the same impression. The two will agree that this thing (the present phenomenon) is this (the word or gesture), which means that for the people expressing an utterance to one another - the word is that which has embodied, at that time, the thing they are experiencing together.

Bialik illustrates his approach with the creation of the word 'ra'am' (=thunder), a word imitating in sound the natural phenomenon that impresses and terrifies people. If we utter it out loud and in the proper intonation, it will sound like rolling thunder, yet on a non-terrifying scale - as reverberation of the natural phenomenon in man's soul. Man then said to himself and the other, this is the thing that happened, and this is what I felt; and upon receiving the other's validation, he could let go of his excitement. He not only indicated the phenomenon, but also identified it through its prominent qualities, and in particular - experienced it reflexively, which granted him consciousness of the quality and emotion that those qualities had evoked in him, enabling the sharing of that experience.

Bialik did not need the terms 'sign' and 'symbol' in his article, but actually, as Schweid describes, he did propose a distinction between them in his own way.[365] He showed how a linguistic symbol is created, and how it brings about the encounter between phenomenon and experience, creating a meaning beyond it; and how it ultimately

---

[365] (Schweid, 1998), pp. 721-729.

becomes a linguistic sign, when the primary experience is forgotten together with the mimetic relation to the word expressing the experience; and yet when we again have the desire to express a similar experience of an encounter with the selfness of things, we must restore the primary mimetic symbolic meaning to the words, and use them not only in the semantic sense, but also in the sense of all the qualities of the mimetic expression inherent in them, as if they had just now been born, at their moment of utterance in view of an event, or encounter, or experience that we wish to express. The ancient meaning is revived in the unique context of the now.

Clearly, the symbol is meant to reveal the secrets of the things around us and the secrets of the soul, but Bialik elucidates that revealment is made possible only by concealing the imperceptible, and by reducing its threatening intensity to a bearable level, and that this is its purpose - to protect us from the fear that takes hold of us. It is clear that this is a divisive act between that which may be identified and surrounded by phenomena, by presenting their impressive qualities, and on the other hand - the incomprehensible "remainder", which is the kernel of their self, whose abyss frightens us. That which we embodied in the words conceals that which cannot be expressed, and remains hidden with mysterious power in the concealed depths; but also the opposite: By concealing the remainder that has no expression, a distance relation was made possible to the hidden abyss, as a perspective of open meaning, beyond that presented in the word.

Let us note, emphasizes Schweid, that Bialik fully defined the symbol's function, as opposed to the sign, which denotes the external object itself. The symbol uses the thing itself to indicate the meanings created by the relation between us and it. It is clear, then, that the symbol too, as does the sign, indicates beyond the word, only in a different way: By embodying the object, and not its the external phenomenon, but rather - intention to the selfness conjoined with the meaning it has for the human aspiring to express his relation to the things, and not merely to deliver objective information. However, it is clear that the example of the word 'ra'am' is not sufficient to explain the function of a language required to express complex human experiences, also in terms of the accordance of things occurring together and constituting the total experience, and its continuity and change, and too - the many levels of experience (sensory, imagery, imaginative, emotional, intellectual), and especially those experiences connected to religion, which expresses man's relation to the mystery of his being in his world, the mystery of the hidden presence of the gods or god as the source of all. This necessitates a rich language capable of offering mimetic expression of various kinds: alliterative, rhythmic, activating, pictorial-visual, associative, conceptual; in other words - a language is required not only to represent objects and complex events between man and the universe surrounding him, but also to represent events occurring as events of the soul, for which language is its tool of thinking and its tool of looking at itself and its surroundings. It is a boundless succession of complex symbols of various levels, each time expressing experiences that are each unique, and which stands alone in the encounter between reflexive man and his surroundings, especially between him and whoever or whatever is beyond the things surrounding man; whoever or whatever - that sees the universe and man himself as the language of expression of its creating, directing and leading power. According to Schweid, Bialik did not develop his contemplation to this level, yet hinted at it through the richness of his illustrative and associative style, complementing in his poetry that which he did not state explicitly in his study.

Bialik's essay and poetic writing is rich with references to canonic literary sources, through deliberate use of imagery and pictorial expressions characteristic of them. The essay too has many allusions to the Bible, legends of the Sages, and medieval literature, and especially of the Kabbalah, which had developed the symbolic religious language to the highest level. In this context, one should particularly note Bialik's use of the Kabbalist word 'blima', originating in the "Book of Creation",[366] which is a primary source of Kabbalist symbolism, and in the metaphor of the story of 'Pardes' - the classic story of ancient Jewish mysticism - to show how symbols reveal the threatening infinity through the concealment that hints beyond them. The allusion to the concept of 'blima' and its meaning in "Book of Creation" are two foundation sources of Kabbalist literature. "Book of Creation" was written as an obscure Mishna, and is an ancient book ascribed to Abraham, copiously interpreted in contemplative medieval literature, as a basic source of symbolic terminology of the theory of Creation, especially in the Kabbalah. There is no doubt then that Bialik's reference to these places, and particularly to the concept of 'blima' with all of its meanings - something whose essence is hidden and must be hinted to mutely, withholding the mouth from speaking - is intentional, and adds a layer of modern interpretation to the ancient term.[367]

Bialik then needed a language shaped through sources, not only as a treasure of individual words, but also as an entire continuum of words, as a unit of a whole expression bearing within it the memory of a unique context, which expressed a primordial and constituting experience of the category of revelation. These sources preserve defined memories together with their contexts, and not anonymous words whose first context is forgotten. Clearly, only this kind of language, which remembers its history and has a rich life within itself, can express experiences of the category of religious revelation. The actual occurrence as an 'event' of these occurrences is conditioned upon operating a linguistic memory that is capable of receiving, containing and expressing them in their occurrence; and it depends upon the ability to rejuvenate these expressions as if they had been created now, in the encounter between presence and the memory constituting its meaning. As mentioned, Bialik hints at this issue; however, in his poems, as Schweid claims, the matters are stated explicitly and while being activated.[368]

---

[366] See: "Book of Creation", Mantua edition, 1562, p.191-192.
http://aleph.nli.org.il:80/F/?func=direct&doc_number=001279369&local_base=NNLALL
[367] (Schweid, 1998), pp. 120-123.
[368] Ibid.

5.3 "Tikkun" - The Mending of the World

Following Ahad Ha'am, Bialik hinted to the "young" Zionist activists that the revolutionary ideas exciting their minds are merely a new transformation of old ideas. In his article "Change of Values",[369] Ahad Ha'am claimed that Nietzsche had taken ideas from Jewish thought, and the young people were now taking from him ground flour with Aryan addition that is not easy to digest, although they were positively sure this is a completely new original theory. Bialik's essays and lectures show that he, as well, did not see innovation in these matters. His writings portray a historical perception that sees the history of humanity as a series of dialectic processes, which repeat themselves in a permanent cyclical order. Each new era commences with a loss of faith in the old, at the end of a gradual process of corruption of the conventions and their being emptied of content. Each new era seeks to get out of its crisis of faith and the void it had left, by dreams and new ideals that make great promises, whereas every dream and illusion ends with disappointment and painful disillusionment, and then all is repeated. The change and progress made from generation to generation originate from the synthesis of old with new, the void with the existing, the thesis and antithesis, the dismal reality and the new shining dream.[370]

According to Bialik's method, the Nietzschian idea of "changing all values", which the young people tempestuously brought into the exiled being, is not a new idea, but rather one often heard from false prophets who had wished to lift the spirits of the people in order to break this vicious circle of destruction, dream, redemption, and painful awakening from the dream - a circle revolving on its axis with permanent hopeless regularity. As a way of coping with this being, Bialik suggests a new solution, which is also a transformation of the old idea of 'tikkun'.[371]

Similarly to the Jews who held 'tikkun hatzot' (midnight prayers), and the Kabbalists who believed in the gathering of the sparks from amongst the broken vessels,[372] Bialik advises the new generation to go forth to hard and continuous labor that does not offer the easy solutions of Herzl and the young ones (a metaphorical attire for Ahad Ha'am's distinct idea of 'qualifying the hearts'). This idea is embodied here in symbols borrowed from sources of Hasidism and Kabbalah, but does not convey admiration of the theory of the occult; rather - it is a sophisticated circumventing way of raising totally modern secular ideas without resorting to the language of abstract study.

The poem ("Shirati" and "Zohar" together) opens, as described by Shamir, with the destruction of the home, and ultimately the personal-national "I" - who had experienced the shadows and dissolution, and the experience of

---

[369] See: A. Z. H. Ginsberg (Ahad Ha'am), "On the Crossroads" (1895) (Hebrew), *The Ben Yehuda Project.* http://benyehuda.org/ginzburg.
[370] (Shamir, 2000), pp. 102-103.
[371] Tikkun Olam - repairing or healing or restoring the world - is based on the Talmudic-contemplative idea dealing with protection and nourishment of humanity's ways of life, and with responsibility for creating improvement, change, and even revolution in the life of humanity.
[372] An idea reverberating as well at the basis of Benjamin's historical-messianic perception.

light, drawing his life poetry from both - awakens to a gray reality, to a world of burden and responsibility containing two contrasting worlds together. This world feeds from the experience of somber poverty, and from the bright light, combining both yet resembling neither.[373] In his poem "To the Volunteers among the People" Bialik suggested gathering the sparks and turning them into a flame.[374] This, claims Shamir, is Bialik's program of 'tikkun'. The poem surveys the circles of history revealed in each generation and every place. Already in"Shirati", before "Metei Midbar" and "Habrecha" had been written, Bialik had hinted at series of phenomena from the history of the Jewish people and their spiritual life, revolving on its axis in a permanent cyclical order, albeit not mechanical. These phenomena are revealed either in an innovative version or an imitative one, a sublime version or as deception. The mystical and scatological ideas of the false prophets are not similar to Herzl's visions, yet one root unifies the various phenomena, as they operate according to the same permanent dialectic regularity that moves history ahead. In every important period a new idea of redemption is born, blinding the eyes of the people. At such a time, the need arises for a chosen person who will take the burden upon himself to bear the mission and bring his people a new song.[375]

The chosen one must be a synthesis of hero of spirit and hero of battle, of Moses and of Samson. One may draw an analogy between the process of secularization and sobriety of the end of the 18th century, in the nation's shift from vacuous beliefs and calculations of apocalypse - to the Enlightenment movement and the processes of the end of the 19th century, with the nation's awakening from promises of the Enlightenment and its slogans, or the sentimental and vague dreams of "Hovevei Zion",[376] to that same naked truth reflected to him from the articles of Ahad Ha'am (called the "Moses of his generation"). According to Shamir, one may draw a line from Ramchal[377] as a mediating man - one foot in the world of Kabbalah and one in the world of Enlightenment - to a mediating man such as Bialik, who had one foot planted in the Hasidic world of his forefathers, and one with the Zionist Enlightenment scholars of Odessa. After all, the poem - as its ending testifies - strives carefully to express the wish that the people quickly awaken from the Herzlian visions, and pass from adolescence to sober maturity, to their stage in life that will be a synthesis between reality and vision, between tradition and foreign influence, between the shadows of home and the imps of the field.[378]

From the descriptions of destruction at the opening of the poem one may understand that in 2000 years of exile, this people had no poetry, only prayers. Now, with their return to action, to actual life, the Jewish people have returned to poetry. Bialik predicts here the short-lived days of the Herzlian revolution, the hopelessness of the rapid and hurried redemption, but also the dazzling beauty of hope. The real solution, he believes, is in the awakening to a gray lusterless routine lacking prestige, yet real and actual. Bialik's world was skeptical and ambivalent, with no extremes. In "Shirati" he reviewed history and offered a program for the future without calling for the downfall of the old, while also not belittling the new ideas.

---

[373] (Shamir, 2000), pp. 104.
[374] Bialik, "Lamitnadvim Ba'am" (1889-1900))Hebrew), BYP.
[375] See: "Sing unto the Lord a new song, for He has done great" (Psalms 98). This 'new', as mentioned, does not deal with casting away the old, but rather a new synthesis - with the old idea appearing in a new way.
[376] "Lovers of Zion": a political organization known as foundation-builders of modern Zionism.
[377] Hebrew acronym of Moshe Chaim Luzzatto (1707-1746).
[378] (Shamir, 2000), p. 711.

"Tikkun" - The Mending of the World

Hence, "Shirati" (together with "Zohar") constitutes a work of multiple directions and paradoxes: The more that the objective reality is impoverished and desecrated, the more the poetic and linguistic reality becomes rich and laden with layers of holy literature; and the opposite - the more the world of the chosen one fills with joy and wondrous transcendental sights, the poorer the language becomes. Moreover: The further the simple referential reality distances itself outward from home to the open field, the more internalized the plot becomes, the more soulful; and the opposite - the reality in the room is revealed to be a simple and external one, not fearful of vision and imagination. This paradox is the result of conjoining two different poetics in one work. As a work written at the turn of the 20th century, "Shirati" looks over the 19th century that was mainly classicist, and the 20th century - mainly of symbolism, and describes the weaving of the new on the ruins of the old. The first part of the poem illustrates the secularization of Hebrew poetry in the 19th century, and the second part - the pursuing of the new being, of the 20th century, of transcendental, idealist and utopian ideas, which distance it from comprehending reality, and do not even facilitate its getting closer to actual deeds.[379]

---

[379] Ibid, p. 107.

5.4 Poetry and Invocation

The language of prayer and the language of prophecy differ from one another, while holding on to each other, yet the language of prayer, of gazing and yearning came first. This, at least, we learn from the development of Bialik's poetry. Schweid finds two types of language of prayer in Bialik's poetry:[380] the prayer of 'shaliach ha'am' (messenger of the people) and the prayer of the individual. Occasionally, his poetry combines the two types, and sometimes confronts one with the other. From the prayer of 'shaliach ha'am', who suddenly felt his loneliness, and with it, the dire need to return to himself and find his way to his god, the language of prophecy developed - whether it be prophecy of reprimand of the people, or the prayer of the individual withdrawing into himself from his people. Although both prayers exclude each other, it seems that the one is not possible without its counterpart. According to Schweid, Bialik's language of prayer manifests, in both types, the problem of its credibility as the language of discourse between man and god, in terms of the certainty of a presence listening and responding. His prayer-poetry is described as a search for a new religious language and a new formulation.

The poem "In the Field" is accepted as the most mature poem of prayer among Bialik's first poems ("Poems of Zion"), in which 'shaliach ha'am' stood before the people. The poem's maturity is expressed in its fullness and complexity of form, style, content and blending between the prayer of the many and the prayer of the individual standing among them. One may note that the same style of prayer will appear later on as the prayer of the secluded individual, who withdraws from the public domain to the domain of his private selfness.[381]

The problem of the credibility of the language of prayer appears as a three dimensional deviation from traditional language, in other words - deviation from the accepted patterns of holy poetry that was continuously bound to the patterns of the permanent prayers in the synagogue; deviation from the place of prayer; and deviation from the form of presenting and intention that embody the basis of the action, the working of god that is in the prayer. The deviation from the version is noted too as distinct detachment from the 'siddur' of prayers, and in the adaptation of modern poetics (rhythm, alliteration, and formal structure) that have no connection to the version of traditional holy poetry. The poem is lyrical-individual, and not poetry speaking in the language of 'we', of a community united around a canonic version of prayer. It is clear, then, claims Schweid, that the one who is praying has chosen to utter new poetry, the poetry of prayer as an individual speaking on behalf of individuals such as himself, who - if his poem reaches them - will pray with him; and if it reaches the nation, it too will unite in his prayer. This is not a prayer in synagogue before the holy ark, but rather as the first and constituting 'evening prayer', which the legends of the Sages

---

[380] (Schweid, 1998), pp. 722-178.
[381] Ibid. p.179.

had attributed to the Biblical Isaac, when he "went out walking in the field toward evening" (Genesis, 24:64).[382] "Isaac said the evening prayer, for they have said: Isaac went out walking in the field toward evening, not discussion but prayer, for they have said: A prayer of a poor man as he faints and before God he pours out his speech", Babylonian Talmud, Tractate Berachot 26:72. In other words, deduces Schweid, this is a prayer in the field, the meaning of 'field' being the field of the homeland, to which the one who is praying yearns to return, and for that reason he prays in his name and the name of the people praying with him.[383]

The work presented in the prayer is a longing for the landscape leading beyond itself, literally, the land to the East, which is the homeland yearned for, and leads to the hidden god, whose revelations of landscape are the language in which he speaks to the human attentive to him; the language of sights, senses, and emotions that the poetry absorbs and internalizes in its words and images, thereby turning the silence of god, who is present through the inducing sights, into the prayer of man to him. Thus, the very intention of the one who is praying is not only to yearn and long, beseech and beg, but also to act and work toward reaching the homeland, to work his god in the field and literally attain the blessing of work. All of these, especially the active element of the action, as well as their sanctification in the prayer of the field and the work, are a complete innovation in the ways of traditional prayer, expressing the Zionist way of thinking. The people are called to mobilize, to leave exile, and to realize the yearning to return to Zion with pity, by building the homeland and redeeming its land.

The poem illustrates this approach when the description opens with expressions of the distress of humiliation and torture, helplessness, and weakness of life in exile. The prayer asks to dissolve the feelings of distress and find comfort. It begins as an escape to an open place, symbolizing a haven from the home that had become a prison for its dwellers, yet during the escape a change takes place, and it becomes the going out to the field, and the going out turns into coming, arrival and attention. This attention, claims Schweid, is that which conveys the prayer. The dramatic course from escape to arrival at a home whose spaces are open to fill the world and lead out to the desired life goal becomes, from here on, the structural logic of the prayer itself. First it is uttered as complaint and supplication, in which the distress still reverberates, but during the weeping - a quasi elevation to a different level of experience takes place. The field and the land remain identical to themselves, but the face turning to heaven absorbs the change in landscape as the evening falls, and creates a perspective exposing visions beyond that which is seen, and attention to the silence beyond voice.[384]

The descriptions in the poem appear as verbal embodiment of a transformation in the landscape from the material-tangible to the spiritual that is even more tangible, or tangible in a different way. The enchanting landscape stands, as it were, in silent evening prayer, and the poet internalizes it, and - according to Schweid - prays the evening prayer through the verbal description, not only in the field, but actually with the field. This is a personal lyrical prayer altering all the accepted ways of expression. Nevertheless, it is easy to see that it is a transformation of tradition and of

---

[382] "Vayeitzei Yitzhak la-suah ba-sadeh lifnot arev"—"and Isaac went out walking in the field toward evening" (Gen. 24:64), "A prayer of a poor man as he faints and before God he pours out his speech", Babylonian Talmud, Tractate Berachot 26.
[383] In the activist branch of Zionism, A.D. Gordon as well interpreted the working in the field as the working of god, as Bialik implies in his poem.
[384] (Schweid, 1998), p. 179.

its language, and not detachment from its sources. On the contrary: As far as tradition is concerned, this is a deliberate return to the primacy of its sources to rejuvenate them. The evening prayer is restored to its literal state, as a source according to the legends of the Sages; in other words, going out to walk in the fields - language of conversing.[385] In his lyrical prayer, Bialik also alludes to the main motifs of the traditional evening prayer, but while doing so - transforms their meaning. Hence, this is not a quote of the sources, nor is it a 'midrash' of the traditional kind, since it is not a secondary usage of things said once to produce more meanings from them, or to serve as reference, but rather it is recharging of the original statement with actual experiencing of now as then. It must be heard today as in its inception, with all of its unique power.[386]

---

[385] The words 'dialogue', 'discourse', 'dialectics', or 'conversation' do not convey the full meaning of the Hebrew word 'siha', which immediately connects to 'bush of the field' and 'walking among the bushes', 'going out for a walk'.
See: Z. Gurevitch, *Conversation* (Hebrew) (Tel Aviv: Babel, 2011).
[386] (Schweid, 1998), pp. 179.

5.5 "Language of Sights"

In his poems, Bialik describes dazzling sights of nature, colorful and vibrant, as the landscape of early primary childhood memories that formed his identity and connections. Bialik blends in with this landscape of memories as he did directly, according to his memory, when he was a child. The language becomes the medium of reflexive remembrance and of actual personal blending with the landscape of memories. In the poem "Zohar", the fabric of landscape is reconstructed in memory as verbal, sensory, and flowing fabric. The peak of movement is intensified in the leap into the pond, in the heart of the fields, reflecting all the sights around it, as the soul reflecting memory.

A dramatic moment of change occurs in the experience described from memory, and in the memory itself, which blends with itself, so to speak, through the reflexive remembrance. It is an encounter of self-reflection of the landscape documenting itself within the transparent pond, and seen from within it in a silent glance; a moment of colorful blending with a supra-physical level, because of the movement of water reflecting the sights when the leaping boy's body hits it. Then there is complete tranquility - not at the end of the movement but rather as its transcendence, as a passing to a different level, of self, of the tangible reality of things gathering inside.

And still is the lake, with her former hue flushed,

Smooth, slumberous and glossy as erstwhile and hushed,

Again then in beamy paths wrinkled is she ,

Beneath her the silent world folds she and lies

In cover of rushes and dim willow tree.[387]

The withdrawing of the landscape into its transcendental selfness, in itself enabling the self-withdrawing of the rememberer into the memory reflecting itself in its primordial universe, the remembrance that becomes tangible and direct - turns into a dream that absorbs into it the landscape of the tranquil pond as a symbol of itself. This is done through an image of a fisherman who raises a net with dazzling sparks of light from the pond. Already at the beginning

---

[387] C. N. Bialik, "Zohar" (1900) in (Beinkinstadt, 1930), p.41.

of the poem there is a hint to the language of the sources that elevates the physical vision to the level of divine revelation. The aspiration to clandestine and silence, the description of the poet longing from the body of the world to its light, and the expression closing the first stanza describing the secrets as revealed to the poet, refer the reader gently but clearly to the level of Kabbalist symbolism. The pond is a Kabbalist symbol, and when the light vision takes place, the poem itself and the title "Zohar" are charged with meaning originating from the Kabbalah. In the description of the group of imps rising and passing, the language used is present tense; there is a mimetic change of poetic rhythm; tangible adherence of imagery of the Kabbalist 'Zohar' to the tangible sights of dazzling light, yet transparent, as the spiritual transparency of the landscapes of memory - all of these rejuvenate the experience of mystic 'zohar' within the completely unique now, symbolizing eternity.

The poem "The Pond" (1902)[388] speaks the same language and reconstructs the same longing for the experience of transcendental unity. One may see it as an example in the context of the function of poetry language as religious language, and the issue of its transformation into modern poetic language. The poem adds a contemplative dimension to "Zohar", and explicitly refers to the revelatory essence of both poems.

We should note that the pond is a reflecting memory, and as such it is a symbol. It appears in this poem as continuation of "Zohar", and in the same function, but this time with explicit indication of the revelatory meaning. Moreover, the revelation is described as the sounding of an ancient voice emanating from mythological landscapes of memory through personal landscapes of memory. The symbol of the pond connects these two landscapes: It is a personal memory, a visual and sound illustration of a mythological memory dwelling deep in the personal memory and turning it into a personal representative myth. Schweid claims that this is a clear continuation of the ancient voice directed to man in the landscape of the myth of the Garden of Eden, as told in Genesis, and reverberating in the mystic legends of the Sages, about the ascension of Moses to heaven. These are the things that the mystic 'midrash' attributes to the ministering angels, who wonder how a man of flesh-and-bones can dare burst into their sanctified domain, and it is a story testifying to the bold mystic scholar who risks himself ascending to the sphere above the human. The poem also has Kabbalist associations connected to mystic revelation: the expressions "revelation of the nearby divine", "revelation of Elijah". The voice calling "Where art thou?" is sounded through the succession of these sources, penetrating the personal memory, and through them filling the space of the now, elevated to eternity.[389]

(...) There is a ghostly tongue unsyllabled,

clandestine, voiceless, and yet rich in tone

in spectacle and image: entrancing forms

that make God manifest to chosen souls

---

[388] C. N. Bialik, "Habrecha" (1902) in *Selected Poems (Bilingual)*, trans. R. Nevo (Jerusalem: Dvir and Jerusalem Post, 1981).
[389] (Schweid, 1998), pp. 185-791.

the tongue in which the world's lord thinks his thoughts

and artists body forth their reveries

or find a semblance of unspoken dreams.

This is the language of visions; it is spelled out

in slit of blue sky and in vast sky space,

in lucent silvery mist and dark cloud mass,

in waving golden corn and cedar height,

in flash of white dove-wing, great eagle-wing,

in stalwart back and eye - enkindling glance,

in sea foam and the sport of laughing waves

in full midnight and silent falling stars,

in clatter of light at dawn, and turbulence

of sunset in an ocean all aflame.

In this, the tongue of tongues the pond disclosed

her universal riddle. Hidden there

concealed in shadow, tranquil, clear and still,

reflecting all things and containing all,

transfigured as she transformation finds,

she seemed to me to be the gazing eye

of the spirit of the forest, deep in thought,

in meditation and in mystery.[390]

The spirit of the forest, the image closing the poem, which in a translation closer to the original Hebrew source would be translated as "The Lord or the Minister of the Forest" is a visionary image of god, the creator hidden in the dark depths of his creation (the darkness of the forest full of secrets), and the quiet language of the gods is the utterance of visions of creation, reflected in the revealing-concealing transparency of the pond. If the pond is "the eye

---

[390] C. N. Bialik, "Habrecha" (1902), stanza 9.

of the Lord of the Forest", then the sights seen there are our world as god created it and sees it, the revelation of the secrets by their concealment.[391]

According to Schweid, when Bialik speaks about the language of languages of the Creation, he does not mean that of the heard words, but rather the sights of landscape perceived as symbols; those sights of foundation that the words induce when they remain in the soul of the man impressed by them. As we've learned in "Revealment and Concealment in Language", god speaks from the Creation in sights and not in words, and in the voice sounding from the ancient depths of the hearing man's soul. However, we should note that Bialik sounds the 'language of sights' in a musical verbal poem, and translates the language of sights into pictorial and alliterative language of speech, and through the voice of the artist he sounds it to the reader, for him to revive the pictures in his imagination, from the depths of his childhood memories, and from within the ancient myth of Creation.

It seems that in the childhood poems Bialik shaped a personal myth connected by Kabbalist symbolism to the myth of Creation. The experience of human existence, man's pondering over the secret of his beginnings, and over the meaning of his existence and destiny, as well as his yearning to return to his origin and be redeemed there of the suffering of existence - all of these are expressed in the prayer of the individual for personal redemption, by returning to the eternal source from which life emanates in the world, and to which it longs to return, to be united at the end.

Contrary to the prayer of the individual that needs the language of sights and is anchored in the myth of Creation, the national prophetic mission - according to Schweid, needs a voice speaking in the language of words, and it is anchored in the myth of the historical purpose and destiny of the Jewish people. Parallel to the personal shaping of the myth of Creation in his childhood poetry, Bialik shaped the myth of the destiny of the 'chosen people', the people wandering in the desert of nations, sinning before the wrathful god of judgment, punished by destruction upon destruction, going out to discover exile, and discover the inners of exile, that each is more difficult than its predecessor and impinges upon the sanctity of life and essence of life.[392]

The nation imprisoned in the foreign countries struggles to return to the Promised Land; it believes and hopes, rebels and despairs alternately. The Zionist endeavor is bound to this myth as it continuation. It is perceived as the last chapter, the final one, after the last final destruction - the destruction of the 'beit-midrash' - which Bialik sees as parallel to the two destructions of the temple preceding it. He sees this destruction as the most devastating one, symbolizing not only the detachment of the people from their god, but also the destruction of the nation itself, and the withdrawal of god from them. Hence, the Zionist endeavor is both a rebelling and despairing hope, a great effort seemingly doomed to fail, to break the ring of the fate of exile, and actualize the vision of the promised redemption by man's own powers - a rebellion against god's sentence in order to return to dwell in his shadow. Yet will the nation achieve its right, be faithful to itself, to its history, in its rebellion against its god? Or does it have - this nation that was destroyed, while passively accepting its fate of exile for so many generations - the necessary powers for such an

---

[391] Here Heidegger's concept comes to mind, discussed in chapter 2 of this essay, of the 'clearing in the forest' (Lichtung) in which Being appears, while at the same time it is also his place of hiding.
[392] (Schweid, 1998), pp. 185-191.

independent endeavor as this? This is the pondering call of the missioned prophet, who has come to lift the spirits of his contemporaries to the heights of the vision of the myth of redemption, and is shocked at the depth of the meaning of the rift embodied in his faith, as his sin.

5.6 Poetry as (Modern) Prophesy

To understand the secret of the Bialikan mission, sounding the ancient voice of the sources in the present of the turn of the 20th century, one must understand, according to Shamir as well as Schweid, the inner connection between the personal myth that draws from representational memories of the individual Jew of his generation, and the national myth anchored in the Biblical story from Exodus on, which continues to reverberate through the legends of the Sages and the Kabbalah. This connection is exposed at the meeting point of the myth of Creation and the personal childhood story, with the national myth and the story of personal maturity, on the background of the tragic life-being of the nation in exile. Just as the story of the forefathers was connected to the Creation story after the expulsion from the Garden of Eden, in the sense of the way toward the vision of wholeness that is to be realized in the future - so the story of the personal-national exile of Bialik is connected to the childhood story, after the personal event of expulsion or fall from the Garden of Eden of the first childhood.

The place of the 'beit-midrash' in Bialik's poetry is portrayed as the first exile of the adolescent boy, parting from his innocent childhood and the perfect landscape of childhood. The 'beit-midrash' denies him the childlike innocence of life in nature, and places him under the burden of 'mitzvah' and the worries of existence in this world. Nevertheless, this is the first exile to a home that still has hope of life and hope of promised redemption in the future, redemption that god guarantees. But then comes the second fall, completely connected to the historical fate of the exiled nation in the present, evoking the feeling that this nation has been completely expelled from the Eden of natural life, from physical adolescence, physical love and from creativity fed by a physical Eros. By yearning to be redeemed in the physical life, with its connection to the myth of Creation, the youth discovers himself in a deserted 'beit-midrash' from which the divinity has withdrawn. However, instead of the dream of returning to the innocence of childhood and the creativity in nature, he finds himself falling into a double-dimensioned exile: On the one hand, an exile from the Garden of Eden of childhood to which he cannot return, and on the other - an exile from the 'beit-midrash', which guarantees future redemption. He must now struggle, and with his own powers, for his present redemption, which has neither innocence nor holiness.

The last hope of the poet is his people, not his god. If the nation redeems itself from the fate of exile with its independent physical powers and return to the lands of the living, to the Promised Land, the exiled individual will find, as well, the way back to the course of life and the physical Eros to which he is destined, and that is the primary hope expressed in the prayer "In the Field".

Bialik created an inner relation between his poetry of prophetic tone and the totality of his poetry, as a source constituting a continuation of a canonic image of the previous sources. He sounded the ancient prophetic voice through actualization of the myth he created, in the sense of a source that he shaped in order to speak about the present to the people of the present. Thus he actually created the source of his prophetic authority by creative connection to previous sources, and thus he created as well the common language between himself and the readers of his nation who saw him as a national poet and prophet, and who internalized the messages of his entire work, absorbed his language, and through it found a renewed connection to the sources from which they had been torn, in their rebellion against the fate of their nation, as Bialik himself had done. This, according to Schweid, is the key to understanding the symbolic shape of the image of the prophet in Bialik's prophetic poetry, which is itself part of the message. Bialik, in his prophecy, created an image of an ideal personal "I", revealed and active on the level of spiritual creation at which he encounters his readers. The voice speaking in the name of god is the mythic "I", which Bialik shaped with material of the sources and material of personal biography, and which was delivered to the people by the poet, who is - as it were - both the prophet of god and the representative of the people.[393]

Bialik's first prophetic poem "A Word"[394] reveals the complex spiritual process in a clear and open way. The poet appeals to the prophet, who is the visionary, mythic "I", his own "I" whom he elicited from the depth of his sources. Thus he presents himself as a poet between his mythic "I" and the people. He speaks to the prophet on behalf of the people, and speaks to the people on behalf of the prophet. It is clear that the language of prophetic authority, from which the people may hear the words of god, is the same language that sounds the myth at the level of the present. The words of prophecy will be heard as prophecy only by those still identifying with the ancient myth through its rejuvenation, and activated by it. One way or the other, the poet elevates the image of himself, in terms of his connection with his people, to the level of myth - where the voice of god is still heard as sounded by the prophets of yore. Here it seems that Schweid assumes a weighty point, when he claims that the reprimand sounded by Bialik to his people from the same source, is no other than the reprimand of their betrayal of this myth, which had shaped their identity as a nation faithful to their god.

Schweid goes on to examine, in this context, the style of the prophetic 'burden' that Bialik shaped to shock his listeners. His connection to the language of the last prophets, especially Amos, Jeremiah, Isaiah and Ezekiel is clear, and evidence to it is the remnants of prophetic language drawn from these sources, but even more so are the rhetorical patterns that sound the same divine pathos - a pathos striving to absolute power, and obligating compulsive operating power, inducing absolute urgency of the need to immediately respond to a supreme caring in a situation of determining life or death. However, again one must note that Bialik does not make secondary use of linguistic materials of the sources, does not quote or interpret them, nor does he imitate them. The formal shape of his prophetic burden is done with tools of modern poetics, in the sense of rhythm, syntax, imagery, and alliteration. Hence, Bialik strived to achieve that same emotional and contemplative activation as did the prophets of the sources in their way, by employing modern rhetoric adapted to the sensitivity and openness of spirit of his contemporaries. The same holds true, according to Schweid, concerning the remnants of language of the sources. Bialik uses them to express the truth revealed to him, and his messages of the present, in deliberate contrast to the language of the sources. Although his purpose is to stimulate the authoritarian memory, to go back and sound it, it is not in the meaning of then, but rather in a different meaning from the meaning of then, to the same extent that the now is different from the then.[395]

It seems that the very awareness of the difference in meaning that had taken place in the consciousness of his generation toward the fate of the nation and toward the compelling authority of its sources, is Bialik's central prophetic message, and one of his most passionate means of evoking regret and responsibility, and generating the answer that every true prophetic vision wishes to achieve, even when it expresses absolute despair of the answer and of the redemption that the answer entails. Bialik's prophetic language is, then, a renewed transformation of the language of the prophets. It sounds the same voice and maintains the same authority, of course only to the ears of the listeners who have internalized the same language, and who are capable of the same renewing transformation, born from the pain of the rift, and from the yearning to bridge it. Whoever does not hear the ancient voice from within, and does not live the historical myth as a memory preceding his own biographical memory, will not hear the voice of the poet-artist who needs prophetic metaphors to shock his readers.

---

[393] (Schweid, 1998), p. 797.
[394] C. N. Bialik, "Davar" (1904) (Hebrew), BYP.
[395] (Schweid, 1998), pp. 794-195.

Poetry as (Modern) Prophesy

After this chapter has examined Bialik's poetic-political course, as well as the connection between the concepts of Bialik's 'awakening', and 'sobriety' of Hölderlin, the question arises regarding the possibility that Bialik's poetic perception will also open the way to a new reading of the place of myth in Hölderlin's poetry, beyond the dichotomy characterizing the dominant interpretational discourse.

The true leader, even if unseen, of the ship of politics is the wind,[396] without it all of history's sails are nothing but dead rags.

(C.N. Bialik, "Culture and Politics")[397]

6. River and Pond - Poetry, Myth and The Political

'Political' is the most general term of political philosophy, however, over the last decades it has come to be known as the concept of 'the political', to be found at the center of philosophical thought, which views it as a basic element of human existence.[398] The concept's meanings (themselves a political act) appear in a semantic space between two extremes: On the one hand, following Carl Schmitt,[399] identification of the political with actual unification under common rule distinguishing friend from foe; and on the other, influenced by Heidegger and Arendt, identification of the political with the very existence of human multiplicity. One extreme focuses the discussion of the political on discussing sovereign government, while the other turns the discussion on the political into a discussion on human existence itself. For the purpose of our discussion we wish to lean on the characterization of the political in connection with the thought of Arendt.

In her book "Between Past and Future",[400] Arendt ponders the circumstances of understanding René Char's "Notre héritage n'est pas précédé d'aucun testament", (translated by Arendt as: "Our inheritance was left to us by no testament"), which had originated in the years of the Resistance, a time when public collective freedom overrode the troubles of private interests. The fact that it is not possible to pass on the richness of moments such as these, the "treasure of the revolution", has - according to Arendt - turned in modern times into a fact of political significance,[401]

---

[396] The word 'ru'ach' appears in the origin in its Hebrew meaning of both 'wind' and 'spirit'.
396 C.N. Bialik, "Culture and Politics" (Hebrew), in *Hagina*, ed. Y. Halperin, August 1918, p.5, http://benyehuda.org/bialik/tarpol.html)trans. Z. Maor).

[398] See: A. Ophir, "The Political"(Hebrew), in *Mafteakh, Lexical Review of Political Thought*, vol. 2, summer 2010, http://mafteakh.tau.ac.il/wp-content/uploads/2010/08/2-2010-06.pdf

[399] C. Schmitt, "Politische Theologie" (1922) in *Political Theology, Four Chapters on the Concept of Sovereignty*, trans. by G. Schwab (Chicago: Chicago UP, 2005).

[400] H. Arendt, *Between Past and Future: Six Exercises in Political Thought* (New York: Viking, 1961).

[401] Ibid, p.17.

not perceived solely as a flaw but rather as potentially positive as well. It is possible that the moments of freedom cannot be delivered on, but they can continue to affect indirectly. Their impact occurs at the time of delivering these attempts into the space of thinking, which must always be struggled over anew - a space enabling their recurrence by each new generation. That which is taken and delivered is not really the contents of these moments, but rather their relation to the continuation of time. Hence it is possible - despite a loss of tradition in the Modern era and the lack of testament stating what the inheritor has by law - to turn the heritage of struggle for freedom, of disrupting the ruthless rush of time, into something that may be experienced every time anew.

Arendt also describes the conditions of delivery of inheritance at times in which the very delivery is doubtful. The space of the present, which in the constant and permanent flow of time enables freedom to be created from the struggle against past and future, Arendt calls "the home of man on earth". The origin of the space of the present, for her, is in man's involvement and action. The concept of 'a gap in time', which she calls 'hiatus', between the old and the new order, appears in order to describe the disruption of the linear chronological sequence of the omnipotent time continuum. In "On Revolution", she notes that the end of the old is not necessarily the beginning of the new, and that freedom can be created only with the creation of a new community.[402] The hiatus between the "no longer" and the "not yet" contains the "moment of truth", of the disruption, in which - as she perceives it - contemplation, politics and freedom occur.

Hence, relation to the concept of 'the political' through the perspective of Arendt, focuses the occurrence of the political in connection with questions regarding the possibility of delivering an idea over time. In other words, the question is: How may one deliver the experience, concepts and culture of past tradition into the future, without dragging along all of the accompanying problems? Or, in our context: Is it possible, and if so then how is it possible, to make room for myths from the past in our times (acknowledging their necessity and involvement in our lives), without dragging along their subjugating dimensions?

The uniqueness of the Modern age, according to Arendt, is that the problem of delivery has turned, with modernity, from that of the limited elite into a comprehensive problem of humanity, hence political.
[402] H. Arendt, *On Revolution* (New York: Viking, 1963), pp. 27-32.

6.1 "Dwelling" - Poetry and Polis

There in the coldest abyss I heard

The stripling moan for liberation,

In floundering rage accuse earth,

His mother, and the thunderer who

Begot him, and they heard him also,

His parents, pitying, yet

Mortals fled the place, for it was terrible,

With him in his chained dark torsions,

The frenzy of the demigod.[403]

Within the tangled dark ivy, hidden in a net of time-space coordinates that are simultaneously realistic and particular, as well as mythological and allegorical, the poet sits to a sudden discourse of his soul with itself. He is facing the coast of Peloponnesus and its voice is the "voice of fate". Then the sound is heard of the noblest of rivers wrestling in the dark with its shackles, and groaning for redemption.

In 1801, Hölderlin began to develop his religious vision in hymns, following the model of the Greek poet Pindar (443-522 B.C.), one of the most outstanding creators of lyrical poetry in Greece. Among Hölderlin's hymns, "The Rhine" (Der Rhein) is perceived by researchers to be the most important, and is dedicated to Isaak von Sinclair, a loyal friend who shared Hölderlin's enthusiasm of the French Revolution and the political dream of a Schwab republic.[404] The poem opens with a meditation on the course of the river, which is demigod, the son of Zeus and of earth, struggling with its chains in its dark prison underground. Hungry for wandering and freedom, and impatient, it is released and swept blindly away from its source, to be exposed and rebel against its fate. The river leaves the bowels of the earth and the mountains, slides toward Asia, and meanders serenely in the land of the Germans, working the land, and maintaining its beloved children. The poem goes twisting on in the Greek tragedy structure passing among

---

[403] F. Holderlin,"Der Rhein" (1798-1800), SPF p.197.
[404] We should mention that in two of Hölderlin's great works, the epistolary "Hyperion", and the tragic drama "Empedocles", the protagonist combines religious or metaphysical intuition of the whole of nature, with the poetic vision of reformation in the political and social order.

gods and the humans seeking to be likened to them, until the titanic primordial energy of the river encounters the boundary where god is. The poem ends in an equilibrium embodied in the apocalyptic wedding ceremony of man and god: Speculation of reconciliation of man with the gods, where - instead of appeasing the gods, for a short while the scales are balanced. The river symbolizes for Hölderlin, "The Poet of the Rivers", the course of history's movement, as well as the course of the creative poetic process. Rousseau, whom Hölderlin considered the epitome of the modern poet, bestows pure language ('Rein' in German is 'pure') as a Dionysian priest divinely foolish and lawless; Rousseau is the stranger in the society of man; he has the divine language that bestows of the holy plenty.

In his article "The Question Concerning Technology",[405] Heidegger connects Hölderlin's poem "The Rhine" to an idea from another text of Hölderlin, "In Lovely Blue",[406] claiming that Hölderlin's poem is what enables the 'dwelling' of the German people in the Rhine valley. "In Lovely Blue" is a prose text in the novel "Phaëthon" (1823), which was written by Hölderlin's admirer and first biographer, F.W.Waiblinger. Despite the lack of distinct references, the text is perceived by researchers as an original work of Hölderlin, and also the basis for the protagonist of the novel, the sculptor Phaëthon, who went mad. The phrase from the text: "poetically man dwells" serves as the title of one of Heidegger's well-known essays,[407] and the concept 'dwelling' slowly became central to his thought. In his essay, Heidegger uses this line of Hölderlin to trace the character of the poetic in its relation to 'dwelling'. Heidegger had already examined these relations in the past in his article "Building Dwelling Thinking";[408] however, in his last article, the point of departure is the question of measure, as it appears in "In Lovely Blue", leading Heidegger to introducing 'measurement' as the nature of poetry, describing poetry as an absolute building, and claiming that man dwells in that which he builds, and that man ultimately dwells in poetry through measurement.

(...) May, if life is sheer toil, a man

Lift his eyes and say: so

I too wish to be? Yes. As long as Kindness,

The Pure, still stays with his heart, man

Not unhappily measures himself

Against the Godhead. Is God unknown?

Is he manifest in the sky? I'd sooner

---

[405] M. Heidegger, "Die Frage nach der Technik" (1954), in HBW, pp. 307-342.
[406] F. Holderlin, "In lieblicher Bläue" (1823), in *Hymns and Fragments*, trans. R. Sieburth (Princeton: Princeton UP, 1984), pp. 248-253.
[407] M. Heidegger, "dichterisch wohnet der mensch" (1951), in *Poetry, Language, Thought* (New York: Harper Modern Perennial Classics, 2001), p. 209.
[408] M. Heidegger, "Bauen Wohnen Denken" (1951), in HBW, pp. 343-364.

Believe the latter. It's the measure of man.

Full of merit, yet poetically, man

Dwells on this earth.[409]

The first moment of measurement, according to Heidegger, occurs when man raises his eyes. He then adds that authentic poetry is precisely when "Man, not unhappily, measures himself against the Godhead".[410] The authenticity presented here results from the possible proximity to the appearance of truth occurring in an intermediate moment. For Heidegger, the upward look, crossing far into the heavens while remaining on earth, stretches as a gap between heaven and earth. This gap is that which is measured for the divinity of man. Man's place appears as inhabiting an intermediate position, whereas in the earlier article relating to this poem, the gap is preserved between the gods, the humans, and the poet, who was seemingly expelled and pushed into this space, where only there may it be determined for the first time who man is, and what his existence is.

The intermediate space seems to take the form of the manifestation of a new temporality:

"The time of the gods that have fled and of the god that is coming ... the No-more of the gods that have fled and the Not-yet of the god that is coming".[411]

This is a space locating the poet as a means of mediation determining together the space and proximity, similarly to the bridge gathering the landscape fourfold:

"gathers to itself in its own way earth and sky, divinities and mortals".[412]

The issue of the relation between man and poet is clarified as well regarding the necessity for 'earth'. The farmer is described as one who needs to be close to the everyday objects, while the poet remains distant to figure the dwelling, or simply to dwell. For Heidegger, the mediating moment is pure poetic experience of being. For Hölderlin this seems to be as a moment of death, since the position of mediator and measurer also bears with it, inherently, the eternal distance from the measured.

In "Hölderlin and the Essence of Poetry", Heidegger adapts the Hölderlinian mythology, while pouring new contents into it. At the foundation of the mythology of the poet, as we have seen, is the 'caesura' between gods and humans. This 'caesura' disrupted an ancient era in Greece in which the gods were united with man and granted him of

---

[409] F. Holderlin, "In lieblicher Bläue" (1823), in *Hymns and Fragments*, trans. Richard Sieburth (Princeton: Princeton UP, 1984), pp. 248-253.
[410] M. Heidegger, "dichterisch wohnet der mensch" (1951) in *Poetry, Language, Thought* (New York: Harper Modern Perennial Classics, 2001), p. 220.
[411] Ibid, p. 289.
[412] Ibid.

their plenty. Hölderlin's era represents a rift and abandonment, and detachment of the gods from the mortals. Humanity's recovery and their redemption from the fall depend upon rehabilitation of the unity, which is the mission of the poet.

In the line from "In Lovely Blue": "Full of merit, yet poetically, humans dwell on this earth", Hölderlin connects between the poetic action and the divinity. The poetic appears as the human way of dwelling. Neither knowledge, nor power, is the way of dwelling, but rather - poetization is that which bestows place to man.

Heidegger, as mentioned, reads Hölderlin's poetry as that dealing with the essence of poetry, and the word 'poetic' is described as bearing a constituting quality, as opening an aperture for the appearance of being. The constituting poetry is perceived as having the character of dialogue, since it is basically discourse with the gods. The act of naming is poetic action directed as discourse, which the poet conducts with the gods when he responds to their demand to be named. The origin of the gift of poetic divinity is neither in the poet nor in the poetry but rather in the gods. The poet appears as exiled into the gap between the gods and mortals. Exposed at the heart of danger, the poet stands to deliver the divine plenty to the humans in order for them to have place and history. The poet thereby unites, as it were, the rift between the gods and humans, granting the latter the place of dwelling that they had lost. Poetry is the poetic giving of the divine receiving; the gift of divinity diverted from its ontological context, and donning theological character. It is the gods who ultimately bestow place, mediated by the poet. The poet translates the gift of divinity into the language of humans, thereby granting them place.[413]

Hölderlin's river hymns seem to Heidegger as flowing from their source, but without forgetting it. His poetry state the holy. The poet, as the river, stands between gods and humans, and as the river - is a demigod. Language, which for Heidegger is the home of being, is given to thinkers and poets who attain its authentic patronage. They receive language and dwell in its home. Their role is to complete the building of the home. Thinking and poetic action provide words for self-exposure of being, or - in other words, words are the way in which being spreads its light. Man as a poet and thinker can call the things by name, and release language from the daily degeneration it is in. Language is not man's creation, but those dwelling in its home may renovate and improve it. Man, dwelling in the home of language, defines himself through it, giving meaning to his existence, and thereby adding to the home and maintaining it.[414]

The origin of language, according to Heidegger, is in 'logos'. It is that which enables language to breathe life into beings. Heidegger interprets 'logos' - usually translated as 'word' or 'speech' - in the Greek sense of 'placed'. 'Speech' means placing beings in the open space, so that they are present. Hence, 'logos' is described not in its regular sense, not as communication between addresser and addressee, and also not as a statement claimed by man about the world, and bearing a value of truth. Both of these are corruption of 'logos', turning it into chatter or logic. In its meaning according to Heidegger, 'logos' is a statement belonging to the world more than to man. The concept of

---

[413] D. Pimentel, "The Gift of Place" (Hebrew), *Bezalel History and Theory Protocols*, vol. 10, October 2008.
[414] (Mansbach, 1998), pp. 93-97.

'logos', as it appears with Heraclites, is in inverse relation to concealment, and bears the ontological values of exposure (Unverborgenheit) and gathering (Versamlung) to exposure. The stating of a thing is therefore not about the thing, but rather is that which grants it its being. The statement is the appearance of the thing in its being.[415] Thus too, in "The Question Concerning Technology",[416] where Heidegger derives the essence of poetry from epistemological study of the Greek word 'poiesis', in its original Greek context as it appears with Plato, the meaning of 'poiesis' is presented as 'creation'. Heidegger understands poetic production in the Phenomenological sense of creation of truth, and as a reason for its appearance. Precisely as with a painting of van Gogh, so too language in general, and poetry in particular, are revealment and exposure of being for Heidegger. Language, in general, and poetry in particular, are a means of 'aletheia', of bringing being to revealment and exposure. The crucial point is that an event of exposing being in poetry and art does not occur in a void. The event of poetry and poetry as an event bear the characteristic of giving. That which is given in the event of poetry and in poetry as event is space. 'Space'. Not empty space or astronomical and mathematical space, but rather human space - space as it appears before the human. In other words - 'place'. The gift of poetry is the gift of place. That which is given to man in the event of poetry is his place, his dwelling and his world, where his life takes place. Time too is given in the event of poetry. Not scientific time, Aristotelian, "vulgar" time, but rather human time; time as it appears for the human and is experienced by him; in other words, history. That which is given to man in the event of poetry is his history, which as the beginning, or the source ('Ursprung') in its original sense, includes the past and the future.[417] Both of these cannot be understood each without the other; only in place does history occur, and history is always of place.[418]

In 1936, the year in which "The Origin of the Work of Art" was written, Heidegger was in the midst of the turning-point through which the concept of 'Dasein' was more greatly perceived in its collective dimension than in its private existential one. Hence, Heidegger's words are directly less to the private person and more to the nation (Volk). The place granted by poetry is less the private personal place, and more the public one: the people and the country. The question of the national identity of the receivers of place remains open in "The Origin of the Work of Art", seemingly at least. Heidegger refers to 'nation' in its general context, but he seems to be speaking increasingly about "our historical nation", namely - the Germans. The question concluding the text is specifically directed to Germans: Will the German nation be able to assume the inhabiting of place that German poetry grants it? The German nation is therefore examined as a test case for the general phenomenon of nation, to which his text presumably refers.

However, in other texts of the same period, and especially the "Introduction to Metaphysics" and the texts dedicated to Hölderlin, his words are less obscure. The collective Dasein appears as 'our Dasein', of the German nation, enjoying preferential treatment of being. In this fashion, when Heidegger speaks of poetry as granting place, he speaks mainly of Hölderlin as granting the gift of place to the German nation.[419]

---

[415] M. Heidegger, "Der ursprung des Kunstwerkes" (1936), in HBW. p. 147
[416] M. Heidegger, "Die Frage nach der Technik" (1954), in HBW, pp. 307-342.
[417] M. Heidegger, "Der ursprung des Kunstwerkes" (1936), in HBW, pp. 139-212.
[418] (Pimentel, 2008).
[419] Ibid.

"Dwelling" - Poetry and Polis

The transformation that Heidegger made from the private existential dimension of being to the collective dimension of people and nation indicates the entailed connection between poetic and political. In the context of the tradition of aesthetic thought, there is an ancient controversy between poetic and political, well-represented by Aristotle and Plato. The two Greek philosophers are of the same opinion regarding the mimetic and emotional character of art; in other words: The main activity of art is the imitation of reality and presenting duplicates, thus it is mimesis. In addition, art is tightly bound to feeling and emotions, namely - to the other of reason. Aristotle wishes to bring art closer to reason by revealing the dimension of reason of art. Although imitation is perceived as a lowly activity since it is not conducted knowingly, it still maintains study and deduction; hence, art may not be seen as the enemy of reason, but rather as that which may assist it in its mission. The same holds true for the emotional dimension in art. Aristotle does not refute it, but does distinguish between emotion and lust: Lust has no dimension of reason, while emotion maintains one dimension or another of reason.[420]

For Aristotle, tragedy - as the highlight of art, constitutes a sophisticated machine of representation whose main purpose is a controlled emotional shaking of the feelings of fear and compassion, which reach their climax at the cleansing moment of catharsis, a purifying moment to which tragedy is directed. The perception of art as a mechanism for public benefit is that which justifies its presence in 'polis'. Hence tragedy is a system in the political field serving as a means of preventing the flaming of passions, which according to Aristotle threatens 'polis', which should be based on reason. In the Aristotelian model, art then is subjugated to 'polis'. The poetic is recruited by the political to become a component in maintaining order.

Plato, for his part, presents a political space devoid of the poetic in his philosophical vision. Contrary to Aristotle, Plato does not attempt to justify mimesis by strengthening its connection with reason, but rather sees in it a direct threat to the foundations of the latter. He perceives art as second-order imitation, namely - imitation of imitation. Since Plato's thought identifies the ideal origin as the origin, art does not imitate the image of the entity in its being, the form, the 'eidos', but only its tangible imitation, while the artisan is presented as 'demiorgos' - he who produces his products for the people (demos) and their benefit, the artisan as producing products for public needs and whose work is beneficial. This is not the case for the artist, whose work has no benefit for 'polis' and its citizens' welfare.

Moreover, art is also perceived as detrimental to the psychological order and to the political order based on it. As a mimetic action twice removed from truth, Plato sees art as a direct threat to reason. Art is perceived as a type of illusion, a spell or soothsaying, diverting man from striving toward the ideals. Furthermore, art also strengthens the passions and lust which are the negative part of the soul that does not act according to measure. The ode, for example, lamenting a deceased loved one, is described as not at all helping one who has lost his son. Instead of listening to his

---

[420] Aristotle, *Poetics*, trans. R. Janko (Bloomington: Indiana UP, 1987), p.57-121.

reason telling him to fortify himself and sally forth, the ode increases his grief, immersing him in it.[421] The removal of art from politics is accepted as the heritage that Plato had left to metaphysics.

Nevertheless, and to be precise, it should be noted that Plato distinguishes between two types of artists: On the one hand, the mimicking artist, known from Plato's reservations in the dialogues of "The Republic", "Laws" and others, and classified as the seventh level, the inferior, of the nine levels of perfection of the soul appearing in the dialogue "Phaedrus". On the other hand, and again in "Phaedrus", the definition of "philosopher or artist" appears again and at the first level, the supreme one of the soul.[422]

While the mimicking artist misses the primal truth, the essence - the artist who creates beauty realizes 'eros', the desire for beauty-good-truth, the highest of the high. The philosopher, the ruler of utopia, is like an artist. He experiences the wonder of the 'look', in the unity of beauty. The experience of beauty heals and regenerates the broken wings of the soul, so that the soaring of the creator of beauty is the philosophical soaring toward the world of ideals from which the soul had dropped. Beauty, in the Platonic sense, is conscious transcendental revealment, in which the (deserving) artist and the philosopher are partners to the process of the soul retracting from the prison of life.[423]

It seems that Plato's approach, in its interpretation of removing art, became the prevailing one (in its Neo-Platonic attire) until F.W.J. Schelling, in 1800, in his book "The System of Transcendental Idealism"[424] generated a revolutionary change in the system of relations between reason (philosophy) and art. Schelling, it seems, got into a philosophical cul-de-sac since he was unable to decide between the Kantian idea of a world-constituting subjective consciousness and the empiricist approach of factual data that obligate the consciousness, due to his indecision as to what comes first - subjectivity of the free consciousness and its immanent patterns, or objectivity of the "necessary", prevalent world contents. His study offers a solution in the image of an assumption of a priori unity between subject and object - one that derives from an other intellectual ability of reason, the intuitive ability. For Schelling, the work of art is such a unity, bridging between freedom and a must, reason and the sensory, man and the world. As far as Schelling was concerned, art will confirm for the world, and always anew, that which philosophy cannot express.[425]

Seven years after Schelling had written his text, F.W.G. Hegel published "Phenomenology of Mind",[426] a book in which he specified art, alongside religion and philosophy, as realms of culture in which the spirit knows itself. Philosophy, religion and art all shape the same content - contents of the "general spirit" seeking to know itself. The three disciplines advance the "general spirit" in history, thanks to the reasoned freedom pulsating at the basis of all

---

[421] Plato, *"The Republic" ("politeia")*, trans. B. Jowett (New York: Cosimo, 2008), pp. 537-558.
[422] Plato, "Phaedrus", trans. A. Nehamas & P. Woodruff, in *Complete Works* (Indianapolis: Hackett, 1997), p. 228.
[423] G. Ofrat, "The Philosophical Miss and the Religious Chance" (Hebrew), in *Studio Art Magazine* 115, July 2000.
[424] F. W. J. Schelling, "System des transcendentalen Idealismus" (1800), in *System of Transcendental Idealism*, trans. P. Heath (Charlottesville: Virginia UP, 1978).
[425] (Ofrat, 2000).
[426] G. W. F. Hegel, "Phänomenologie des Geistes" (1807), in *Phenomenology of Spirit*, trans. A. V. Miller, (Oxford: Clarendon, 1977).

three. They are committed to the logic of dialectics, and the only difference between them is in their dependence upon material and imagery. Art depends on medium and imagery for its existence, more so than religion's relative dependence (particularly on mythic images), and surely more than philosophy, which is a purely spiritual act of the "general spirit" knowing itself. Hence, one may say that art is philosophical. The philosopher is interested in art as long as art is purposeful, and its purpose is supreme or absolute truth, beauty and good.

In Heidegger's ontology, his connection to the second interpretation of Plato is clear - that which enables the artist and philosopher accessibility to the ideal. He sees the political and poetic as sharing a common source. The origin of the word 'politics' is the Greek word 'polis' - city-state. 'Polis' is the first human political organization, combining urban organization with state. However, the original meaning of 'polis' did not necessarily derive from the political. Heidegger claims that to understand the concept one must seek its pre-political meaning. According to the principle of ontological priority, precisely as logic is the corruption or impoverishment of 'logos' in its original sense, and 'ethics' is the degeneration of 'ethos' in its original one, so too is 'politics' the degeneration of the original meaning of 'polis'. Hence, the first meaning of 'polis' is connected less to politics and more so to ontology. He adds that this is also the way in which the Greeks themselves, and first and foremost Aristotle and Plato, considered 'polis'.[427]

Heidegger derives the ontological meaning of 'polis' etymologically, through the linguistic connection that he exposes between the word 'polis' and the word 'pelein', which means 'to be', 'to arrive', 'to appear'. Thus, 'polis' in its original Greek context is the arena of appearance. The ancient Greeks also identified 'pelein' with being in its pre-Socrates and pre-metaphysical sense. Hence, 'polis' is presented as the arena of appearance of being. 'Polis' then is but another name for 'aletheia', namely - the arena of appearance of beings in their true being, preceding and enabling any reasoned representation. In its ontological sense, 'polis' may be considered an axis of being, around which beings appear in their truth. There is a primary connection between 'polis' and being; 'polis' is but the site of appearance of truth, of being, and of being as truth.

'Polis' gathers man around itself, granting him position and history, as the one who stands in the center of being. Man dwells precisely in the arena of the appearance of being, which is 'polis'. The dwelling place of humans is not arbitrary, nor does it derive from geographical or strategic reasons. Heidegger explains the location of 'polis' ontologically: 'Polis' dwells in the arena of appearance of being. 'Polis' is but the arena of appearance of being. This appearance is that which constitutes 'polis', and which renders unique its location as the worthy dwelling place of humans.[428]

---

[427] M. Heidegger, "Hölderlins Hymne Der Ister" (1942), trans. W. McNeill & J. Davis (Bloomington & Indianapolis: Indiana UP, 1996), pp. 79-83.
[428] Ibid.

"Dwelling" - Poetry and Polis

The poetic therefore appears as that which is at the basis of the political, as constituting the political, as granting the political its place of occurrence. 'Polis' is itself a site of appearance of being, however, in order for the appearance to occur it needs poetry. Poetry is an event of appearance of the truth of being, an event of 'aletheia'. The literal meaning of truth is the 'non-concealed' (a-lethe), in other words, the appearance of truth as active release from the elementary state of its concealment. The revealment of truth and the release of being to its appearance are not conducted then by reason, but rather by the other of reason, which is poetry. Being is revealed through poetry as a gift, the gift of foundation, the gift of place. Its appearance in poetry grants man place and history, in other words, 'polis' and its political existence.[429]

In "Hölderlin and the Essence of Poetry",[430] the gift of dwelling is described as entailed from terms of Hölderlin's mythology, singing the rift between man and gods, and the yearning for its mending. Here too the claim is reiterated that the poetic word conveys a constituting quality, as it is the one to reveal an opening for the appearance of being. However, it is emphasized here that the constituting poetry conveys a character of dialogue, since its essence is in discourse with the gods, expressed in the action of naming, which in itself is response to the call of the gods to be named. Hence, the origin of the gift of poetic dwelling is not in the poet nor is it in the poetry, itself a means of delivery, but rather in the gods. The poet is exiled into a medium 'Zwischen' - between the gods and mortals, and in his poetry mediates (in the heart of danger) between the divine plenty and the mortals. Poetry, then, appears as poetic giving of divine receiving, in other words - as conveying character that it is difficult not to call 'mythic' or 'theological'.

In "Introduction to Metaphysics",[431] Heidegger describes the constitution of 'polis' through his reading of the first ode in "Antigone" by Sophocles. The first stanza of the ode describes man:

"There are many strange and wonderful things (Deinon), but nothing more strangely wonderful (Deinotaton) than man,"[432] where the adjective Deinon in Greek means both 'wonderful' and 'terrible'. Heidegger ascribes this adjective both to man and to being: Being is Deinon since it is violence itself, and man is Deinon since he draws his essence from being, and belongs to it. Heidegger reads the ode as a description of the struggle of human Deinon with the Deinon of being; a description of man's violent struggle to dwell in being. As man is Deinon, he belongs to being, and therefore does not flinch from its overwhelming violence, working with all his might to conquer and control the elements of nature with his reason and to create within them a place for himself. Polis. The ode describes man as one who defeats the waves with his ships, carves furrows in the earth, and catches animals in the net of his 'teche'. 'Teche' is neither technique nor technology in their customary sense, which to Heidegger is corruption of the original meaning of the concept. 'Techne' in its original Greek meaning should be understood as knowledge of that which is present,

---

[429] (Pimentel, 2008).

[430] M. Heidegger, "Hölderlin und das Wesen der Dichtung" (1936), in *Elucidations of Holderlin's Poetry*, trans. K. Hoeller, (New York: Humanity Books, 2000), pp. 51-56.
[431] M. Heidegger, "Einführung in die Metaphysik" (1935), trans. G. Fried and R. Polt (New Haven: Yale UP, 2000), pp.147-165.
[432] Sophocles, *Antigone*, trans. J. E. Thomas (Clayton: Prestwick House, 2005), p. 19.

knowledge of being. 'Techne' as knowledge is the releasing of being toward appearance and revealment. It is the useful human look, enabling the appearance of being. 'Techne' is understood here, phenomenologically, as the intention of man, enabling him to produce being from beings. Trade, hunting and farming are all ways of 'techne' in the sense that they are conducted by knowledge of being. Art too is a way of releasing being toward appearance; hence it is a type of knowledge as well, a type of 'techne'. 'Techne' is but a different name for human Deinon, the power of gods operating against the violence of being in order to conquer place in it. From this point of view, the event of 'aletheia' is perceived as an event that man is to generate decisively. Thought and language seem to lead being forcefully into appearance and revealment. Violence appears, and is based in this text of Heidegger, together with doubtful political declarations, as a basic means of man's action in the world, and ontologically justified.

The struggle, according to Heidegger, is between that which may be called the order of man manifest in 'techne', in other words, knowledge/art - and the order of being, manifest in 'dike', meaning 'justice'. Dwelling and conquest of place are conducted through pitting 'techne' against 'dike'. Man is but the event of pitting these two one against the other.

Since the power of 'Deinon' of being is greater than the power of human 'Deinon', man is condemned to leave the struggle ever defeated, as he is finite and mortal. Man's inevitable crashing on the rocks of being is a tragedy or catastrophe. The ones who conduct 'techne' - the thinkers and poets - are those who stand up to the power of being, and through language and thought grant man place in which to dwell. This dwelling assumes an image that is different than the divine gift of plenty described in other places, and appears here as overpowering conquest. Dwelling is acquired poetically, yet violently.

Despite the essential difference between Heidegger's two articles regarding the way of poetic dwelling of man, the poet in both is destined to the same fate. In both descriptions the poet, who grants dwelling, is kept away from it. In "Hölderlin and the Essence of Poetry" the poet is described as exiled to the gap between divine and human, and -granting dwelling - he is left in the gap outside of it. In "Introduction to Metaphysics" as well, the fate of those who grant and create 'polis' is to remain 'a-polis'; to remain without place, lonely, strangers and hostile, with no endurance or boundary, no structure and order, since they themselves, as creators, must first of all create all of these.

In "Introduction to Metaphysics" Heidegger sees Germany as the forerunner, who must release being subjected to the modern era in nihilistic distress, and lead the Germans to a new and promising future, which is but a return to their forgotten past. Thus will man's humanity be restored, and thus will Germans return to their privileged place intended for them in history, as those standing at the heart of being.[433] The text, claiming that the fate of those creating place is to be left outside of place, actually appears as recruiter of ideologies and saturated with nationalist rhetoric, as if intending to buy its creator the place of leader at the heart of the events.

---

[433] M. Heidegger, "Einführung in die Metaphysik" (1935), *Introduction to Metaphysics*, trans. G. Fried and R. Polt (New Haven: Yale UP, 2000), p. 153.

"Dwelling" - Poetry and Polis

The perception of 'art', as seen in the discussion of 'polis', is threshold space, as Janus-faced, dwelling inward and outward together, in the gap between 'polis' and 'a-polis', differentiated between interior and exterior, known and stranger, public and private, human and being; differentiated between other and responsibility. Otherness, as described by Dror Pimentel, is the 'desire' of art (following Jacques Lacan) - everything that has of the hybrid and futuristic in it, that is beyond law and economics. Loss of this 'desire' means loss of the artistic in art - stagnation. At the same time, however, art cannot abandon its connection to that which has of the community and common existence in it, everything that has responsibility.[434]

The danger lurking at the door of art is the double danger of losing its connection to the otherness on the one hand, and to responsibility on the other. The first danger, the Aristotelian, is the danger of losing the connection to the otherness following its subjugation to discourse, authority, and mission. With these, the connection of art to responsibility is preserved, yet its otherness is lost, and art can deteriorate into recruited, pamphlet art. The second danger, the Platonic, is that of art losing its connection to responsibility. By virtue of its otherness, art is kept away from the political body, thereby becoming indifferent to the being of life. This art, preserving its otherness while abandoning its responsibility, might lose its connection to the primary and immediate, to the community and to time. It might deteriorate into vacuous mannerism, and be swallowed as a consumer product in the market economy. Abandonment of the difference - whether loss of otherness by assimilating into 'polis', or loss of responsibility - is the danger that art faces. Dwelling in the difference enables art to maintain its otherness without losing its responsibility, and to maintain its responsibility without losing its otherness, to avoid indifference to place without assimilating in it, which are its two dangers.[435]

The thinker, calling for 'a-politicalness' of creators, to their granting the gift of place while they are left outside of it, recruits his philosophical qualifications to the Nazi polis, in exchange asking of them a place of honor in it. Thus, as described by Lyotard, "the greatest thought gave itself to the greatest horror".[436]

---

[434] (Pimentel, 2008).
[435] Ibid.
[436] J. F. Lyotard, *Heidegger et les Juifs* (1988), *Heidegger and the Jews*, trans. A. Michel & M. Roberts (Minneapolis: Minnesota UP, 1990), p.5.

6.2 "Sechinah" - "Dwelling" in Hebrew

I recall a forest: in the forest

I recall a single hidden pond

secluded from the world and deeply set

in shadow of a tall oak blessed by sun

and learned in the discipline of storm.

Alone, she dreams a world turned upside down,

and fishes for her golden fish in silence.
And no one knows what is within her heart.[437]

During the first five years of the twentieth century, Bialik wrote and published most of his big poems, one after the other, starting with "My Song" and "Zohar" (1901), through "The Dead of the Desert" (1902), "In the City of Slaughter" (1903), to "The Pond" and "The Scroll of Fire" (1905). In "The Pond" one sees the conclusion, perhaps the climax, of the poetic course of Bialik's poetry. The two contrasting trends of his poetry, the autobiographical and the epic, as clearly revealed in "Zohar" and "The Dead of the Desert", seem to have met in "The Pond" - an encounter from which this great and complex ars-poetic poem was created. In this work Bialik created the most concentrated expression of the profound core of his poetic ambivalent world - the enigma of two worlds, twin worlds, without knowing which came first. It is no wonder then that this sophisticated and enigmatic poem drew, over the years, interpreters, critics and researchers of a variety of disciplines.

Almost all of Bialik's interpreters saw in "The Pond" an element of gazing, or an element of dream, of the poet standing vis-à-vis the world as a quasi embodiment of the act of poetry itself.[438] Baruch Kurzweil, as part of his

---

[437] C. N. Bialik, "HaBrecha" (1902), in *Selected Poems, (Bilingual)*, trans. R. Nevo (Jerusalem: Dvir and Jerusalem Post, 1981). Nevo translated the poem's title as "The Pool", but here "The Pond" is suggested as a more suitable translation of the Hebrew source.
[438] (Hirschfeld, 2011), p. 143.

comprehensive perception of the I-world relations in Bialik's poetry, saw an egocentric element in "The Pond", of the 'I-poet' separating him from the world, and supposedly preventing real contact.[439]

"The Pond", to Kurzweil's perception, is a purified visionary dream element, yet it is contrary to real contact through actuality, both revealed and metaphysical. He determined a type of perceptional convention, in his criticism, in connection to "The Pond", as an element differentiated from the world - an ideal element contrasting it.[440]

Dan Miron sees the poem as presenting a developmental process from romantic childishness to symbolic maturity: In the first part of the poem, the pond is the manifestation of the childlike soul that does not distinguish between the world of objects and the world of sights, and only in the second part, which shapes the process of revealment and mature insight, does the image of the mature "I" become shaped, well-distinguished from the world. Poetry, claims Miron, derives not from man's connection to nature but rather from his intellectual metaphysical processing of that connection, so that nature is to be interpreted as language. A complex system of correspondences must be created between its components and spiritual truths of the soul.[441] The second part of the poem is interpreted by Miron as construction of a symbolic perception of reality, purifying the "language of sights" in the last stanza of the poem - a step representing for him a stylistic change that Bialik had undergone in his work, from its romantic foundations (in which Kurzweil's interpretation is immersed) to modernist contemplative realms.

According to Ariel Hirschfeld,[442] Miron's perception of the concept of "I" continues the Kurzweilian perception of its object-subject relation. For Hirschfeld, the great bold statement of "The Pond" is the claim that the most remote, the absolute-other, the divine (to be found in the "heaven of heavens") is to be found as well in the depths of the "I", at the deepest extremities of its subjective being. This, according to Hirschfeld, is the revealment occurring at the heart of the hidden pond; a revealment containing, through dream, knowledge that can be touched only through 'non-knowledge'; knowledge touching the absolute-other, not derived from empirical experience of the "I" in its sensory contact with the world, but rather encompassed in it, by virtue of being alive, born to a mother in the chain of life.

This approach is described as drawing its basis from the Kantian perception of 'universal subjectivity' of the 'genius'. The pond as a mirror - sees; it is the opening of a dimension whose being is speculative (mirror - speculum), in other words, it is the opening of a world built on reflection, while at the same time also conducting an act projected onto the future. This is the introduction of the mirror into consciousness. This is also the definition, according to H.G. Gadamer, of the poetic message distinguished from the discursive one; in other words, the creation of 'being' whose status is undefined by conditions of reality, while also not opposed to them. This is the element that frequently expects its completion.[443] This two-faced situation, joining the pond's silent and clandestine being and its supra-time activity ("fishes for her golden fish in silence..."), constitutes, for Hirschfeld, an element and solution for the comprehensible

---

[439] B. Kurzweil, "I-World Relations in the Poem Habrecha" (Hebrew), in *On the Edge of the Pond*, ed. U. Shavit and Z. Shamir (Tel-Aviv: Hakibbutz, 1994), pp. 47-57.
[440] Hirschfeld, 2011), p. 143.
[441] Dan Miron, "Space as Language" (Hebrew), in *On the Edge of the Pond*, ed. U. Shavit and Z. Shamir (Tel-Aviv: Hakibbutz, 1994), pp. 165-75.
[442] (Hirschfeld, 2011), p. 144.
[443] H.G. Gadamer, *Truth and Method*, trans. J. Weinsheimer & D. G. Marshall (New York: Crossroad, 2004), pp. 60-76, 412-433.

life of 'knowledge', similarly to the Platonic element of 'place' (khora); in other words - the dimension of containment found between 'being' and 'being created'.

Julia Kristeva turned this dimension into a central concept in the perception of the semiotic level of the poetic message. To her perception, the pond may be described as a state preceding 'symbolic' activity, a quasi primary generator, preceding words as a grammatical conscious system, the 'content' appearing before every sign and desire to speak and connect.[444] The power of this primary language, distinguishing it from ordinary language, is its being 'non-linguistic language' with no system of signs; differentiated from the system of signified, and from the world of phenomena and experiences. It becomes language due to the moments of creation of sight in the chaos of being. The thing is 'seen', hence becoming the subject of meaning. The 'sight' is then the totality of connections in relation to "I".

Here Hirschfeld accepts Miron's perception regarding the symbolist quality of the implied perception about the element of reverberation, the mutual response, the correspondences - not because a symbolist claim is made here about the existence of parallel elements in a world where poetry wishes to expose their secret existence, but rather because a symbolist occurrence is drawn here between "I" and "world". However, as opposed to the symbolism approach, this language has no parallel, there is no place there to translate one thing into another, and it is entirely enigmatic. This step, which may be called 'arrested or failed symbolism', presents Bialik's 'language of sights' as empty language; as an enigma with no solution and no meaning beyond the sight embodied in it. The pond is therefore not a romantic symbol expanding into the infinite, and likewise, there is no revealing of a network of symbolic parallels of meanings, but rather - a focusing on 'thing' and its sight, which creates a moment of encounter in the poet - that which Hirschfeld calls 'solution' or 'coitus', in which the poet's soul is embodied in the sight.[445]

Hirschfeld further claims that the perception manifest in Bialik's poetry may seem as a mystic one, assuming an ephemeral reception of divine sights; however, the speech of the poem is not mystic, and is not interested in a halo of mystery surrounding an esoteric realm in which super-natural powers play. Hirschfeld perceives the poem as distinguished from mystics since the poem's speech is "revealed and open to reading that is not reserved for the few alone."[446]

At this point we beg to differ with Hirschfeld's approach. One may agree that Bialik's perception is not only mystic, and this matter is not related to the justifications connecting mysticism with textual exclusivity. The fact that Bialik's approach is not mystic - although this poem and his poetry in general are full of mystic elements and allusions - derives from Bialik's approach representing, as we've seen, a more complex tension regarding myth; in other words , that which Hirschfeld calls 'absolute-other'. The mystic dimension, related to exceeding boundaries of the self in the desire to assimilate into that absolute otherness, is indeed present in Bialik's poetry, but together with the dimension of 'blima', which blocks this assimilation from becoming realized. Thus ambivalence is manifest (as will be expounded

---

[444] Kristeva, 1984), pp. 30-59.
[445] (Hirschfeld, 2011), pp. 155-156.
[446] Ibid, p.156.

further on), so that while it does not assimilate into the mysterious, it not only does not flinch from it, but is even supported by and is based upon it.

Hirschfeld's approach, which denies a mystic dimension to Bialik's poem, seems to us as hinting at a somewhat broader denial; in other words, his step - which describes Bialik's 'language of sights' in terms of 'arrested or failed symbolism', and presents it as enigmatic, with no solution that has meaning beyond sight - actually seeks, as is customary in the interpreter's times, to deny a mythic dimension pulsating in the poem. Hence the interpreter has to go quite far in explaining, for example, how "a clandestine tongue" is one that is common in the world and open to all. In this context we wish to claim here that "a ghostly or Godly tongue unsyllabled, clandestine" is actually no more and no less than "a ghostly or Godly tongue unsyllabled, clandestine", and that "in this tongue God manifest to chosen souls", in other words - it is the language of his knowing the chosen, as the example of "artist creator" who, in this language, embodies the thoughts of his heart, where a solution for a dream will be found. In this context, the following also comes to mind: "The Holy spirits, that walk up in the light and the Shining god-like breezes", as Hölderlin describes in "Hyperion's Song of Destiny".[447]

Further on in his article, Hirschfeld quotes an excerpt from Bialik's autobiographical writing (written at the request of Klausner), where Bialik describes his personal development, which was mainly outside of the 'cheder' (traditional Jewish school), and away from the eye of adults, and that during these lonely hours Bialik the child would narrow himself into a hidden corner, contemplate, day-dream, ponder, build worlds and construct visions clandestinely, as the little pond hidden in the forest, where the whole world is there silently and in a different hue.[448]

In this excerpt, Bialik notes his main development as extending through states of loneliness, withdrawal, and intensified reception. The pond is the embodiment of the broad passivity outwards. The inner realm where the "I" slowly grows is presented as the holiest of holies, as the innermost sanctity. In this context, Hirschfeld quotes a version that Bialik wrote of this letter, and which was not published, where he relates to the feminine quality of being passive: "I am an activated man by nature, in the sense of 'nokba' (from Aramaic: nekev - feminine, affected, passive), and did not participate in my acts of creation."[449] This feminine state according to Hirschfeld became, in "The Pond", the clandestine element of the "I" and its source of vitality, a quasi being with the quality of both a nursing mother and a feeding infant. And in particular - that which grips the "I" is not the vessel that he is in, but rather the inner dual tension pulsating in him from within: "The relations of the forest and the pond, the exchange of power and protection between them, the vital dependence binding them - are the focus, the kernel holding and defining the "I". The "I", even in its final narrowing down, is not one but two".[450]

This reading seems to clarify Hirschfeld's trend, hinted at earlier, which denies a mythic dimension of the poem. A conceptual net is implied here, as if spread over the text to trap and read the text through it. If we follow the cues of that approach, then the refutation of myth constitutes a basic layer there.

---

[447] F. Hölderlin, "Hyperions Schicksalslied" (1799), SPF, p.25.
[448] C. N. Bialik, *Letters* (Hebrew), ed. F. Lahover (Tel-Aviv: Dvir, 1937), p. 162.
[449] C. N. Bialik, *Chapters of Life in Four Versions* (Hebrew) (Jerusalem: Tarshish, 1943), p. 37.
[450] (Hirschfeld, 2011), p. 157.

Hence, if we reject - according to his approach - that which was called here 'absolute-other', or 'divine' (to be found in "heavens of heaven"), as the poet's reflected image in the twin world, what then may replace it? Hirschfeld replies by the way in which he identifies the pond with the embodiment of "passivity open outwards". The conjunction of this passivity with Hirchfeld's description of the revelation occurring at the heart of the pond, so that touching it is only by 'non-knowledge', brings to mind Hölderlin's 'Blödigkeit'. And when Hirschfeld concludes that the forest and the pond, the exchange of power and protection between them, the vital dependence binding them - are the focus, the kernel holding and defining the "I", it seems to clarify as well that which looks like a connection to the interpretational field, of which Benjamin's reading of Hölderlin is one of its main axes.

In Hirschfeld's reading, it seems that in "The Pond" as well 'Blödigkeit' becomes the authentic position of the poet; that nothing is left for him except for the immobile experience, total passivity, which is the essence of courage, nothing but giving himself completely to relations. In this context it is easy to understand this de-mythologization approach, although one may not ignore the fact that the price of silencing the mythic dimension of the Bialikan text seems to generate a narrow reading here, which is not conducive to understanding the richness of the text.

According to the dialectics of myth (through which the interpretational field of Hölderlin's poetry was earlier examined), Hirschfeld's reading of Bialik appears as a de-mythologizing approach. The outlines of the interpretational field of Bialik's poetry are demonstrated through a polar position manifest in Asaf Inbari's reading of Bialik's poetry, as poetry which deals mainly with the experience of revelation or even epiphany.

While Kant and Husserl thought that subjectivity is the state of man, that there is no way to break through it and observe, even for a moment the 'thing-in-itself', Bialik, according to Inbari, thought differently.[451] He believed in the possibility of revelation, which he identified in the action of revealment and concealment of language - identification of the action of language with exposure, which in itself preoccupied, in similar aspects, some of the researchers of the period, such as Heidegger and his perception of exposure of being revealed in language; V.B. Shklovsky, who dealt with the role of 'defamiliarization' of art;[452] and Benjamin, whose ambivalent critical-messianic approach saw language as redeemer.

The desire for an experience of revelation, according to Inbari, is not a desire for an ongoing experience, as an up-scaling of the 'level of consciousness' described by mystics, but rather it is the desire to experience revelation while acknowledging the temporality of any revelation. It is the desire to experience it again and again, and that means repeatedly experiencing the concealments that come before and after every revelation. The dialectic of concealment-revealment is a flash, not a permanent beacon. The believer and the artist, according to Inbari, are not deterred by concealment (as opposed to the mystic, who abhors concrete reality as it conceals the transcendental, according to his approach); they do not perceive concealment as the odious contrast of revelation, but rather as a necessary component,

---

[451] A. Inbari, "On the Language of Revelation" (Hebrew), in *Hadarim 14*, ed. H. Yeshurun)Tel Aviv, winter 2002(, pp. 56-86.
[452] V. B. Shklovsky, "Art as Technique", in *Literary Theory: An Anthology*, ed. J. Rivkin and M. Ryan, (Malden: Blackwell, 1998).

of equal value, in the flashing dynamics containing both. The seekers of revelation are the believer and the artist - and not by chance does Hebrew derive the words 'emuna' (belief) and 'omanut' (art) from a common root.[453]

In his article "Between One Concealment to the Next, the Abyss Flickers",[454] Asaf Inbari deepened the description of the 'religious frequency' of Bialik's poetry and of the visionary aspect appearing from every line of the poet, and determined that Bialik's poetry is an accurate report of ecstatic experience. He further stated that the music, weeping and laughing are pure reactions that inevitably follow revelation. To his perception, poetry does the opposite, it does not respond to revelation - it generates it.[455]

Regarding Hirschfeld's approach earlier presented, which may be described as de-mythologization of Bialik's poetry, or at least as minimizing the mythic dimensions and the role of myth in this poetry, Inbari's approach is clarified as polar. According to him, Bialik's poetry is no less than a report of transcendental experience, an experience of revelation. These two approaches, which we have set opposite each other, seem to us to be far-fetched interpretations pressing the complex poem into an absolute position - at the price of denying its tense and ambivalent dimension.

Inbari, as notes Haviva Pedaya,[456] does not take into account the distinction that Bialik himself tried to determine between the non-verbal and the verbal. The dimension of the non-verbal, the language of languages (and this evokes the concept of primordial or Creational language, of Benjamin and Heidegger), is always connected in Bialik's work with moments of muteness touching muteness, music touching music, picture touching picture. Occasionally speech is an evolving part of this event, and then that is poetry.

According to Pedaya's approach, one does not ask whether the poet experienced identification with being, or only the rift between "I" and being, as in the example of Kurzweil's binary positioning, which describes Bialik as shifting between language and silence; and Inbari as well, who despite his criticism of Kurzweil, depicts tension between blending with being and non-removal of the concealment - while according to Pedaya the moment of revelation, completely saturated, is the very moment of the feeling of mystery.[457]

One may not say then that there is a moment when being is divested of its concepts and revealed as it is, but rather that there is a moment when the intensity of the feeling of being, with all the weight of its mystery and revelation, propels all the words, and from this moment of shocked muteness all the words erupt as if created anew, as if placed side by side for the first time, as had occurred initially. And this is revelation, or poetry. It is a moment in which the sense of being is experienced in its full weight unto the feeling of bursting; a moment of standing muteness against muteness. This experience of revelation does not mean removing the veil that is cast over being, but rather - as

---

[453] (Inbari, 2002), p. 6.
[454] A. Inbari, "Between One Concealment to the Next, the Abyss Flickers" (Hebrew), in *Hadarim 13*, ed. H. Yeshurun, (Tel Aviv, winter 1999(, pp. 21-32.
[455] Ibid.
[456] H. Pedaya, "The Mute Language of Sights and the Speech of Darkness" (Hebrew), in *An Offering to Menachem*, ed. H. Amit, A. Hacohen, H. Be'er (Jerusalem: Hakibbutz, 2007), pp. 427-442.
[457] Ibid, p. 435.

Bialik implied - it is a step of being in which the eye sees through the eyes of being. The experience of revelation is the experience of mystery.

> *Seated then at the border of the pool,*
>
> *considering the riddle of two worlds,*
>
> *twin worlds (but which one prior, to me unknown)*
>
> *I bend my head beneath the mossed old trees*
>
> *which drop upon me blessed light and shade,*
>
> *resin and song, and feel most sensibly*
>
> *a silent influx freshening my soul,*
>
> *and feel within my unslaked thirsting heart*
>
> *which seeks the mystery of holiness,*
>
> *the pressure of an insatiable demand*
>
> *and overflowing mute expectancy*
>
> *of certain revelation near at hand,*
>
> *or imminent appearance of Elijah.*
>
> *While still in expectation my ear strains,*
>
> *and heart expires in fear and in desire,*
>
> *the echoed voice of God in hiding speaks,*
>
> *breaking the silent deep with "Where art thou?"*[458]

The pond in this poem appear in continuation to the pond in "Zohar" and in the same role, as a reflecting memory and a symbol, but this time with explicit mention of the revelatory meaning. Revelation is described in the poem as the sounding of an ancient voice rising from mythological landscapes of memory, and through personal landscapes of memory. The symbol of the pond connects these two landscapes - it is tangible personal memory and it is a known Kabbalist symbol.

---

[458] C. N. Bialik, "Habrecha" (1902), stanza 8, in *Selected Poems (Bilingual)*, trans. R. Nevo (Jerusalem: Dvir and Jerusalem Post, 1981).

"Sechinah" - "Dwelling" in Hebrew

The motif of 'shechina' that appears in "The Pond" and reappears in other poems of Bialik, as we shall see, serves as a channel for Bialik's approach both to the issue of the revealed and concealed, and to the action that we shall call 'political' - that is, intention and action for the people, or to be more precise, for their culture. We should emphasize that this does not refer to Bialik's public endeavors (which in themselves fit the described trend), but rather to the political act manifest in the Bialikan poetics. Moreover, 'shechina' is also no less than a worthy Hebrew translation for 'dwelling'. The basis of the concept of 'shechina' in Hebrew is the root (sh.ch.n.) whose meaning is 'dwell' or 'be in'. The traditional place of appearance of 'shechina' is in 'mishkan', which is the Temple in Jerusalem, which - similarly to the Greek temple described by Heidegger - is the site of appearance.[459] Furthermore, both of the concepts together are characterized by the same special mixture of meanings, binding ontology with theology, or physics with metaphysics. The same mixture of meanings characterizing 'dwelling' and 'shechina' derives in both concepts from their connection to a third one - 'place'. The Hebrew word for 'place' (makom) well-demonstrates the ontological-theological binding, which is not at all foreign to Jewish thought, since the word 'makom' itself - in addition to signifying space, or area, or the volume that a body takes up, or could take up - is also a name of god: "That he is the place of the world, and his world is not his place" (Genesis Rabah, 68:10). This concept constitutes a conceptual blend of space and experience which grants sites their 'wholeness' or 'selfness' - an opaque concept expressing the epistemological tension between subjectivity and objectivity.

The term 'shechina' first appears as an independent concept in the legends of the Sages, where 'shechina' describes the presence of god in the world: "Two that are sitting and there are words of Torah between them - shechina is between them" (Mishneh Avot, 3:2), and also "man and woman were granted shechina between them" (Babylon Talmud, Soteh, 17:71). The shechina which descends, ascends or disappears represents the appearance of the abstract god in the world of man's reality. 'Shechina' appears as a divine being found in the gap, between the worlds and reflecting, in its essence, the connection between the divine and human. Although the word 'shechina' indicates female, this fact is not prominent in the literature of the legends of the Sages, which does not expound on the feminine characteristics of 'shechina'. This, however, changes in the literature of Kabbalah, where 'shechina' is identified with one of the divine spheres, and there its femininity gains broad and deep development.[460]

The Kabbalist 'shechina' has many faces, varied and contradicting. 'Shechina' is the present aspect of divinity in the world, and its many faces express the complexity and multi-aspects of human reality. In portions of the Kabbalah literature, 'shechina' is described as the divine image closest to life, history and the soul. The names 'soul', 'spirit' and

---

[459] According to Heidegger's step one sees, for example, King David's acquisition of the threshing floor of Araunah the Jebusite, in order to erect an alter for god (Samuel 2, 24:18), as a release of being and its meaning for use. The location of being in its meaning, as a place of sacrifice for god, constitutes its historical meaning delivered both in deed and in myth.

[460] In the literature of "The Zohar" for instance, 'shechina' is described with all of her physiological, functional, sociological, sexual, and psychological characteristics. The texts deal with her body structure and attribute to her the ability to receive, contain, and even give birth, nurse and feed. Her sexual connections are expressed in situations of desire and awakening, as opposed to moments of distance during menstrual cycle or divorce. Socially and sociologically, her relations are described vis-à-vis home and the world of speech, as well as the world of rule and monarchy. In terms of her personality, she is connected to opposites and variations of reality: on the one hand, shechina is associated with the aspect of judgment, fire, and annihilation of the world - she is called 'ilna demuta' (the tree of death), thus connected to judgment, night and destruction; on the other hand, she is described as a protective image, supportive, benefactress, compassionate and advocate.
See: B. Roi, "Shechina", in *Devarim Ahadim* 8 (Jerusalem: Hartman Institute, June 2010).

"Sechinah" - "Dwelling" in Hebrew

"I" are associated with 'shechina', and corroborate its closeness to the being of existence and to inner structures in man's soul.

As described by E.E. Urbach,[461] the term 'shechina' in the literature of the Tana'im indicates presence in place, and this place is usually associated with the 'mishkan', the house in which god dwells, which is the 'house of the shechina'. After the destruction of the Temple, 'shechina' is chosen to indicate the divine presence that is not connected to a certain place but rather to the people: "In every place that the People of Israel exiled, supposedly the shechina exiled with them" (Mechilta of Rabbi Yishmael 110, Pascha 94). The Kabbalah intensified the identity of 'shechina' and people; the 'shechina' went with the People of Israel into exile and stayed there with them. The Kabbalists are the sons of 'shechina', but they - as is she - are the whole of the Jewish people. Their troubles are hers, and their sufferings are hers. With the shift from presence in the place of the Temple to presence in the people, the new dimension in which 'shechina' takes part is intensified - the dimension of time. When the 'shechina' exiles with the Jewish people after the destruction of the Temple, she becomes an entity living in time, with its flow and turbulence. In other words, 'shechina' changes from a concept indicating a philosophical necessity to something identified with changes, with the possibilities and variations that history provides.

The status of 'shechina' as a powerful myth in the cultural consciousness served for the creation and strengthening of an ethos around the revival of 'shechina' from its ashes, expressing an aspiration to bringing closer in time the act of redemption. This ethos was a central component in the lives of the Zafed Kabbalists, and around it various customs were conducted, such as 'midnight prayers', study of Torah, a call to live in poverty to imitate the present state of the 'shechina', and charity - intended to redeem the 'shechina' from its destruction. Moreover, a unique image of divinity in crisis was developed, whereby alongside the sublime god, whole and compassionate, the 'shechina' is revealed as an impaired image, residing in rift and fall. This image is the embodiment of a divinity that is not at its best, but rather at its weakest. This picture of rift is an invitation to mend.

> *All gone with the wind, all swept away by the light,*
>
> *a new song filled with song and morning of their lives*
>
> *and I, a tender chick, was quite forgot*
>
> *alone under the wing of the Divine Presence. ('shechina')*[462]

The central image in the poem "Levadi" is of the tender chick sheltered last in his nest, under the wings of the 'shechina'. The image develops with the growing of the chick, which feels that its sheltering under the protective

---

[461] E. E. Urbach, *Hazal* (Hebrew), (Jerusalem: Magnes, 1982), pp. 33-35.
[462] C. N. Bialik, "Alone" ("Levadi"), in *Songs from Bialik: Selected Poems*, trans. A. Hadari (Syracuse: Syracuse UP, 2000), p. 23, stanza 1.

wings of the 'shechina' is becoming trouble and a burden, and it seeks to fly to the light, in other words, to the realms to which its brethren have already flown. As the chick grows stronger, so the 'shechina' grows weaker and ceases to be necessary. The light seems to signify the Enlightenment, and the "new world". The chick appears as the last believer in the beit-midrash, and the 'shechina' - a metaphor for the traditional Jewish world whose grip is faltering. The expression "under the wings of the shechina" is used in two meanings. In one, the 'shechina' protects the poet physically as well as spiritually, but in the second the expression implies death, as taken from the memorial prayer for the soul of the deceased: "Find the proper rest under the wings of the shechina" ("Yizkor" prayer).

The motif of loneliness develops in the poem as the status of the 'shechina' grows weaker:

"...and the Divine Presence (the 'Shechina') herself shook her broken right wing over my head."[463]

The poet is aware of the 'shechina' weakening, and beyond his own concerns over loneliness, he is also aware of the concern of the 'shechina' that she will be left alone when the chick, her only son, flies away from the nest. One may note the Biblical foundation serving Bialik in this stanza. As in the case of Abraham, who was told to take his only son whom he loved, so too the 'shechina' is apparently asked to give up the only son who has remained behind. The image of the 'shechina' is depicted here as human, as a mother anxious about her son's abandonment. The motif of the broken wing develops into a symbol of the rift of the Jewish world.

Further on the 'shechina' is described as "already driven from all corners"[464] and pushed into a hidden corner in the beit-midrash, and the chick's yearning to fly out of the window grows. The 'shechina' is described in her sorrow; she clings and weeps, and now tries to stop the chick from leaving, seeking to shelter him with her broken wing. The loneliness now is not that of the chick but rather of the 'shechina'. At the end of the poem the sound is heard from afar of the weeping of the 'shechina', whose abandonment was perhaps inevitable, but seems to have been accompanied by mixed feelings of the poet. She is described as a mother abandoned by her children. The Book of Lamentations (which it is customary to read on the 9th of Av) serves as the Biblical foundation here for Bialik, as Jeremiah's lament over the destruction of the Temple: "How doth the city sit solitary, that was full of people. How doth she become as a widow". Bialik creates a connection to the rift of his time regarding the crisis of history of the Jewish people, who according to Bialik, do not learn from past events, and each time again follow promises that will most likely fail.

Hence, it seems that the concept of 'shechina' fits Bialik's method, which we spoke of earlier, and which re-activates a myth from the past in the present times of the poet. The 'shechina' appears to the readers of the poem, Hebrew readers of his times, first of all, as a known and familiar concept of Jewish mythology (to be precise - mysticism). The very appearance of a concept such as 'shechina' entails a train of meanings, implications and hints derived from its being a 'transforming concept', which - as we have already seen - has taken meanings on and off

---

[463] Ibid, stanza 2.
[464] Ibid, stanza 3.

throughout the tradition of delivery;[465] a mythic and transcendental concept based on the Bible and generations of Jewish thought and mysticism. The 'shechina' represents the divine dimension, which similarly to Hölderlin's gods before their withdrawal, is to be found in the world of man. It is the divine sphere found among people, and - like Hölderlin's gods - so may Bialik's 'shechina' forsake and hide.

However, here in the poem "Levadi" it is not the departure or hiding of the 'shechina' which leaves man lonely, but rather it is the agonizing man who leaves his broken-winged 'shechina'. Bialik takes the familiar myth of the 'shechina' as mother, as a feminine element signifying as well the area in divinity that resides with man, and he generates a transformation which brings about a reversal in the status of the 'shechina'. In other words, if traditional Jewish history represents a constant aspiration to be under the wings of the 'shechina' of god, and if periods of departure of the 'shechina' or its hiding are perceived as times of distress and disaster, then here it is the 'shechina' which is abandoned. The autobiographical story of a young Jew standing "At the House of Study's Threshold" (as the title of another poem of Bialik)[466] and attracted to a new and tempting freedom, conjoins with the question of the historical fate of a people on the threshold of a rift in time between dying tradition and spell-binding revolutionary ideas that are destined to fail.

---

[465] We should mention an essential closeness in Hebrew between 'masoret' (tradition) and 'mesira' (delivery).
[466] C.N. Bialik, "Al Saf Beit ha-Midrash" (1894), BYP.

6.3 Radical Knowing of the Unknowable

The concept of 'shechina', apart from being a myth re-activated in a prophetic context, that is, political - embodies an addition role. 'Shechina' as the trails of divinity, as a divine dimension found as it were in contact with man, and residing in being of humans and in history, is - for Bialik - a factor that the poet wishes to have revealed to him, as in the poem "The Pond", which seeks the "revelation of the shechina", and where the concept indicates a quasi gap between real and metaphysical, between that which is known and that which is unknowable.

It will not be far-fetched to describe the tension between revealed and concealed as a central motif in Bialik's perception of language as well as in his poetry. "The Pond" as an ars-poetic text dealing with the essence of poetry and its mission demonstrates the tension between the two twin worlds, the revealed and the concealed, the known and that which cannot be known. In thought and in poetry, says Gilad Bareli, there is a repeated motif of a deliberate effort toward knowledge, toward explanation or toward expression of that which may neither be known, nor explained or expressed.[467] These matters have been presented by various philosophers, poets and thinkers as the essence of life and of man's experience, whose very existence is not worthy but for reaching there and peeking. The god known only by his negative aspects in the philosophy of Maimonides and the mystic in Wittgenstein's Tractates are examples of it, and many more may be added from the annals of thought and poetry.

These statements about things that are not known and are not knowable have, of course, a paradoxical tone, and one must distinguish, according to Bareli, between knowledge supported by or derived from an epistemological framework which distinguishes, such as that of B. Russell, between 'knowledge by acquaintance' and 'knowledge by description', and the knowledge relevant to our study, which is radical knowledge. In other words, regarding knowledge about things that are not radically known, their knowledge, explanation and even description are blocked to us in principle, yet nevertheless - and this is the wonder claims Bareli - they are implied and peek out, as it were, to those seeking them.

Russell and many others following him thought that knowledge by description and knowledge by acquaintance are the two ways to explain knowledge (objectual).[468] According to this, the horizon of our knowledge can reach the scope of our acquaintance and our conceptual ability. Speaking about things beyond this becomes not only impossible but also senseless. Regarding this approach, Bareli claims that any epistemological system by its very nature limits the field of knowledge in a certain way, so that any claim regarding the existence and nature of things

---

[467] G. Bareli, "Bialik: Revealment and Concealment in Love and Language" (Hebrew), in *Jerusalem Studies in Hebrew Literature*, vol. 15 (Jerusalem: Mandel Institute, 1995), p. 137-160.
[468] Bareli's words here relate to the knowledge of things, objects, and not the knowledge of truths or statements. The relation between these two and the very interpretation of the first type of knowledge are complex matters preoccupying many philosophers, and will not be deliberated on here.

beyond the field of knowledge is left with an accompanying flavor of the inexplicable or meaningless. And yet, even within the framework of the most rigorous methods, the claim is reiterated of things existing which are considered of supreme importance, and beyond the realm of human reach and knowledge. There are those, especially philosophers, who derive the matter from the structure of their method, such as with Kant and the 'thing-in-itself', the knowledge of god in Maimonides' work, and Wittgenstein and the structure of the world and of language.

Presumably, claims Bareli, Bialik - as did many other writers, poets and mystics - speaks of an experience that cannot be known and cannot be described in words. A peek into the delivered content and the allusion to it are, of course, within the scope of human experience, but this matter may be interpreted in two ways: The first is mainly the experience of the special 'peek' into a realm concealed in the course of ordinary life, while the other is a quasi hint at the hidden and unattainable side of the ordinary experiences and knowledge of man.[469]

From a methodical point of view it is difficult to explain this talk about experience whose content is in principle beyond the scope of attainment of man, and beyond that which may be described in language. This problem has preoccupied many philosophers, yet it seems that the main reasoning was given by Wittgenstein, and was a basic motif in his thought, from the Tractates and to his later writings. Is there room and explanation for speech (peek) about this mystic experience? Is there a twilight area encompassing, as it were, the realm of possible knowledge, and that which may be given meaningful description in language?

It was the philosophers who were strict in distinguishing the knowledgeable realm and in distinguishing that which is given to meaningful description, who found room for an appeal to knowledge of the beyond, and this for methodical philosophical reasons. Philosophers such as Maimonides, Kant and Wittgenstein, according to Bareli, deal with theoretical philosophical knowledge of something that cannot be known, and is not in the realm known to man. This is a quasi hidden side whereby the knowledge of its existence is necessarily wished for on the revealed side. God in Maimonides' method, and the 'transcendental formal' concepts of Wittgenstein's Tractates are of this type. The philosopher's position does not lean on specific experience but is valid in accordance to the validity of his methodical claims.

A moment of peeking, its concealment and disappearance, as well as the question of the limits of language's ability, are the central subject of "The Pond", and the essay "Revealment and Concealment in Language", from which we learn that language with all of its combinations does not at all introduce us into the inner place or absolute essence of things, but rather separates us from them and from the scope beyond that of language. So what is there? Bareli asks: What is the real essence from which language separates us? And Bialik replies: 'Blima' - "Blom picha midaber" ('close your mouth from speaking'). If man does indeed get to the point of speech and his mind is frozen, this is only due to his fear of remaining one moment with that 'chaos'. "No man can see me and live", said god (Exodus, 33:20). The metaphor of separation and peeking, according to Bareli, hints to this being a realm of holiness. Yet language of chaos and 'blima' is a language of death and nullification.

---

[469] (Bareli, 1995), p. 138.

Radical Knowing of the Unknowable

This combination of obscure and wondrous of the realm of holiness, actually of god himself, with the realm of absolute darkness, chaos, blima and death, is paralleled in the emotional dialectic position of man, who yearns and desires the hidden, while fearing and escaping it at the same time. This is implied in "Revealment and Concealment in Language",[470] in the way in which Bialik concludes the paragraph describing language and words as a device for diverting attention from the great fear, as a means of sealing and separating from the threatening chaos. It is this eternal darkness which casts such horror; it alone has always secretly attracted man's heart, evoking in him hidden longing to peek there a moment, so that all fear it and all are drawn to it.

Kurzweil, who did not discern the described dialectic, according to Bareli simplifies the meaning of the essay, turning it into a defense of language and knowledge, against the failing mysticism. Thus, it seems that in the cartography evolving in the interpretational field of Bialik's poetry, there is a connection between Kurzweil and Hirschfeld, who interpret Bialik in a simplifying de-mythologizing interpretation. The place of 'blima' is interpreted by Bialik as a place of universal pondering, the inner space and absolute essence of the things. The combination of 'chaos' and 'blima' is taken from Job, 26:7, "He stretches out the north over the void and hangs the earth on nothing". The traditional interpretations interpret 'bli+ma', as 'that has no real in it' (Metzudat David), or: 'that which has no reality in itself and it is the center of the country' (RLBG). However, the use of 'blima' for a mystic indication of the hidden divine realm is connected to the "Book of Creation", and to Kabbalah uses. All of these do not reconcile with Kurzweil's thesis of the victory of poetry and knowledge over the secret and mystery supposedly opposing them.

There are non-language sources of peeking into the abyss, such as music, weeping and laughter, which - as Bialik describes it - are the rising of the abyss itself, and any creative work that has no reverberation of one of them has no life and would be better not having come into the world. However, Bialik does not thus deny language and its ability to express our knowledge and experiences. His position, according to Bareli, is much more radical: There is no knowledge without language, and no knowledge except with language. Knowledge and language are gripped together as "the flame is connected to the ember" (this expression itself is taken from the "Book of Creation"). Ten spheres of 'blima' - their end in their beginning and their beginning in their end, as the flame is connected to the ember: A Kabbalah allegory uniting the idea of holding the revealed realm with the concealed from which it feeds, together with the idea of revealment of the concealed realm only through the revealed. However, both knowledge and language are concealment of chaos, 'blima' and separation from it. The candle of knowledge and speech, the ember and the flame, is the everlasting candle that will never be extinguished; however, the very area that from here on is in the realm of artificial light - what is it worth as opposed to the sea of infinity of darkness of worlds that still remains, and always will remain, outside?[471] Knowledge and speech both appear as the function of man's great fear of the terrible chaos before him. Thus too belief itself, it too is but a diversion, and even life. They all appear as but a desperate attempt of separation, concealment and escape - the whole flow of life, its entire content, is but an exhausting constant attempt of diversion. Every moment of pursuing after - is at that moment a rejection from -.

---

[470] C. N. Bialik, "Gilui ve-Kisui Balashon" (1917) (Hebrew), in *Literature* (Tel Aviv: Dvir, 1977), pp. 24-31.
[471] Ibid, par. 4.

What then are the sources of peeking, of which all of our lives, thought, knowledge and language are but an attempt to conceal and escape it? Bareli locates guidelines for this question in Bialik's writing. One line of thought deals with sources of experience that are of the self, neither language nor knowledge, as is too the 'language of sights' at the end of the poem "The Pond".[472] Another line of thought, the most important one for Bareli, is the implied inner dialectic in revealment and concealment in language (and in life). Concealment and constant escape, like the fear feeding them, are connected in a quasi perception, peek, or knowledge in a hint of chaos. The darkness and 'blima', concealment and sealing are not merely objective states that seem such to the outsider looking in, but rather they are intentional acts of man, and as such they are connected and conditioned upon a certain perception, peek or knowledge in a hint - of that from which they are concealed and escape. This matter is emphasized by Bialik as the main essence and meaning of the language of poetry and of the people interpreting the secret; those who their whole lives pursue the very point that makes the sights and the combinations of language directed toward them - as one unit in the world, after their one soul and the self essence of things. The language of these too is concealment in Bialik's eyes. Yet it is as primary concealment, which has in it the power to hint at that which it conceals; therefore in the language of these, "between revealment and concealment, the abyss flickers".[473]

The appeal to the unknown abyss is presented here not merely as a separate mystic experience (peek) but rather as an accompanying aspect of the very act of concealment and escape, of the very life (hint). The perception reached by the poet is mainly in its implied character. This is another perception of entire reality with all of its variety of details, as hinting at that which is beyond them, to that which is perceived as their source and the essence of their being. This unified perception enables the poet to feel a hint in every detail seen and every sound heard.

Bareli characterizes Bialik's experience of love as connected to its being an experience inside life, expressing and reflecting an essential aspect of that hidden thing, which if we could, we would perceive as the experience of life itself. This essential aspect is but that dialectic tension between the hidden and the revealed. The hidden is a condition and basis of the revealed, yet we have no attainment of the hidden or contact with it except through hinting and peeking, embodied in the revealed. The matter of hinting, by which the familiar and the known hints to hidden and unattainable content, becomes - as described by Bareli - the basis of the perception of language, knowledge and life, in "Revealment and Concealment in Language". The realm of darkness, chaos and 'blima', the realm of that which is beyond the revealed world, is the realm containing unattainable fullness - fullness at which the artist, the poet and the holder of the secret succeed in attaining a momentary peek, while language, knowledge and life themselves are based on a hint of it. This is a hint which turns them paradoxically into directed toward it, if only in the way of escape, fear and yearning for the unknown hinted.

The hidden reality is an ideal reality, the source and purpose of the entire reality - a reality to which the heart is drawn, to which all of man's life is directed while it is unattainable and the yearning for it is never satisfied. It

---

[472] (Bareli, 1995), p. 749.
[473] C. N. Bialik, "Gilui ve-Kisui Balashon" (1917) (Hebrew), in *Literature* (Tel Aviv: Dvir, 1977), par. 4.

causes a sense of barrenness and metaphysical loneliness, of whoever suddenly perceives his life and reality around him as hinting to a hidden source of fullness and vitality that is in principle beyond his reach.

6.4 "Holy Sobriety"

The river in Hölderlin's poetry, as history or the process of creation, constitutes in its course a continuation from the source onward, to the future; striving, through crises, to a comprehensive balance manifest in an apocalyptic wedding ceremony. Speculation of reconciliation of man with the gods when instead of appeasing the gods, the scales will be balanced at least for a short while. The poet, in the image of Rousseau, is the one who, as a Dionysian priest, grants the language of purity (Rein - pure in German). The poet has of the divine language that bestows of the holy plenty.

Hölderlin's poem "The Rhine"[474] and the fragment "In Lovely Blue"[475] were a point of departure, in this chapter, for studying the concept of 'dwelling', as it appears in Hölderlin's writing and develops in the Heideggerian interpretation. If, in earlier chapters, it could be seen that the two poets perceived 'poetics' or poetic language as the basis, or 'lebensraum', or as the means of the historical movement of myth, which - as mentioned - was discerned as a certain type of literature, then the discussion on the concept of 'dwelling' in this chapter (through discussion of the concept of 'polis') has sharpened the status of 'poetic' as constituting 'the political'. Through this, the connection is also established between the mythic (via the poetic) and the political in Heidegger's writing, as a slope where his claims are prone to slip into submission to the temptations of the 'absolute', a road-sign warning about the dangers apparently manifest in a step which gives myth room as political power.

Bialik's poems "Alone",[476] "The Pond",[477] and the essay "Revealment and concealment in Language"[478] were the point of departure for discussion of the concept of 'shechina' in Bialik's writing, a concept that is a proper translation of 'dwelling' into Hebrew, while at the same time also indicating an expression of divinity.

Studying the meanings of the concept has led to a sharper understanding of two poetic-political steps in Bialik's poetry: The first is the poet's methodical use of myth, when he takes the concept, with its train of meanings, and re-activates it as an authentic prophetic myth, combining the rift of the individual being of the poet with the miserable historical fate of the people. The second deals with Bialik's perception of the experience of revelation, as a dialectic lingual experience of revealment and concealment. In the essay "Revealment and Concealment in

---

[474] "Der Rhein" (1798-1800), SPF.p 197.
[475] F. Holderlin, "In lieblicher Bläue" (1823) http://www.hoelderlin.de/quellen-druck/d-31-03.html
[476] C. N. Bialik, "HaBrecha" (1902), in *Selected Poems (Bilingual),* trans. R. Nevo (Jerusalem: Dvir and Jerusalem Post, 1981).
[477] C. N. Bialik, "Levadi" (1902), in *Songs from Bialik: Selected Poems*, trans. A. Hadari, (Syracuse: Syracuse UP, 2000), p. 23, stanza 1.
[478] C. N. Bialik, "Gilui ve-Kisui Balashon" (1917) (Hebrew), in *Literature* (Tel Aviv: Dvir, 1977)

Language"[479] Bialik presents the concept of 'blima' (the traditional interpretations interpret: bli+ma, 'that has no real in it'), as a realm not radically known to man and blocked to language in principle. And yet, and surprisingly, it is hinted at and peeks to those seeking it. The language of poetry (as that of mystics) is but additional concealment; however, this is as a primary concealment with the power to hint at that which it conceals. This unifying perception constitutes the basis, for the poet, of sober poetics of mediation, attentive to a hint from the abyss, in every detail seen and every sound heard.

In the poem "Half of Life"[480] Hölderlin presents the concept of 'holy sobriety', which appears in the spirit of Bialik's concept of 'blima', as a measure of judgment and as an element divesting myth of its authority (by way of 'sobriety'), while not denying the myth's vitality, which grants man place (by way of 'holiness'). Thus, myth is set in a new and tense context of sober holiness. Denial (as in Heidegger's case) of the divesting dimension of sobriety is the danger lurking in submission to the historical power of myth; it is submission that had enabled a stretching interpretation of Hölderlin's poetry unto indicating a "new mythology" (down the slope to the absolute). On the other hand, denial of the dimension of 'holiness' of myth might easily lead sobriety to non-action and to melancholy.

By synoptic positioning of the poets and the encounter between their concepts, 'holy sobriety' and 'dwelling' of Hölderlin, and respectively, Bialik's 'awakening' and 'blima', we shall claim that a different reading appears of the poets' mission in relation to the dialectic of myth - a mission that may be located beyond the dichotomy characterizing the cartography of the polar interpretational discourse, as mentioned, between de-mythologization and re-mythologization. The two poets' intersecting concepts may be seen as mechanisms of judgment, as embodying an approach of 'mediation' between the withdrawal of myth to its return, and as the ones that expose, each in its way, the illusion of the binary contrast between de-mythologization and re-mythologization as the full view of the world. In the encounter between the poetics, 'mythic' appears as 'meaningful', at least for the fact that approaches seeking to divest themselves of myth transform, apparently of necessity, into an appeal to that which diverges from the meaning (and is destined to quickly transform into new meanings).

Hölderlin's poetics, stretched between contrasts, as a heroic attempt to deliver a Greek past into a German present, and to blend idolatry polytheism with Christian monotheism unto an idyllic future in Hesperia, Schwab of his homeland; and Bialik's poetics, which re-activates mythic materials of the past in order to deliver them as an 'event' of the present, as the endeavor of 'tikkun' within the rift between the old and new - both poetics sing the crisis of traditional myth as part of its own story continuum, thereby constituting 'caesura' and continuation of the sequence simultaneously.

Hence, the encounter between the poetics presented by this essay draws outlines of the poetic-political approach[481] of the poets, diverting the matter from the source of authority to the ways of delivery,[482] an approach that

---

[479] The essay in itself demonstrates considerable similarity to Heidegger's perception of language, which developed later, as shown further on.
[480] F. Hölderlin, "Halfte des Lebens" (1803-1804), SPF, p.171.
[481] In connection to the poetic, as constituting the political (Heidegger), and in relation to the perception of the concept of 'the political' in connection to the questions about the possibility of delivering an idea over time (Arendt).

acknowledges the 'present loss' of the myth and seeks to add and convey its memory in culture, and deliver it, if only as broken failed delivery, as an event of the present - a step of 'rift' and 'fall', in itself locating their poetry anew as part of a continuum of accumulated delivery in history.

This approach, possibly expressed by 'holy sobriety', acknowledges on the one hand the subjugating potential of myth, and the liberties born of its weakened historical authority; while on the other, its vitality that has no substitute, as a text constituting 'place' and 'history' for individuals and communities (and one may add our current awareness of the latent presence, apparently inevitable historically and theoretically, of myth, in the institutions of culture and state).

The two poets may then be read as ones presenting myth in their poetry as a poetic-political factor of regenerative quality in relation to culture, and the poet's image as a prophet, bearing the failure of his mission to his people, as the lightning rod of history. The question that arises at the end of the discussion is in relation to a possible contribution of the approach, entailed by the encounter between the poets (found, as mentioned, beyond the dichotomy between advocates and deniers of myth), regarding questions of our times, or, in other words: Who wants poets at all in lean years?[483]

---

[482] A world view attributing the main importance to the accumulated historical sequence ignores the basic question of the source of authority of the text. If indeed it is a revelatory text, then its authority is clear, but if it is a human creative work, then one cannot associate holiness with a man-made text, hence - what will justify its authority? Both for Hölderlin and for Bialik, it is possible to identify a step of diversion, transferring the center of gravity from the question of factual validity of the delivered myth to the ways of delivery and interpretation; a diversion of the validity of the myth from validity derived from the past to that derived from the present.
[483] ("Wozu dichter in dürftiger zeit") "Brod und Wein" (1800-1801), stanza 7, in SPF, p. 151.

> *"Yesterday I postponed my study of Ontology and went to see Geulah (so you see I took your advice finally), eventually finding her. We sat together till after midnight, and I came to see how much messianic yearning roils behind her nationalist thinking. I said, "The goal should not be to reach the kingdom [Malchut], but first to produce a man worthy of it." . . . Geulah answered, "The empty vessel is ready to accept the wealth of sacredness [Shefa Kodesh]."*
>
> *(Jacob Taubes in a letter to Samuel Hugo Bergman)*[484]

7. Conclusions

In conclusion of this essay, it seems that the primary hypothesis of the research regarding the existence of conceptual connection and poetic similarity between Hölderlin and Bialik has been sufficiently corroborated, since there is considerable similarity in their basic questions about the mission of the poet and the purpose of poetry - issues at the heart of their ars-poetica.

In the presented cartography of the interpretational field and criticism dealing with the two poets, the issue of 'myth' has been found to be the central factor around which the various interpretational approaches polarize. Most of the interpreters and critics, both of Hölderlin and of Bialik, despite their variety of differences, take a stance on either side of the dichotomist divide regarding the question of the status of 'myth' of the past in present times. On the one hand, the re-mythologizing approach (well-represented by Heidegger) grants "privileged rights" to myth, identifying with its power and desiring its return, while on the other, as its dialectic contrast, the de-mythologizing approach warns against its subjugating power and wishes to be freed of it and to have it eradicated from cultural institutions.

A genealogical survey of the concept of 'myth' in its historical transformation shows that trends of negativity and rejection of myth appear in a quasi dialectic cycle, after which come times requiring myth and its re-activation. The historical dialectic of the movement of myth embodies as well an inherent paradox, according to which steps of de-mythologization, in the course of time, themselves turn into myths. Studies in this chapter also reveal the vitality

---

[484] J. Taubes, in a letter to S. H. Bergman (1951), tells his frend about a meeting with Bergman's philosophy student Geulah Cohen, an ex-terrorist and later on a parliament (Knesset) member and the "Mother of the Jewish Settlers".
See: N. Lebovic, Introduction *New German Critique*, Duke UP, fall 2008, 35 (3 105): 1-6.

and the historical and theoretical necessity of rejuvenation of myths, apparently due to their necessity from the aspect of the consciousness, and their and social and cultural importance.

The two dichotomous approaches, sharpened in the interpretational discourse of the poets' poetry - the approach advocating myth and the one denying its influential presence - appear then as problematic, each in itself, and as insufficient, since the re-mythologization approach granting "privileged rights" to myth entails the danger, as we have seen, of yearning for the absolute and sliding into political theology, while the de-mythologization approach entails inaction and melancholy, and the danger of abandoning politics.

Synoptic reading and comparative study show the poets as embodying in their writing (and considerably in their lives) the crisis of tradition of their cultures, namely - the problem of delivery into the present of myth from the past and its continuation from a source divested of its authority; or in other words, the problem of inheritance, at a time when the very possibility of delivery is doubtful. Hence we shall claim that the synoptic approach and intersection of the poets' concepts delineate outlines of a reading born of the encounter between their respective poetries. This reading remains in the background and is not necessary when each of the poets is read on his own and within the framework of the interpretational field surrounding him. In this reading, their intersecting concepts (such as 'holy sobriety' and 'dwelling' of Hölderlin, and 'shechina' and 'blima' of Bialik) are seen as mechanisms of judgment, and embody a poetic (and political) approach of 'mediation', between the withdrawal of myth and the possibility of its future return. This approach views myth as a type of literature, and diverts the focus of the historical matter from the question of the validity of myth to the conditions of possibility or impossibility of its delivery. This is poetics that sings the crisis of tradition as part of the story sequence of tradition itself, thereby conducting simultaneously a step of 'caesura' and continuation of the sequence. This approach, found to be close, if not common, to both Hölderlin and Bialik, actually constitutes the poetic response (failing/succeeding) of each of the poets, in his own way, to the crisis of tradition from which their respective poetries derive. Hence we shall claim here that their approach exposes the illusion of the binary contrast between de-mythologization and re-mythologization as a full world view, and presents possibilities suitable for our times, for re-thinking the idea of 'tradition' and the status of 'myth' in culture.

Hölderlin and Bialik sing their private individual songs, yet, at the same time, they also sing to their people, and employ, both of them, a tone of prophetic reprimand (as failing prophets agonizing over their mission). Through the perspective of Heidegger,[485] the poetic appears as constituting the political, and through that of Arendt,[486] the definition of the political is connected to the question of possibilities of delivery of past inheritance into the present, or, in the language of this essay - of the archaic myth into our times. The encounter between the two poets, who appear as those who had elaborated on this dilemma in their writing, is - in conclusion of the essay - a point of departure of theoretical speculation, seeking to study the possibilities manifest in their approach regarding (poetic-political) re-activation of myth of the past, as an opening for cultural rejuvenation from within a crisis, or at least as a potential means for re-coping with political questions of our times.

---

[485] M. Heidegger, "Hölderlins Hymne Der Ister" (1942), trans. W. McNeill & J. Davis (Bloomington & Indianapolis: Indiana UP, 1996), pp. 79-83.
[486] (Arendt, 1961).

7.1 Tractatus Poetico-Politicus

Despite the distance between their worlds in time and space, the connection between Hölderlin and Bialik is at the heart of the poetics of the two poets. In their reflexive ars-poetic writing, which deals with the ideal of poetry and the mission of the poet, one may draw an analogy between the process of secularization and sobriety of Hölderlin's period at the end of the 18th century, in the shift toward Enlightenment, and the awakening from the promises of the Enlightenment and its slogans in Bialik's period at the end of the 19th century. Both poets sing the being of their times as the song of the whole and its rift; the song of the crisis of faith and the crisis of the sobriety.

The question of the ideal of poetry, as well as the question of the poet's mission under conditions of multi-dimensional crisis, shaking the old definitions of identity and identification, are the focus around which is woven, each under its own circumstances, the poetry of the two poets, as well as their theoretical writing. The approach (or to be more precise: the movement) of the poet in relation to these questions is examined in his writings, as well as through the main controversies of the dominant interpretational discourse. The study shows that both in the case of Hölderlin and in that of Bialik, as read by their interpreters, the issue under dispute - at the basis of the way in which the poet's mission is perceived and the purpose of his poetry - is the issue of 'myth' and the question of the possibility of its delivery.

Hölderlin's image appears, in the study, as one who, from within the rift of a world emptied of divinity, presents a negative theology of absence, aspiring to a redeeming vision of mythological blending of a (Greek) past with a (Christian) present unto a comprehensive German unity and future. The poet appears as one who fell and landed in the gap, the empty present between the glorious past, when the gods were to be found in the world of man, and the future of their return/absence. In this gap, the mission of his poetry is manifest, measuring the distance for man; mediating the memory of the divine plenty. In this gap, the failing of the mission is also manifest, a failing constituted in sobriety and madness together. On the one hand, the inherent failure of the poet's mission may be viewed as based on 'sober' acknowledgement of the distance from the source as being unbridgeable; on the other, there is the failure of the mission of the poet, who appears as a martyr hit by the lightning of madness while emptying into man the gift of the saturated plenty of the gods; or - due to the madness disintegrating poetic authority - as an expression of the weakening of the reasoned control in the first stages of mental illness.

Hölderlin's failed mission may also be seen as appearing in a renewed transformation as a myth of 'fall', combining the private and personal dimension of the poet with the national German myth constituted by virtue of the claim of connection attributed to the (Greek) source lost and the lament over its loss, since German culture, in the continuum of its historical thought, presents a line of melancholic consciousness identifying its lost source in Classical Greece, and does not cease indicating the 'caesura' and the rift from the source.[487]

The melancholy is borrowed from the psychoanalytical discourse: Sigmund Freud, as known, distinguishes between normative and pathological mourning.[488] In normative mourning, the loss of the object is compensated for by its replacement in time with a new object. In pathological mourning, however, the bereaved refuses to enable any possibility of substitute, and fixates with hopeless yearning on the lost object. The melancholic approach is based on the principled refusal to allow for compensation and substitute of the lost object. The coping with the loss is described as universal, as loss of the first object when separating from the mother's body - a loss compensated for in turn by the alternative object of the body of the beloved. The melancholic approach opposes this exchange in principle. Melancholy as a pathological reaction to loss becomes a world view, based mainly on opposition to the principle of an alternate object. It is in this sense that German culture appears as melancholic.[489]

Walter Benjamin seemed to have internalized Hölderlin's approach when he saw his current reality as a fall into a damaged and cursed being, a world view entailing depression and melancholy. In the fall, the eternal purity of naming was desecrated.[490] The words lost, as result of the sin and expulsion, their primordial power to express reality, and became mere means of communication. Our language already lacks the mythic dimension that enables intuitive recognition of the world; hence, language is in quasi exile and cannot achieve knowledge of the world. Language then has fallen into a mediating function of chatter; hence, man's ability to know nature is lost, thereby condemning nature as well to silent sadness.

This, according to Benjamin, is the first flash of reasoned, distinctive and separative thinking at the base of existing language. This is also the step that pushes man into the world of doubt and duality. The very creation of distinction between things creates the seed of existence of multiplicity and confusion, and superfluity of language, since "multiplicity of names is the deepest lingual reason for melancholy".[491]

Hence, a dialectic relation seems to be dividing Hölderlin's interpreters. Heidegger, according to his system (which itself developed considerably in connection with the concepts of the poet), reads Hölderlin as embodiment of the poet as 'conveyer of the tension' of myth; the poet-prophet, as mediator between the gods and man; as expressing in his poetry the power of language to expose being, and as the one who with his language grants the people place and history. This approach of Heidegger views myth as a constituting element and necessary factor in bestowing meaning, a sense of place, and history. Hölderlin is perceived as one who has put himself at the heart of danger for his people

---

[487] See: (Pimentel, 2008).
[488] S. Freud, "Mourning and Melancholia" (1917) in *The Standard Edition of the Complete Psychological Works of Sigmund Freud* (London: Hogarth Press), vol. 14, pp. 239-260.
[489] We should mention Schelling's view point regarding melancholy (Schwermu), as the human eternal yearning for divinity, a yearning that never forgets. This yearning is based on the tension between the identification of man with god and, on the other hand, his separation from him.
  See: F. W. J. von Schelling, "Philosophische Untersuchungen über das Wesen der menschlichen Freiheit" (1809), in *Philosophical Investigations into the Essence of Human Freedom*, trans. J. Love and J. Schmidt (New York: State UP, 2006).
[490] W. Benjamin, *Reflections: Essays, Aphorisms, Autobiographical Writings* (New York: Schocken, 1986), p. 328.
[491] Ibid, p. 329.
Also see: M. Sluhovsky, "The Beauty of Failure" (Hebrew), *Amirot*, February 2012.

and for man, facing the overwhelming plenty of the gods/being, until hit by the lightning of madness, thus fulfilling his destiny as martyr. Heidegger's approach - active and decisive by character - transformed into actual political attire, which was harnessed to the mytho-ontological establishment of Nazism in his call to create a "new mythology" for the Germans.

Contrary to Heidegger's approach there stands Benjamin's interpretation, according to which Hölderlin's writing is actually a step of de-mythologization of the 'hymn'. His interpretation presents the image of Hölderlin as a prophet whose mission has failed; whose poetry is divested of its mythic elements, and of any sources of authority - divested of any mission. In other words, the mission of poetry is the divesting of mission in order to submit to openness and to complete giving to relations. Benjamin emphasizes Hölderlin's concept of 'sobriety' as a key to protecting against that which he called the 'romantic desire to the absolute'. Hölderlin, to him, was the one who sang with sobriety the gap between man and his gods, and the helplessness of language.

Lacoue-Labarthe, examining the interpretations of Heidegger and Benjamin vis-à-vis Hölderlin's poetry, stands to Benjamin's side, claiming that Heidegger failed to fathom the deconstructive and de-mythologizing dimension of Hölderlin's poetry, and that the privileged status Heidegger grants myth is that which inevitably led his method to the temptations of the romantic absolute.[492] Despite the different readings and view points presented by Jean-Luc Nancy[493] and Avital Ronell,[494] one may see their readings of Hölderlin as placed at the polar dialectic of Heidegger's interpretation, and as to be found with Lacoue-Labarthe in Benjamin's camp. The critical poetics of Blanchot, of inherent duality, fluctuates between both poles without affixing itself easily to either, yet seems to favor the approach of viewing poetry as metaphysical activity - hence, according to the dialectic of 'myth', tending toward Heidegger's camp. Our study of Hölderlin then leaves us basically with two polar possibilities to understand the place of 'myth' in the concept of poetry and in the mission of the poet. One possibility is based on the mytho-ontological approach of Heidegger, which sees in 'myth' the power of 'dwelling', bestowing connection to source, place and history; while the opposite approach, based on Benjamin's criticism, is constituted on 'sobriety'. 'Myth', according to Benjamin, turns out to be a subjugating power, and 'sobriety' is that which makes it possible to be extracted and liberated from the hold of 'myth'. Poetry appears as open submission and passivity, which divests itself of any dictate, thereby reaching disintegration, which turns poetry into prose.

In the interpretational field of Bialik's poetry, the dialectic of 'myth' draws a similar cartography, albeit more varied and extreme, actually presenting a process of shaping the self-awareness of modern Hebrew literature as part of contemporary Zionist culture. At one end is Inbari's approach, viewing Bialik's poetry as reporting an event of revelation, where the more complex interpretations tending to this wing are Kurzweil's approach, viewing the abandonment of faith and Jewish tradition as the central spiritual question of Hebrew literature, which described Bialik as the one who perceived the degree of rift and tension between the collapse of the old world of belief and the strong need to revive it; and Eliezer Schweid's approach, according to which there is a conscious mechanism in Bialik's

---

[492] (Lacoue-Labarthe, 2007).
[493] (Nancy, 1999), p. 44.
[494] (Ronell, 2002), pp. 11-14.

poetry of re-activating myths from Jewish tradition together with personal and authentic-prophetic myth. Ziva Shamir's reading of Bialik as Hebraic-Hellenistic synthesis transfers us to the opposite pole, where Miron's approach lays,[495] according to which Bialik constituted the autonomous subject of modern Hebrew literature as an exemplary model of national poetry: "A two-aspectual or three-aspectual narrator, connecting the individual with the public, and emotion with contemplative abstraction".[496] In proximity lays the de-mythologizing reading of A. Hirschfeld, identifying in Bialik a post-romantic national approach, and describing Bialik's religious-revelatory dimension as representing a subjective experience of the inner element of the other as an element containing divinity.

Hence, the study raises two extreme possibilities of reading the poetry of the two poets, in relation to the question of delivering myth in tradition. One is the active approach of mythologization in Heidegger's spirit, proposing a "new mythology" which has the power to grant political 'dwelling'. This approach presents a response to the question of tradition as a call to return to the origin, but at the price of actualizing the danger lurking from the mythic-political blending, in the form of the temptations of the absolute.

The second alternative is the 'sober' approach - a secular, de-mythologizing approach in the spirit of Benjamin, and currently preferred by interpreters. According to this approach, the crisis of tradition is in a hopeless rift from the logic of the 'primordial'. In an era of historical-retrospect, the past, inseparable from myth, has been forgotten and cannot be produced. The mythic function, as a mechanism of activity-identification, is that against which politics must now be re-invented. Ultimately, this approach seems to formulate practicalities of inactivity, of passive submission to relations, of attentiveness, which may entail the discernment of event or events, in which the future is inaugurated.[497] Giorgio Agamben's step, for example, seems to present an illustration of a development of the Benjaminian approach. On the one hand, Agamben (inspired by Benjamin) emphasizes the urgency of liberating intervention at specific present times (Jetztzeit), while on the other, he also justifies inactivity and extreme passivity, empowering helplessness, which neutralize his call to action, leaving without answer the question of "How?", at the exchange point between politics and theology.[498]

Reading Bialik's writing and the interpretational field surrounding it, through the dialectic of 'myth' and with the concepts of discussion of Hölderlin, raises an approximation of those two trends presented, namely, the re-mythologization which reads Bialik as expressing a yearning for the forgotten past and his desire for its revival, an approach that retroactively turned Bialik from a prophet of the Revival movement into a herald of forceful political institution;[499] and the de-mythologization approach, seeking to expose Bialik's nationalism and the myth in his poetry as expressing the central trend in theological-political Zionism.

It seems that such a polar dialectic arising from the discussion is not sufficient to allay a sense of dissatisfaction, since both of the possibilities examined in relation to myth - the one seeking its return and that denying

---

[495] See: D. Miron, *Farewell to the Poor "I"* (Hebrew), (Tel Aviv: Open University Press, 1986).
[496] Ibid, p. 100.
[497] See: P. Lacoue-Labarthe, J. L. Nancy, "Le Mythe Nazi" (1981) in *The Nazi Myth*, trans. B. Holmes, *Critical Inquiry*, vol. 16, No. 2 (Winter, 1990) Chicago UP, pp. 291-312.
[498] See: V. Liska, *Giorgio Agambens Leerer Messianismus* (Wien: Schlebrügge.Editor, 2008).
[499] (Hirschfeld, 2011), p. 144.

its necessity - are limited and problematic, each in its own way, and neither may be taken as a fertile source for coping with the questions of our times.

The approach supporting 'myth', appealing to it or indicating the need for its revival raises considerable problems. Since the collapse of Christianity, as described by Nancy and Lacoue-Labarthe,[500] this approach appears in the image of the return of the past as imitating the ancients, and as such, 'myth' operates as serving an exclusive identifying function, whose historical transformations, as we have seen, are found in a highly developed way in German romanticism, and in a more modern and decisive way in the theory of G.E. Sorel, and the theory and practice of Nazism. The presence of myth in our times is philosophically problematic as well (in the spirit of the Platonic rejection), since as we have seen in the paradox of 'myth' - the very perception of 'myth' as such prevents the possibility of establishing its authority. There is grave danger inherent in 'myth' - the danger of its advocating a political theology and sliding into one or another genre of Fascism.

On the other hand, advocating the 'sober' approach in itself raises questions, the first being: Is rejection of 'myth' at all possible? Does this approach (in itself denying the sociological and psychological dimensions of the phenomenon of 'myth') not have a form of transformation of the Cartesian approach, which - in the name of freedom and reason - demands purification of bias, thereby becoming dogmatic? Is not this approach (or in its accepted expression as an effort to expose 'myth' in places where it does not declare itself) the transformation of a new myth? Moreover, the elements of inactivity, passivity, submission and openness at the base of this approach (as the dialectic opposites of any authority) raise a question about the path that may lead from submission and passive openness to the ethics and politics of justice.

As a result of the encounter created here between the poets, and in continuation of the observations entailed by the cartography of the interpretational fields of their poetics, the outlines are drawn of a reading born of the search for the common or similar between the poets, and from the very intersection and synoptic positioning of their concepts side by side or one above the other; a reading that remains in the background and is not necessarily required when each of the poets is read separately and in the framework of the interpretational field surrounding him.

Hölderlin's noble failure is viewed from the synoptic reading as an attempt to overcome crisis by continuing myth in his way, as an event that joins the previous story and re-interprets it. This step represents the vitality of myth, as well as the danger manifest in the yearning for it. At this focus of the perception of myth as a vital source, on the one hand, and as something upon which one can no longer lean, on the other, Hölderlin presents the concept of 'holy sobriety', appearing as measurement, as an element that divests myth of its authorities (by way of 'sobriety'), while not denying its unique power (by way of 'holiness'), thereby placing myth in a new context of sober holiness. Denial (as in Heidegger's case) of the divesting dimension of 'sobriety' is the danger lurking in acknowledgement of myth, which had enabled stretching Hölderlin's poetry unto a "new mythology"; on the other hand, denial of the 'holiness' of myth, and its rejection, only leads to silent melancholy.

---

[500] (Lacoue-Labarthe and Nancy, 1990)

As to Bialik, the blend of traditional materials of myth examined through the prism of personal experiencing, in itself perceived as 'typological', and in this sense as prophetic, places his entire oeuvre, and especially the mythic parts, within an expansive context of traditional Jewish literature as its dialectic continuation. However, the uniqueness of this continuation, from the aspects of content and form, lays in the embodiment of the crisis of faith or the crisis of traditional myth, as part of the story continuum itself,[501] since the consciousness of the crisis of faith entered myth as a central event of dramatic 'fall' into an abyss of disappointment and despair. Moreover, the story of the 'fall' is the generator in myth of transforming the intensity of religious experience into national experience; or, in other words: Traditional myth received limited "life extension" as revolutionary national myth.

Bialik's approach seems to have been shaped under the impact of the thought of Ahad Ha'am, according to which at the base of every religious idea there is truth derived from unmediated life experience, which the religious person dresses with theological attire. The challenge set by Ahad Ha'am was to find the human truth behind the religious practice. For example, his 'Moses' is a man of truth and justice, and the meaning of the statement that "Moses speaks with God" is no more than an expression of the idea of loyalty to absolute truth. Actually, Ahad Ha'am conducts a reduction of the idea of god into truth in the Kantian sense, thereby enabling rediscovery of (Jewish) religious content in secular terms. This sort of step, conducting actual transformation of every cultural meaning, despite its acquiring considerable supporters in its day, cannot by any means be accepted by the believer, who rejects outright as false the notion of god being truth in the Kantian sense.

Influenced by Ahad Ha'am, Bialik actually took a different step. According to his method, the inner sequence of Judaism is not connected to dogma or a world view, but rather to an inner continuum of human expression - linguistic and textual continuum, anything that grows from the inner life of the creative work in ongoing actions of infinite interpretations. Since Judaism, according to Bialik's method, was never one unified world view, but rather arguments and constant interpretational conflict, then that which turns it into one whole is its continuum within its sources. The importance of the Bible then is not only by virtue of that which is said in it, but rather - and especially - that which may be said due to it; in other words, that which may be created within its conceptual sequence. Hence it is less important to study that which is written, and more important to interpret the written, since interpretation creates a new connection to the continuum, thereby creating original identity. This, as we have seen, is the heart of the renaissance step taken by Bialik. Bialik created the "Book of Legends" with this approach, in order to bridge the language of the sources and Jewish secular language in the Hebrew education system,[502] and acted to revive the Hebrew language, which is the basis for the lively and vibrant existence of the continuum.

Ensuing from the encounter between the poetics of Hölderlin and Bialik and the interpretational fields surrounding them, there may be delineated outlines of the poetic-political approach of the poets, which - as we shall

---

[501] (Schweid,1998), p. 179.

[502] C.N. Bialik and Y.H. Ravnitsky ("Sefer ha-Aggadah"), *Book of Legends,* trans. W. Braude (NY: Schocken Books, 1992).

wish to claim - divert the focus of the poetic discussion from the origin of authority to the ways of delivery;[503] an approach acknowledging the "present loss" of myth, and which seeks to continue conducting its memory in culture, delivering it, even a broken failed delivery, as a present event, in a poetic step of 'caesura', 'rift' and 'fall', which in itself re-locates their poetry as part of the sequence of tradition.

The intersecting concepts of both poets of Hölderlin's 'holy sobriety' and 'dwelling', and Bialik's 'awakening' and 'blima', are viewed as mechanisms of judgment; as embodying an approach of 'mediation' between the mythic withdrawal and its return; and as those exposing, each in his own way, the illusion of the binary contrast between de-mythologization and re-mythologization as the full world view. Hölderlin's poetics, stretching between opposites, and Bialik's poetics which re-activates materials of myth from the past in order to deliver them as an 'event' in the present - both poetics sing the crisis of traditional myth as part of its story continuum, thereby constituting at the same time 'caesura' and continuation of the sequence.

Hölderlin and Bialik appear from the encounter as those singing the crisis of tradition and agonizing, each in his way and under the circumstances of the presence/absence of mythic in a world that no longer has a winning method. Furthermore, both poets present this agony, based on the 'fall' of the language of myth, as a poetic-political response to the challenges of their times and world; a response that in itself places their poetry anew as part of the chain of delivery of 'myth' in the accumulated history of their traditions.

This poetic-political approach of the two poets acknowledges, on the one hand, the submissive power of 'myth' and the liberties born from the weakening of its historical authority, and on the other hand - its irreplaceable vitality, as a text constituting 'place' and 'history' for individuals and communities.

It seems that at this stage of the discussion, after having discussed as well the genealogy of the concept of 'myth' and examining its dialectic historical movement, it is difficult to deny that myths renew and are destined to renew by virtue of that which may be seen as theoretical and historical necessity; in other words: A significant perception of reality, capable of granting human beings general orientation, and stimulating in them the necessary energies for a purposeful enterprise of historical dimensions, is not possible without myth. In this context, it is possible to view the current global crisis of culture and politics, on the one hand, as connected to the difficulty in accepting comprehensive and extensive collective explanations such as those that myths had provided humanity for so long a time; and on the other, as the dialectic pole of that difficulty, or as direct reaction, there is intensification of fundamentalist myths in a mimetic, separationist and enforcing interpretation.

---

[503] A world view attributing the main importance to the accumulated historical sequence ignores the basic question of the source of authority of the text. If indeed one speaks of revelatory text then its authority is clear, but if one speaks of human creation then it is not possible to locate holiness in the man-made text, and what may justify its authority in this context? Both for Hölderlin and for Bialik it is possible to identify a step of diversion, transferring the center of gravity from the question of the factual validity of the delivered myth to the ways of delivery and the interpretations, a diversion of the validity of myth from one derived from the past to one deriving from the present.

The crisis of sobriety (dealing too with a sober examination of the illusions that the sobering raises), from which the poetry of the two poets derived, in a gap of a hundred years, may be seen then as continuing to pulsate and reverberate, even more strongly, in our times as well. It does not seem possible to blunt the strength of the dichotomy (whose limitations we have presented above) between subjugation to myth and escape from its claws. However, the approach of the poets, as viewed from the encounter, shifts the matter from the mythic origin to its ways of delivery, and its 'caesura', so that by its breaking of the accumulated sequence of tradition it appears as a theoretical movement opening a way beyond the polarity between those rejecting myth and those yearning for its return. Thus, their approach constitutes an invitation to rethink, through it, the idea of 'tradition'.

7.2 Tradition and Speculation

On the way to rethinking the idea of 'the traditional', one must overcome a lack of clarity of terms, since the term (in its appearances as 'traditionalism' or 'traditionalization') has often been used by those identified with a conservative, fixating approach of tradition. This matter is exemplified by Alain Badiou's approach, presenting tradition by way of repetition, as the pole opposing change.[504]

The term 'tradition' or 'the traditional' discussed here, will then be charged with other meanings, as will be described further on. Actually, this step will constitute an attempt to delineate - as a continuation of the approach entailed by the encounter of the poets, and with the aid of the view points of Meir Buzaglo[505] and Yaacov Yadgar,[506] the outlines of that which may be described as a "modern traditional approach".[507]

This approach is formulated in the intermediate space between conservative approaches or even subjugating ones opposed, as mentioned, to change (and the need for their criticism seems clear), and on the other side, the approaches celebrating freedom of all restrictions and limitations. This type of approach is expressed by Wolfgang Schirmacher in his concept of 'homo generator'.[508]

For Schirmacher the human being is that animal which is artificial by nature.[509]

What marks humans as human is its capacity to generate life techniques. Homo generator begins to fulfill the artificial existence of humanity, as generator of human reality and tomorrow's artificial world; "homo generator" is a Dasein beyond metaphysics, a new human being which needs no Being, no certainty, no truth.

Schirmacher states that the task before humanity is to reformulate what it means to be human: mortality as well as natality are called into question again. With openness as our existential taste and co-evolutionary power as our

---

[504] Alain Badiou, *The Philosophical Concept of Change*, Seminar at the European Graduate School , Saas Fee , 08/10/2012 .http://www.egs.edu/faculty/alain-badiou/videos/the-philosophical-concept-of-change/
[505]
[506] Y Yadgar, Masortiut, (Hebrew), *Mafteakh, Lexical Review of Political Thought*, vol. 5, summer 2012, http://mafteakh.tau.ac.il/wp-content/uploads/2012/06/5-2012-07.pdf.
[507] This is also an attempt to rise to the challenge that Badiou sets in the above seminar, regarding the philosophical need to develop 'modern tradition'. See there.
[508] See: W. Schirmacher, *Homo Generator: Media and Postmodern Technology* (New York, 1994).
Also see: W. Schirmacher, "Homo Generator in the Postmodern Discussion" from "A Conversation with Jean-François Lyotard" in *Poiesis, A Journal of the Arts & Communication*, ed. Stephen K. Levine (Toronto: EGS Press) vol. 7. 2005, pp. 86-99.
[509] W. Schirmacher "Indirect Communication and Aesthetic Ethics: An Ironic Reading of Kierkegaard" Poeisis 9 (2007).

design, Homo generator favors eternal revisions and safeguards the freedom of creation. What we clone is exactly this attitude of open generating and never a mere copy of anything.[510]

The traditional approach may be seen as formulating itself in polemic with Schirmacher's perception; indeed, the challenge of confronting his perception was among the factors leading to the present research. One may view the traditional approach as questioning the very possibility of 'homo generator' being free of history in the Nietzschian sense, and in relation to the price of 'absolute' freedom. Based on Schirmacher's concept, we shall describe the possible movement of 'myth' as 'regenerative' in culture. The term is presented here as a biological metaphor to describe movement of rejuvenation within restrictions. 'Regeneration' indicates a process of renewal with dynamic connection to the source, as an impaired genetic code operating faithfully according to memory of the past, yet involving in its movement also reaction to trauma.

The meaning of 'tradition' presented here is of a perception based on the inner continuum of expression, a linguistic and textual continuum through which 'myth' appears, as mentioned, as a particular type of literature. According to this view, 'tradition' is everything that grows from the inner life of the creative work in constant actions of infinite interpretation, canonization, forgetting, and remembrance. That which turns it into one is its sequence within and around its sources. The 'delivery' involved in the idea of 'tradition'[511] is perceived as a central element in Judaism, and is the space within which the language of Judaism and the world it conveys develop. In 'delivery', as described by Buzaglo, the relation of a priori loyalty or faithfulness rules. This relation is not imitation of preceding generations but rather the willingness to propose an interpretation and to fight for it.[512]

According to this perception, loyalty is not a limitation of rationality, a submission of autonomy or a hindrance to be suspected and to see as threatening, but rather a condition for the beginning of a process of debate with heritage and distant traditions. Tradition cannot be rectified by suspecting the world delivered to us. Conversely, loyalty and love are that which give strength to overcome trends of freezing of tradition, and to prevent it from becoming obstinate tribalism.[513]

'Tradition', as described by Yadgar,[514] appears then as a quasi 'language' into which man is born, and in and through which he grows up, becomes a member of a community, becomes acquainted with the world around and constitutes as a subject. 'Tradition', which is ever current (as opposed to its image, accepted by both sides of the secular-religious debate, which see it as a type of frozen remnant of the past, whose image, content, and - in part of the claims - even its meaning, are closed and sealed), is simultaneously that which enables us to perceive reality and interpret it, and also that which sets the boundary and horizon of the same perception and interpretations. Through its

---

[510] W. Schirmacher. "Cloning Humans with Media: Impermanence and Imperceptible Perfection." *Poeisis*, no. 2 (2000).
[511] In Hebrew the word 'mesirah', translated into 'delivery', and the word 'masoret', 'tradition', derive from the same linguistic root.
[512])Buzaglo, 2008), p. 13.
[513] Such a perception of traditionalism evokes Heidegger's perception of the poet and thinker as dwelling in the house of language, hence their status as renovators of the house.
[514] (Yadgar, 2012(.

institutional and symbolic structures, tradition shapes social, cultural and political reality, and charges it with meaning, while remaining far from being a closed, eternal, one-sided dictate, since its deliverers are its interpreters.

This type of understanding of tradition, or at least the main outlines of this perception, may be found (under various names and concepts), inter alia, in the discussion of Ludwig Wittgenstein, "language games", "forms of life" and "background knowledge";[515] in Clifford Girtz' post-Wittgensteinian claim about the public and community character of thought, and his ensuing reconstruction of the concept of 'culture';[516] Thomas Kuhn's concept of 'paradigm';[517] and the ideas of Charles Taylor about the roles of the 'inter-subjectivity meanings' and 'language' in constituting the lives of humans.[518] This perception has gained methodical and extensive formulation in the thought of H.G.Gadamer,[519] and has also gained the careful attention of social scientists such as S.N. Eisenstadt[520] and Edward Shils.[521]

Although these thinkers are from various schools of philosophy and use a wide variety of investigation methods, it is not difficult to see that they conceptualize tradition in similar and complementary ways, all directed toward the basic idea that tradition should be perceived as a narrative found in the background; a dynamic, textual, practical and symbolic narrative, constituting both the individual and the community. This idea emphasizes that tradition, which is collective in essence, is not only inevitable but necessary for the construction of reflexive subjectivity.[522] This perception of tradition also emphasizes that there is no meaning to the apparent contrast between tradition (the collective) and liberty (the individual), since the very ability to perceive the subject as an independent acting-agent is itself dependent upon a constituting tradition, in which such formulation is a priori possible. In this spirit, the afore-mentioned thinkers propose to re-examine, positively, the value of earlier perceptions and knowledge delivered to us by 'heredity', regarding historical and social reality. Such an understanding of tradition succeeds in exposing as well the blind spots of positivist-rationalist thinking - the intellectual element from which the thesis of modernization and secularization grew, and proposes ways to go beyond the boundaries of empiricist rationalism through emphasis on the importance of other ways of knowledge, first and foremost practice - since rather than being a theory seeking application, traditionalism is a practice worthy of theorization.[523]

Emphasizing the constituting role of tradition also sheds light on the place of authority, which appears as a pre-condition to the accumulation of knowledge and reflexive examination of reality; all of this vis-à-vis the contention of enlightenment that any pre-condition to knowledge is blatant bias. As mentioned, this is a 'textual' perception of tradition, since it comprehends tradition as that which, similarly to any 'text', is actualized and receives

---

[515] See: L. J. J. Wittgenstein, "Philosophische Untersuchungen" (1953), *Philosophical Investigations* (Oxford: Blackwell, 2001).
[516] C. Geertz, *The Interpretation of Cultures* (New York: Basic Books, 1973).
[517] T. S. Kuhn, *The Structure of Scientific Revolutions* (Chicago: Chicago UP, 1962).
[518] C. Taylor, "Philosophy and the Human Sciences" in *Philosophical Papers* (Cambridge: Cambridge UP, 1985).
[519] H. G. Gadamer, *Truth and Method* (New York: Crossroad, 1989); *Philosophical Hermeneutics* (Berkeley: California UP, 1976).
[520] S. N. Eisenstadt, *Tradition, Change, and Modernity* (New York: Wiley; S. N., 1972).
[521] E. Shils, *Tradition* (Chicago: Chicago UP, 1981).
[522] (Yadgar, 2012).
[523] (Buzaglo, 2008), pp. 59-77.

meaning and content only when we, its deliverers, understand it, in other words - interpret it, charging it with meaning (which is ever "current"), internalizing it and applying it; that is: The understanding of tradition (which requires, on its part, interpretation of tradition) is a condition for the existence of tradition, and this understanding is embodied, lived, in practice.

Although we do not choose the tradition into which we are born and grow, whether as individuals or as community, the ongoing project of shaping our identity is conducted through dialogue between us, the deliverers of tradition, and our tradition. This dialogue brings about a broadening of our horizons, as well as renewed understanding and interpretation of tradition itself (hence, of course, 'language' too is not finite and closed, and is also undergoing a continuous process of interpretation, shaping and updating). In other words, tradition is a basic condition, in which (and in its boundaries, which are in a continuous process of shaping and definition) the liberty of its deliverers is constituted to build their identity as individuals and as members of a community (so that the distinction between these two 'roles' or 'identities' dissolves).[524]

A clarifying way of understanding the nature of the interpretational dialogue between tradition and its deliverers is the idea of 'game' that was developed by Gadamer[525] and Wittgenstein[526] each separately: From the beginning, the existence of the game depends upon us, the players, who choose to participate in it; however, from the moment we enter it, its rules become a code guiding our behavior; the game exists in us, the ones who answer to its rules. We accept a role in the game, become characters in it, and the game - on its part - exists by virtue of the very fact that we take part in it and obey its basic rules; the game is not an independent action of the subject (the player), but rather an 'activation' of the subject by the game. In this respect, the encounter between tradition and its deliverers may be described as 'appropriation' - not of ours, its deliverers appropriating it, but rather the opposite - we become characters of the game, which is tradition. As emphasized by Paul Ricœur,[527] the implication of this approach is the relinquishment of a perception that is so central to secular rationalist enlightenment, of the subject as independent agent. This relinquishment is a pre-condition to the expansion of our personal consciousness under the guidance of 'text' (in this case - tradition).

It is the tension between strangeness and alienation on the one hand, and acquaintance and belonging, on the other, which characterizes the constituting, dialogue-oriented understanding of tradition, which interprets and appropriates us, while we are "applying" it. As mentioned, this is not a dialogue between equals; we belong to tradition before it belongs to us. Tradition and its residues have lasting power that determines that which we develop into being. Our conditions of existence are such that we are born and grow up into tradition. We already convey with us a certain past from the moment we are born, and this basic condition is the (inequity) context in which our dialogue relation with it is conducted. This dialogue relation is as an ongoing attempt to understand tradition and interpret it, in

---

[524] (Yadgar, 2012).
[525] (Gadamer, 1989), pp. 102-110.
[526] (Wittgenstein, 1953/2001), paragraphs 198-242.
[527] P. Ricœur, *Hermeneutics and the Human Sciences: Essays on Language, Action, and Interpretation* (Cambridge (UK): Cambridge UP, 1981), pp. 182-198.

the same process that Gadamer calls "Fusions of Horizons". This is not, then, a simple one-directional scheme of tradition "influencing" us; tradition fulfills a role in the very constitution of our identity as individuals and as a collective.

Jewish tradition appears as anchored in 'myth'. It is customary to see, as its foundation, the "Event of Mount Sinai" as the event of divine revelation delivered from generation to generation in the collective memory. The perception of tradition as an interpretational continuum lays void the question of the validity of 'myth' as constituting tradition, and focuses on the accumulative dimension of interpretational reference to 'myth' and the ensuing meanings of the revelation 'event'.

Delivery, writes Buzaglo,[528] is the transferring from generation to generation, such as the delivery of Jewish heritage, while in reporting - one describes to another something he considers true. The distinction between delivery and report does not relate to the delivered content but rather to the act of speech in which the content appears. Report is a certain type of speech action, whereas delivery is another type of speech action. The difference is that delivery is based on loyalty of the receivers to the deliverers, and loyalty of each generation to the preceding one, and not only regarding the reliability of inter-generational report. In Wittgenstein's terms, delivery is a language-game. Contrary to report, delivery entails an intimate connection between the deliverer and his addressee. The addressee is loyal to whoever delivers to him. He is loyal to him and not only believes him.[529] The deliverers are not necessarily aware of their being deliverers rather than reporters (in this sense, delivery is different, for instance, from telling a joke - a situation in which the deliverer and the receiver know it is a situation of telling a joke). Loyalty is expressed in withstanding attempts to refute the delivered content. In withstanding such attempts at refutation, the receiver will try to re interpret differently the content delivered to him so that it sounds meaningful.

Ultimately, we are loyal to a collection of words delivered to us by tradition, and not to certain claims. By adopting the words, we are not committed to holding an opinion whose purpose is the transferring of true or false claims. We receive messages and we may render a different interpretation not only of the content but also of their "power of claim" (an idea of Frege's which Wittgenstein subsequently developed as 'language games'). The difference between delivery and report is expressed in the connections between the deliverer and the receiver, and in the relation of the receiver to the sentence inherited from his parents or forefathers (this difference may be demonstrated as well by the distinction between a priori and post-priori sentences). The term 'custom' is supported by the term 'traditional'. The traditional person follows the custom of his forefathers; he does not live by the book.[530] The relation between traditionalism and criticism is demonstrated by Buzaglo's use of Kant's "Light Dove":[531] The dove thinks that the lighter the air is, the better it will fly, and it also thinks that without air its flight will be perfect. Is this not the case as well with those thinking that if they are rid of past tradition (albeit not devoid of problems) and bring

---

[528] (Buzaglo, 2008) pp. 28-29.
[529] Ibid, p. 29-46.
[530] Ibid.
[531] I. Kant, "Kritik der reinen Vernunft" (1781), *Critique of Pure Reason*, trans. P. Guyer & A. Wood (Cambridge: Cambridge UP, 1999).

themselves to infinite openness, they will be more critical and better reach the truth? And as in the fable of the dove, is it not this wrestling with tradition which provides the necessary friction for movement and dialogue? Eliminate it and you will find yourself a tourist wandering in the land of opinions.[532]

'The traditional' is not an a-modernist phenomenon. On the contrary, it is actually shaped by confronting competing understandings and interpretations of tradition which are clearly modern, and as a concept it becomes clearer in the light they shed. One may identify those competing approaches (by way of generalizing, of course) under the names of secular Rationalism and romanticist orthodox Conservatism.[533] If these two approaches build themselves as two polar categories or as two contrasting members of a binary construct (while denying the ambivalence characteristic of modernism), then 'the traditional' is as a 'stranger', one whose position in relation to that same group is defined by the fact that he has not belonged to it from the beginning, so that he "brings to it qualities that have not derived nor could derive from the group itself". The presence of the stranger impairs the binary structure and weakens it.

The concept of 'holy sobriety', of Hölderlin's poetry, seems to better represent here the blending that tradition offers between the memory of myth from the past and its re-interpretation in the present. The concept of 'holy sobriety' appears in the dialectic of 'myth' that we have surveyed, as the 'stranger', exposing the lie of the contrast between de-mythologization and re-mythologization as the full world view; as the difference which contains all the differences and thereby leaves nothing outside but itself. Since this contrast is the basis upon which stand social life and the differences that maintain and stabilize it, the 'stranger' weakens social life itself - since the 'stranger' is neither friend nor foe; and since it may be anyone. The 'stranger' is one of the family of 'undecidables'; one of those confusing unities, yet present anywhere, as described by Jacques Derrida; they can no longer be contained within a philosophical (binary) contrast, when they oppose and impair this contrast without constructing a third concept.[534]

---

[532] (Buzaglo, 2008), p. 18.
[533] 'Conservatism' or 'orthodoxy' will refer here to the approach upholding tradition as eternal, permanent and authoritative - an approach which Yadgar calls 'fundamentalism' (Yadgar, 2012).
[534] J. Derrida, *Dissemination*, trans. B. Johnson (Chicago, IL: Chicago UP, 1983), p. 71.

7.3 On Myth and Political Imagination

The hermeneutical encounter between Hölderlin and Bialik has been found in this essay to open a discussion on the question appearing as basic to the poetic mission of the two, which is the question of myth and its possible poetic delivery from the past, beyond the modern rift regarding its transcendental authority.[535] The images of the two poets emerge from the encounter as those who represent, in their writing, an alternative to the dichotomy between that which has been described as 're-mythologization' and 're-mythologization' of culture; or between that which may be called (in creative generalization) "liberal rationalism" and "romantic fundamentalism". This alternative is manifest as a poetic-political approach, essentially textual, relating the central importance to historical sequence; shifting the center of gravity from the question of the validity of delivered myth to the ways of delivery and to interpretation. In other words: Shifting of the source of validity of myth from that which derives from the past to that deriving from the present. This approach, characterized here by closeness to the idea of 'the traditional', maintains a mission of its meandering continuation through interpretation and poetic re-activation of myth from the past, into culture of the present.

The encounter between Hölderlin and Bialik and the study of the question of the delivery of myth in tradition invite, at conclusion, the question of the political relevance of their poetic approach, and of the possibilities of its application in relation to urgent questions of our era. At the conclusion of this essay, an attempt will be made to speculate about the transformation of (the poetic) 'myth' into a regenerative or innovative element in the culture of our times. Speculation about the possible contribution of re-activation of poetic myth in current politics (without denying the dangers involved in such a step) is presented in outline, within the context of the Israeli-Palestinian conflict - in itself a "tragic laboratory" of relations between myth and politics.

Zionism, as an idea that became a national liberation movement for the Jewish people, anchored the Jewish people from all over the world - in consciousness and in deed - in the Israeli place. Stories of various Jewish Diasporas in various places were woven into a narrative of exile and revival, dispersal and independence. The Zionist ideology was built on the myth of the return to Zion, whose meaning was perceived as return to history. The constitution of the renewing nation necessitated as well a return to symbols, rituals and myths of Jewish nationalism, religion and history. An active return to history through a renewed sovereignty in the Land of Israel often required of the individual to sacrifice his name, profession and home, for something bigger, for the story framework to which he belonged. The act of sacrifice of the pioneer immigrations from the beginning of the 20th century, which sought to be the vanguard of the

---

[535] Kristeva claims that poetic language is that which enables change and mending of the fragmented subject. Poetic language not only shatters meaning but also diverges from it, enabling the creation of new meaning. Poetic language grants passion to suppressed urges; it does not refine them but rather grants them renewed form with meaning.
(Kristeva, 1984), pp. 163-164.

Jewish nation, had an unexpected continuation: The Zionist prophecy was fulfilled tragically, when instead of redemption, the constitution of Jewish sovereignty appeared as a blood-shed conflict with the Palestinian inhabitants of the country, a conflict which gave birth to the image of a conquering and discriminatory rule. Refugees of the Holocaust and of Eastern countries reached the state-in-creation. The story of their sacrifice was not a legitimate part of the Zionist pioneering ethos: The "dust of man" had to be turned into a "new man", the 'tsabar'. The purpose then was to constitute a collective having a common sociological destiny, for the sake of which myths of heroism were constructed, with national rituals and melting-pot ideology.[536] Over the last few decades it has become accepted by many researchers of Israeli historiography and sociology to doubt Zionist 'myths'. The "new historians" conduct de-mythologization of Zionist images that are shattering - not due to historical research, since, as mentioned, corroboration, or refutation, are irrelevant to the growth or destruction of 'myth'. 'Myth' and 'history' may exist in parallel to one another. Refutation of myth is possible only at the proper time, when the ethos, or normative value, has changed. Israeli society has shifted from an ethos of a heroic pioneering society to an ethos of a consumer and communication-oriented society - and accordingly, the myths constituting its values have changed.[537]

The reduction of the status of the Zionist endeavor and the increasing weight of the communications experience seem (by way of generalization, of course) to be leading two polar processes connected to each other and shaping the space of Israeli identity, two processes inherited from the Zionist revolution: On the one hand, reduction of Judaism to nationality, expressed in the creation of the secular Israeli leading to cultural pluralism which lacks a unifying connection, and the disintegration of the Israeli collective experience as known until now; and on the other hand, the strengthening (with political empowerment) of religious elements (some of which are fundamentalist) which identify worthy Judaism with life according to the Halacha. These processes are advancing, while connected by the umbilical cord to the conflict between Israel and her neighbors and the ongoing conquest of the Palestinians, and seem to be leading Israelis through a process, in which the word 'fall' well-describes the horror and despair of those who had believed that a Jewish nation could don a different image.[538] It seems that Zionism has appeared in our times as a utopia that failed.[539]

The Israeli-Palestinian conflict has long been charged, and more intensely over the last few decades, with values and symbols of religion binding together the sanctity of the land, the religious command to rule and settle it, the holy sites, and the war, terror, and sacrifice for religious ideals.

---

[536] (Ohana and Wistrich, 1996), pp. 11-37.

[537] In contemporary historical research, perceptions that were accepted in the past are under examination and criticism, undergoing re-evaluation, sometimes even up to blatant refutation of their measure of truth. A new generation of Israeli historians views Zionism as 'meta-narrative' ('myth', in the language of Jean-François Lyotard), creating an 'invented tradition' of national unity or of historical anti-Semitism. The Zionist settlement endeavor is perceived as colonialist take-over of Europeans against authentic Palestinian nationality.
See: (Ohana and Wisetrich, 1996), pp. 11-37.

[538] J. Rose, *The Question of Zion* (Princeton: Princeton UP, 2007).

[539] In contrast, for instance, to the American (USA) world view as described by Jean Baudrillard, which at least until the events of September 2011 "considered itself" a utopia that had succeeded.
See: J. Baudrillard, *America* (New York: Verso, 2010).

On Myth and Political Imagination

Proposals of bridging and of solution developed and presented from both sides of the conflict, as well as other international factors, have all been based on a political discussion that avoids the mythic dimensions of the conflict and views myth of both sides as "barriers" for it solution.[540] It is becoming clearer that "barriers" such as these are well-entrenched on both sides of the conflict, and furthermore, since the 90s,[541] the same 'mythic discourse' has intensified and taken hold of large populations that were not considered religious in the past.[542] And it seems that the active political discourse, desperately denying the mythic dimension in the discussed conflict, is far from providing an answer for the needs and demands that are seen to be essential to both conflicting sides.

The avoidance of mythic-theological discourse within the context of the political conflict is understandable, since this discourse appears today as appropriated by the religious-fundamentalist factions of the conflict,[543] based on ancient militant theological-political myths that have inherent difficulties with compromise, and do not even recognize the legitimacy of bridging discourse, suspecting its motives and accusing it in one way or another of colonialism. Similarly, the mythological discourse is appropriated by the political theology of the rulers, who make use of reductive interpretations of myth in order to justify forceful policy. And if this is not enough, the opening of the gate of legitimacy of the political discourse to myth, so claim the opponents, may also awaken from their slumber Jewish-messianic trends that have lay at the base of Jewish zealotry for generations, subversive to the elements of the Zionist endeavor as well, glimpsing through its so-called secular attire.

The encounter between Hölderlin and Bialik brought to the discussion two concepts whose meanings are close - 'holy sobriety' and 'blima'. Hölderlin's 'holy sobriety' represents, as a paradoxical poetic expression, a powerful theoretical tool as well, which - if not for its denial, may have served Heidegger as a brake in his slip into the absolute. This indicates the dangers of reductive interpretation, in addition to the passive elements of Hölderlin's poetry which enabled "capturing" him.[544] Similarly, Bialik's concept of 'blima' with its roots in Jewish Kabbalah,[545] and its re-introduction in poetics of the times of the poet, as man's muteness and barrier at the boundary determined for him, appears as a theoretical means that may brake the slipping into the Jewish absolute; to the mythic-messianic element in its narrow hegemonic reading. The concept of 'blima' reminds one (whoever chooses to listen) of human

---

[540] See: Y. Bar-Siman-Tov ed., *Barriers to Peace in the Israeli-Palestinian Conflict* (Jerusalem: The Jerusalem Institute and Adenauer Stiftung, 2010).
[541] Actually since the "Oslo process" in 1993.
[542] (Bar-Siman-Tov, 2010).
[543] This context brings to mind the approach of Quentin Meillassoux who criticizes the abandonment of metaphysical studies (and within the context of our issue: the study of 'myth') to fundamentalism in its various forms.
See: Q. Meillassoux, *After Finitude: An Essay on the Necessity of Contingency*, trans. R. Brassier (New York: Continuum, 2008).
[544] In 1964 Ernest Simon published an essay called "Heilige Nuchternheit" (Sacred Sobriety) where he sought to describe a middle path that does not deny the Jewish messianic idea on the one hand, while limiting its political power on the other.
See: E. A. Simon, "Heilige Nuchternheit" (1964), in *Brucken* (Heidelberg: Lambert Schneider, 1965), pp. 468-470.
[545] "Tole shamayim al blima" ("Hanging land on blima"; Job, 26:7) and in "Book of Creation", which is an important source for understanding the spheres, it is written about the spheres that they are "ten that have no end" - that since they are sublimated from infinity they must reflect its infinity, hence they are called there the "ten spheres of blima", as interpreted by Ramak (Pardess Rimonim) "bli+ma" - with no essence, as he says: "They have essence attained for humans, as they are not limited or attainable, for they have no boundary or actualization", which necessarily entails that "They appear as the sight of a flash and their purpose has no end", and in the interpretation of the Ramak, prophecy is not affected by them, they are not attainable even for the prophet, who only sees their reflection in other things (Ramak, Book of Creation).

limitations, and that acknowledgement of god is meant to be greater than the horror of man ("God is with me, I shall not fear what man does to me"; Psalms, 118:6).

We shall claim then that the approach of 'holy sobriety' in the spirit of the concepts of Hölderlin and Bialik as characterized here, granting place to myth, may be a considerable contribution to an encounter and legitimization of conflicting traditions, based on the mythic foundation common to both sides (which nowadays appears as the main thing in common for them).[546]

In the introduction to the issue of "New German Critique", 2008, devoted to political theology,[547] Editor Nitzan Lebovic demonstrates the polarization of the controversy by presenting the approaches of Mark Lilla and John Gray:

Lilla's observation is that "today, we have progressed to the point where our problems again resemble those of the sixteenth century… Theological ideas still stir up messianic passions, leaving societies in ruins." According to Lilla, much of the current trouble in the world is a byproduct of this political theology: "So long as a sizable population believes in the truth of a comprehensive political theology, its full reconciliation with modern liberal democracy cannot be expected."[548]

Gray proceeds, however, from an opposite direction. He diagnoses a contemporary apocalyptic mood and, simultaneously, turns his political-theological emphasis into an analytic tool: "The world in which we find ourselves at the start of the new millennium is littered with the debris of utopian projects, which though they were framed in secular terms that denied the truth of religion were in fact vehicles for religious myths."[549] He notes that destructive images of the apocalypse or prophecy imply an urgent need for radical change through an extreme shift in political language, as demonstrated by the pioneer of modern political theology, Carl Schmitt, Whose work and stark critique of liberalism inspire both the radical left-wing critique of liberal imperialism and its neoconservative opposite.[550]

The question to be asked is whether in the polarized controversy of the political theological discourse there is room and benefit for a mediating poetic-political approach such as presented by Hölderlin and Bialik?

---

[546] The development of the idea of 'traditionalism', as well as its 'mytho-political' implications, is described in this essay through a Jewish-Israeli prism. For parallels of this approach in Islam, as well as the possibilities of discourse between traditions, see:
C. Geertz, *Islam Observed Religious Development in Morocco and Indonesia* (Chicago: Chicago UP, 1971).

[547] N. Lebovic, "Introduction", *New German Critique* 105, vol. 35, No. 3, Fall 2008.

[548] M. Lilla, "The Politics of God," *New York Times Magazine*, August 19, 2007. The article
is part of a wider project Lilla develops in his book "The Stillborn God: Religion, Politics, and the
Modern West" (New York: Knopf, 2007). Cited in: (Lebovic, 2008).

[549] J. Gray, *Black Mass: Apocalyptic Religion and the Death of Utopia* (New York: Farrar,
Straus and Giroux, 2007), 1. Cited in (Lebovic, 2008).

[550] Schmitt famously claimed that European political history from Thomas Hobbes's Leviathan to the French Restoration proved that liberalism "had no political content and was only an organizational form." See: Carl Schmitt, "The Crisis of Parliamentary Democracy", trans. Ellen Kennedy (Cambridge, MA: MIT Press, 2001), 8n4. His negative conclusion of course led to "decisionism" based on a moment of crisis, when the sovereign must take responsibility and act as an absolute and sole ruler, equal
in power to any divine entity . See: (Lebovic, 2008).

On Myth and Political Imagination

Political philosophy is inherently connected to political crises of its time of development, and from history one may learn that political crises bear changes and revolutions in political thought; and that theory is considered one of the factors generating or exacerbating a crisis. It is difficult not to view the global political situation - especially in Israel - as in crisis, and it seems that the need for paradigmatic changes is even more emphatic at present.

Are the political categories and concepts, provided to us so far by Western political tradition in all of its variations and avoiding mythic discourse in general, appropriate for the local crisis? And if not, how would local political thought look - being endemic, having grown from within the unique political crisis, and intending itself, first of all, for its conceptualization, understanding and solution? It is possible that the theoretical discourses active these days in the political arena (shaped in general abroad) limit the political imagination, thereby reducing the possibilities of action open to us. Hence, it is possible that the political situation in Israel has unique characteristics, as the shaping presence of myths of the past at the basis of the current political discourse, which make it difficult to be understood with the aid of existing theoretical political concepts, so that the lack or the creation of local political language or thought, emerging from the characteristics and practice unique to the conflict, may have implications on the way in which we perceive the characteristics of the crisis and the possibilities of its solution.[551]

To conclude, we shall claim that the Israeli-Palestinian conflict at its basis is not a "civilian" conflict, but rather mythic-religious. Hence, its solutions should be sought from within that same mythism - neither in its arrangement or denial, nor in its regulation to a "healthier" or more "controllable" level, but rather in the fermenting action of mythic potential, that is often releasing.[552] Archaic myth has long been neglected, in favor of factors enflaming the conflict, and it is now appropriate to examine a new use of myth that will change the field of meaning. It seems appropriate to develop politics that examines the potential of new poetic interpretation of myths and their re-activation in our times as regenerative power.

The question[553] left open at the conclusion of this essay is: Can reflexive and self-aware consciousness (of its dialectic movement, of its necessity and of the dangers embodied in it) indeed be capable of activating and regenerating reliable and authentic myth? The entailed conclusion, at the end of this essay, is that if hope exists for it, it should be sought for from the poets.

---

[551] See: The Van-Leer Institute, Jerusalem: Toward a Local Political Thought, research group statement, 2010. http://www.vanleer.org.il/he/node/806
[552] See: I. Binyamini, Toward a Critical Theology of the Contemporary Political (Hebrew), 2011, http://haemori.wordpress.com/2011/09/19/theology/
[553] Inspired by E. Schweid (Schweid, 1996).

Abbreviations used in Footnotes

SPF   F. Hölderlin, *Selected Poems and Fragments,* trans. M. Hamburger (London: Penguin Books, 1998).

BYP   *The Writings of Chaim Nachman Bialik,* (Hebrew) in: The Ben-Yehuda Project, http://benyehuda.org/bialik/

BSW   W. Benjamin, *Selected Writings*, vol.1-4 (Cambridge: Harvard UP).

HBW   M. Heidegger, *Basic Writings: From "Being and Time" (1927) to "The Task of Thinking" (1964)*, ed. D. F. Krell (New York: Harper Collins, 1993).

Bibliography

Adorno, T.W. (1992) "Parataxis: On Hölderlin's Late Poetry", in Notes to Literature vol. 2, trans. S.W. Nicholsen (New York: Columbia University Press), pp. 109-149.

Arendt, H. Between Past and Future: Six Exercises in Political Thought (New York: Viking, 1961).

Aristotle, Poetics, trans. R. Janko (Bloomington: Indiana UP, 1987), p.57-121.

Beinkinstadt, B. An anthology of poem translations: From the Hebrew and the

Yiddish (Cape Town: City Printing Works, 1930).

Badiou, A. *Manifeste pour la Philosophie (1989) Manifesto for Philosophy*, ed. N. Madarasz, (Albany: New York UP. 1999).

Baeck, L. *Wege im Judentum* (Berlin: Schocken, 1933), pp.90-103.

Baudrillard, J. *America* (New York: Verso, 2010).

Barthes, R. *Mythologies* (Paris: Editions de Seuil, 1957), trans. A. Lavers (London: Paladin, 1972), p.8.

Barthes, R. *Image, Music, Text. "The Photographic Message."* ed. and trans. Stephen Heath (New York: Hill, 1977), p. 15-31.

Barthes, R. *Le Neuter (The Neutral)*: Lecture Course at the Collège de France (1977–1978), (New York: Columbia UP, 2005).

Beiser, F. C. *German Ideals: The Struggle against Subjectivism, 1781-1801* (Cambridge: Harvard UP, 2002).

Benjamin, W. *Selected Writings*, vol.1, 1913-1926 (Cambridge: Harvard UP, 1996); vol. 2, 1927-1934 (Cambridge: Harvard UP, 1999);vol. 3, 1935-1938 (Cambridge: Harvard UP, 2000).

Benjamin, W. *Illuminations: Essays and Reflections*, ed. H. Arendt, trans. H. Zohn (New York: Schocken Books, 1969).

Benjamin, W. *Berlin Childhood around 1900,* trans. H. Eiland (Cambridge and London: Harvard UP, 2006).

Benjamin, W. *Moscow Diary* (1926–1927), ed. G. Smith & R. Sieburth,

trans. G. Scholem (Cambridge and London: Harvard UP, 2006).

Benjamin, W. *The Origin of German Tragic Drama* (1928), trans. J. Osborne (London, New.York: Verso, 2003).

Benjamin, W. *The Arcades Project* (1927–40), ed. R. Tiedemann (Cambridge, Harvard UP, 1999).

Berman, A. *L'épreuve de l'étranger. Culture et Traduction dans l'Allemagne Romantique: Herder, Goethe, Schlegel, Novalis, Humboldt, Schleiermacher, Hölderlin* (Paris: Gallimard, Essais, 1984).

Bialik, C.N. and Ravnitsky, Y.H. *Book of Legends*, trans. W. Braude (NewYork: Schocken Books, 1992).

Bialik, C.N. *Aftergrowth and Other Stories*, trans. I. M. Lask (Philadelphia: Jewish Publication Society, 1939).

Bialik, C.N. *Selected Poems,* trans. R. Nevo (Jerusalem: Magnes Press, 1981).

Bialik, C.N. *Songs from Bialik: Selected Poems*, trans. A. Hadari (Syracuse: Syracuse UP, 2000).

Blanchot, M. "Hölderlin et la Parole Sacrée" (1946), in *The Work of Fire (La Part du Feu)*, trans. C.Mandel (Stanford: Stanford UP, 1995), p. 111-131.

Blanchot, M." La folie par excellence" (1591), *Critique. 45* (February 1951), pp. 99-118. Revised version as preface in: K. Jaspers, *Strindberg and Van Gogh*, trans. O. Grunow, D. Woloshin, (Tucson: Arizona UP, 1982).

Bibliography

Blanchot, M. "*L'Espace litteraire*"(1955), trans. A. Smock (Lincoln: Nebraska UP, 1989).

Breslauer, S. D. *The Hebrew Poetry of Hayyim Nahman Bialik (1873-1934) and a Modern Jewish Theology* (Edwin Mellen Press, 1991), p.185.

Bruford, W.H. *The German Tradition of Self-Cultivation: Bildung from Humboldt to Thomas Mann* (London: Cambridge University Press, 2010).

Buber, M. *The Kingship of God* (Jerusalem: Bialik Institute, 2000).

Buber, M. *Moses: The Revelation and the Covenant* (New York: Humanity, 1998), pp. 14-16.

Cassirer, E. *An Essay on Man: An Introduction to a Philosophy of Human Culture* (New Haven: Yale University Press, 1944).

Coetzee, J.M. *Holderlin, the Poet in the Tower*, NYRB e-edition, October 19, 2006, http://www.nybooks.com/articles/archives/2006/oct/19/the-poet-in-the-tower/?pagination=false

Constantine, D. *Hölderlin* (Oxford: Clarendon Press, 1988).

De Man, P. *Critical Writings 1953-1978*, ed. L. Waters (Minneapolis: University of Minnesota Press, 1989).

De Man, P. "Heidegger's Exegeses of Hölderlin", *Blindness and Insight* (Minneapolis: University of Minnesota, 1983), pp. 246–66.

Derrida J. "Le retrait de la Métaphore" (1978), in *Poesis*. No. 7, 1978.

Derrida, J. *Dissemination*, trans .B. Johnson (Chicago, IL: Chicago UP, 1983), p. 71.

De Saussure, F. *Writings in General Linguistics* (Oxford: Oxford UP, 2006).

Di Giovanni, G. and Harris, H.S., ed. *Between Kant and Hegel: Texts in the Development of Post-Kantian Idealism* (Indianapolis: Hackett, 0222(.

Donelan, J.H. Hölderlin's Poetic Self-Consciousness, *Philosophy and Literature* 26, (2002) pp. 125-142.

Durkheim, E. *The Division of Labor in Society*, trans. L. A. Coser (New York: Free Press, 1997), pp. 39, 60, 108.

Eisenstadt, S. N. *Tradition, Change, and Modernity* (New York: Wiley S. N. 1972).

Eliade, M. ed., *Encyclopedia of Religion* (New York: Macmillan, 1987).

Fichte, J.G. *Introductions to the Wissenschaftslehre and Other Writings* (1797-1800), ed. and trans. D. Breazeale (Indianapolis/Cambridge: Hackett, 1994).

Fichte, J. G. *Addresses to the German Nation* (1121), trans. G. Moore (Cambridge: Cambridge UP, 2008).

Fioretos, A. ed. *The Solid Letter: Readings of Friedrich Hölderlin* (Stanford: Stanford UP, 1999).

Förster, E. (1995) "To lend wings to physics once again": Hölderlin and the 'Oldest System Program of German Idealism', *European Journal of Philosophy* 3(2), pp.174-198.

Freud, S. Mourning and Melancholia (1917) in *The Standard Edition of the Complete Psychological Works of Sigmund Freud* (London: Hogarth Press, 1956-1591).

Fromm, E. *The Forgotten Language (1951)*, (Austin: Holt, Rinehart & Winston, 1976).

Gadamer, H. G. *Truth and Method*, trans. J. Weinsheimer & D. G. Marshall (New York: Crossroad, 2004), pp. 60–76, 412–433.

Gadamer, H. G. *Philosophical Hermeneutics* (Berkeley: California UP, 1976).

Geertz, C. *Islam Observed Religious Development in Morocco and Indonesia* (Chicago: Chicago UP, 1971).

Geertz, C. *The Interpretation of Cultures* (New York: Basic Books, 1973).

Gethmann-Siefert, A. "Heidegger and Hölderlin: The Over-Usage of Poets in an Impoverished Time", *Heidegger Studies* (1990), pp.59-88.

Gosetti-Ferencei, J. A. *Heidegger, Hölderlin, and the Subject of Poetic Language* (New York: Fordham University, 2004).

Bibliography

Gray, J. *Black Mass: Apocalyptic Religion and the Death of Utopia* (New York: Farrar, Strauss and Giroux, 2007).

Hanssen, B. and Benjamin A. E. ed., *Walter Benjamin and Romanticism* (New York: Continuum. 2002), pp. 140-141.

Hegel, G. W. F. *Phänomenologie des Geistes (1807), Phenomenology of Spirit*, trans. A. V. Miller ([Oxford: Clarendon, 1977).

Heidegger, M. *Sein und Zeit* (1927), trans. J. Stambaugh (New York: State UP, 1996).

Heidegger, M. *Basic Writings: From "Being and Time" (1927) to "The Task of Thinking" (1964)*, ed. D. F. Krell (New York: Harper Collins, 1993).

Heidegger, M. *Introduction to Metaphysics* (1935), trans. G. Fried and R. Polt (New Haven: Yale UP, 2000).

Heidegger, M. *Off the Beaten Track* (Holzewege), trans. J. Young & K. Haynes (Cambridge: Cambridge UP, 2002).

Heidegger, M. (1998), in *Logic As the Question Concerning the Essence of Language*, trans. W. T. Gregory and Y. Unna (New York: SUNY, 2009).

Heidegger, M. *Elucidations of Holderlin's Poetry*, trans. K. Hoeller, (New York, Humanity Books, 2000).

Heidegger, M. *Poetry, Language, Thought* (New York: Harper, 2001).

Heidegger, M. *Hölderlin's Hymn "The Ister"*, trans. William McNeill and Julia Davis (Bloomington, In.: Indiana UP, 1996).

Heidegger, M. "Hölderlins Hymnen Germanien" und "Der Rhein", Freiburger Vorlesung, Wintersemester 1934/35, ed. S. Ziegler (Frankfurt a.M.: Vittorio Klostermann, 1980).

Bibliography

Henrich, D. *Der Gang des Andenkens: Beobachtungen und Gedanken zu Hölderlins Gedicht.* Stuttgart: Cotta, 1986; *The Course of Remembrance and Other Essays on Hölderlin*, ed. Eckart Förster (Stanford: Stanford UP, 1997).

Hewson, M. "Two Essays by Blanchot on Hölderlin", *Colloquy Text Theory Critique 10* (November 2005). http://arts.monash.Ed:u.au/ecps/colloquy/journal/issue010/issue10.pdf . p. 221-230

Hölderlin, F. *Hyperion or the Hermit in Greece*, trans. R. Benjamin (New York: Archipelago Books, 2008).

Hölderlin, F. *Selected Poems and Fragments*, trans. M. Hamburger (London: Penguin Books, 1998).

Holderlin, F. *Hymns and Fragments*, trans. R. Sieburth (Princeton: Princeton UP, 1984).

Hölderlin, F. "On Judgment and Being", in H.S. Harris, *Hegel's Development: Toward the Sunlight 1770-1801* (Oxford: Clarendon Press, 1971), pp. 515 - 516.

Hölderlin, F. *Essays and Letters on Theory*, trans. and ed. T. Pfau (New York; University of New York Press, 1988).

Horkheimer, M. & Adorno, T. W. *Dialektik der Aufklärung (1944), Dialectic of Enlightenment*, ed. G. S. Noerr, trans. E. Jephcott (Stanford: Stanford UP, 2002).

Hutchens, B.C. *Jean-Luc Nancy and the Future of Philosophy.* (Montreal & Kingston: McGill-Queen's UP, 2005).

Inwood, M. ed. *Heidegger Dictionary* (Oxford: Blackwell 1999).

Israel, J. *The Radical Enlightenment: Philosophy and the Making of Modernity 1650-1750* (Oxford: Oxford UP, 2001), pp.258-274.

Jung, C. G. *Psychiatric Studies 1902–1905*, vol. 1. (London: Routledge, 1953).

Kant, I. *Kritik der reinen Vernunft (1781), Critique of Pure Reason,* trans. P. Guyer and A. Wood (Cambridge: Cambridge UP, 1999).

Bibliography

Kleinberg-Levin, D. M. *Gestures of Ethical Life: Reading Hölderlin's Question of Measure after Heidegger* (Stanford: Stanford University, 2005).

Kristeva, J. *Black Sun: Depression and Melancholia* (New York: Columbia UP, 1989).

Kristeva, J. *Language: the Unknown: An Initiation Into Linguistics* (1595) trans. A. M. Menke (NewYork: Columbia UP, 1551).

Kristeva, J. *Revolution in Poetic Language* (New York: Columbia University Press, 1984).

Kuhn, T. S. *The Structure of Scientific Revolutions* (Chicago: Chicago UP, 1962).

Taylor, C. "Philosophy and the Human Sciences", *Philosophical Papers* (Cambridge: Cambridge UP, 1985).

Laplanche, J. *Hölderlin et la Question du Père* (Paris: PUF, 1961); *Hölderlin and the Question of the Father*, trans. Luke Carson (Victoria, BC: ELS Editions, 2007).

Lacoue-Labarthe, P. & Nancy, J. L. *Le Mythe Nazi (1981)* in *The Nazi Myth*, trans. B. Holmes, Critical Inquiry, vol. 16, No. 2 (Winter, 1990) Chicago UP, pp. 291-312.

Lacoue-Labarthe, P. "Poetry's Courage", in *The Solid Letter: Readings of Friedrich Hölderlin*, ed., A Fioretos (Stanford: Stanford UP, 1999), pp.74-93.

Lacoue-Labarthe, P. *Heidegger and the Politics of Poetry*, trans. J. Fort. (Urbana: Illinois UP, 2007).

Lebovic, N. ed., *New German Critique* 105, Vol. 35, No. 3, (Fall 2008).

Lévi-Strauss, C. *Structural Anthropology*, trans. C. Jacobson (New York: Basic Books, 1963).

Lévi-Strauss, C. *Myth and Meaning* (New York: Schocken Books, 1978), p.3.

Lernout G., *The Poet as Thinker: Hölderlin in France* (Columbia USA:Camden House, 1994).

Lilla, M. "The Politics of God," *New York Times Magazine*, August 19, 2007.

Lilla, M. *The Stillborn God: Religion, Politics, and the Modern West* (New York: Knopf, 2007).

Liska, V. *Giorgio Agambens Leerer Messianismus* (Wien: Schlebrügge.Editor, 2008).

Lyotard, J. F. *Heidegger et "les Juifs" (1988), Heidegger and the Jews*, trans. A. Michel and M. Roberts (Minneapolis: Minnesota UP, 1990), p.5.

Malinowski, B. *Myth in Primitive Psychology* (London: Norton.1926), p. 216.

Mcluhan, M. "Myth and Mass Media", in Daedalus, vol. 88, No. 2, *Myth and Mythmaking* (Spring 1959), pp. 339-348.

Meillassoux, Q. *After Finitude: An Essay on the Necessity of Contingency*, trans. R. Brassier (New York: Continuum, 2008).

Miron, D. H. N. *Bialik and the Prophetic Mode in Modern Hebrew Poetry* (Syracuse University Press, 2000).

Murray, G. *Five Stages of Greek Religion* (London: Courier Dover Publications, 1935).

Nancy, J. L. "The Calculation of the Poet", in *The Solid Letter: Readings of Friedrich Holderlin*, ed. A Fioretos (Stanford: Stanford UP, 1999), p. 44-73.

Nancy, J. L. *The Ground of the Image*, trans. J. Forth (New York: Fordham UP, 2005).

Nancy J.L. *Corpus*, trans. R. A. Rand (New York: Fordham UP, 2008).

Nietzsche, F. *The Birth of Tragedy from the Spirit of Music* (1872), trans. Douglas Smith (Oxford University Press, 2008).

Nietzsche, F. "On the Use and Abuse of History for Life", (1191) in *Unfashionable Observations: The Works of F. Nietzsche*, trans. R. T. Gray (Stanford: Stanford University Press, 1995).

Ohana, D. and Wistrich, R. S. ed., *Myth and Memory* (Jerusalem: Van Leer - Hakibbutz Hameuchad 1996), pp. 11-37.

Plato, "Phaedrus", trans. A. Nehamas and P. Woodruff, in *Complete Works* (Indianapolis: Hackett, 1997), p. 228.

Bibliography

Plato, *The Republic ("politeia")*, trans. B. Jowett (New York: Cosimo 2008), pp. 537-558.

Ricœur, P. *Hermeneutics and the Human Sciences: Essays on Language, Action, and Interpretation* (Cambridge UK: Cambridge UP, 1981).

Ricoeur, P. *Symbolism of Evil*, trans. E. Buchanan (Boston: Beacon Press 1986).

Ronell, A. *Stupidity* (Urbana: Illinois UP, 2002).

Rose, J. *The Question of Zion* (Princeton: Princeton UP, 2007).

Rosenzweig, F. *Der Stern Der Erlosung (1921), The Star of Redemption*, trans. B. E. Galli (Madison: Wisconsin UP, 2005).

Schelling, F. W. J. *System des transcendentalen Idealismus (1800)* in *System of Transcendental Idealism*, trans. P. Heath, (Charlottesville: Virginia UP, 1978).

Schelling, F. W. J *Philosophische Untersuchungen über das Wesen der menschlichen Freiheit (1809)*, in *Philosophical Investigations into the Essence of Human Freedom*, trans. J. Love and J. Schmidt (New York: State UP, 2006).

Schelling, F.W.J. *Zur Geschichte der neueren Philosophie (1833–4)*, in *On the History of Modern Philosophy*, trans. A. Bowie (Cambridge: Cambridge University Press, 1994).

Schiller, F. *On the Aesthetic Education of Man* in a series of letters, ed. & trans. E.M.Wilkinson & L.A. Willoughby (Oxford: Clarendon Press, 1982).

Schirmacher, W. *Homo Generator: Media and Postmodern Technology*, New York, 1994, in http://www.egs.edu/faculty/wolfgang-schirmacher/articles/homo-generator-media-and-postmodern-technology/

Schirmacher. W. "Cloning Humans with Media: Impermanence and Imperceptible Perfection." Poeisis, no. 2 (2000).

Bibliography

Schirmacher, W. "Homo Generator in the Postmodern Discussion: From a Conversation with Jean-François Lyotard" in Poiesis, Journal of the Arts & Communication, ed. Stephen K. Levine (Toronto: EGS Press, 2005), vol. 7, pp. 86-99, ISSN 1492-4986/2005.

Schirmacher W. "Indirect Communication and Aesthetic Ethics: An Ironic Reading of Kierkegaard." Poeisis 9 (2007).

Schirmacher, W. ed. *Philosophy of Culture, Schopenhauer and Tradition* (Atropos Press, 2008).

Scholem, G. *Major Trends in Jewish Mysticism* (1941), (New York: Schocken, 1995) p.490.

Schmitt, C. "Politische Theologie" (1922) *Political Theology. Four Chapters on the Concept of Sovereignty*, trans. by G. Schwab (Chicago: Chicago UP, 2005).

Schmitt, C. *The Crisis of Parliamentary Democracy* (1923), trans. by E. Kennedy (Cambridge/MA: MIT Press, 1985).

Shils, E. *Tradition* (Chicago: Chicago UP, 1981).

Simon, E. A. "Heilige Nuchternheit" (1964), in *Brucken* (Heidelberg: Lambert Schneider, 1965), pp. 468-470.

Shklovsky, V. B. "Art as Technique", in *Literary Theory: An Anthology*, ed. J. Rivkin and M. Ryan (Malden: Blackwell, 1998).

Sophocles, *Antigone*, trans. J. E. Thomas (Clayton: Prestwick House, 2005), p. 19.

Sorel, G. *Reflections on Violence* (1908), trans. T. E. Hulme and J. Roth (New York: Collier, 1950).

Sparks, S. ed. *On Jean-Luc Nancy: The Sense of Philosophy* (London: Routledge, 1997).

Veyne, P. *Did the Greeks Believe in Their Myths,* trans. P. Wissing (Chicago: Chicago UP, 1983).

Warminski, A. *Readings in Interpretation: Hölderlin, Hegel, Heidegger* (Minneapolis: University of Minnesota, 1987).

Bibliography

Wittgenstein, L. J. J. *Philosophische Untersuchungen (1953), Philosophical Investigations.* (Oxford: Blackwell, 2001).

Wordsworth, W. "My Heart Leaps Up" (1802), in *Poems by William Wordsworth*, (New York: Ginn & Co., 1897), p. 409.

Wordsworth, W. *The Complete Poetical Works*, ed. J. Morley (London: Macmillan and Co, 1888).

Bibliography

Hebrew Bibliography:

Amit, H., Hacohen, A., H. Be`er, *An offering to Menachem* (Jerusalem: Hakibbutz, 2007).

Azoulay, A. *Once Upon A Time: Photography in the Footsteps of Walter Benjamin* (Hebrew), (Ramat Gan: Bar-Ilan UP, 2006).

Bar-Siman-Tov Y. ed. *Barriers to Peace in the Israeli-Palestinian Conflict* (Jerusalem: The Jerusalem Institute and Adenauer Stiftung, 2010).

Bareli, G. "Bialik: Revealment and Concealment in Love and Language" (Hebrew), in *Jerusalem Studies in Hebrew Literature*, vol. 15, (Jerusalem: Mandel Institute, 1995), p. 137-160.

Bialik: C.N. *All writings of Chaim Nachman Bialik* (Hebrew), in *The Ben Yehuda Project,* http://benyehuda.org/bialik/

Bialik, C.N. "Revealment and Concealment in Language" (Hebrew) (Tel-Aviv: Dvir, 1977) pp. 24-31.

Bialik, C. N. *Letters* (Hebrew), ed. F. Lahover (Tel-Aviv: Dvir, 1937).

Bialik, C. N. *Yiddish poems*, trans. A. Zeitlin (Tel Aviv: Dvir, 1956).

Bialik, C. N. *Things by Heart* (Hebrew), (Tel Aviv: Dvir, 1935).

Bialik, C. N. *Life Chapters: In Four Versions* (Hebrew), (Jerusalem: Tarshish, 1943).

Binyamini, I. *Toward a Critical Theology of the Contemporary Political* (Hebrew), 2011, http://haemori.wordpress.com/2011/09/19/theology

- Buber, M. *Te'udah Ve-yi'ud* (Hebrew), (Jerusalem: Bialik Institute, 1984).

Buzaglo, M. *Language for the Faithful* (Hebrew), (Jerusalem: Mandel and Keter, 2008).

Bibliography

Ginsberg, A. Z. H. (Ahad Ha'am), O*n the Crossroads* (1895), The Ben Yehuda Project http://benyehuda.org/ginzburg.

Gurevitch, Z. *Conversation* (Hebrew), (Tel Aviv: Babel, 2011)

Hirschfeld, A. "Bialik's Habrecha: I - as a World" (Hebrew), in *Jerusalem Studies in Hebrew Literature*, vol. 24 (Jerusalem: Mandel Institute, 2011).

Holtzman, A. *Chaim Nachman Bialik* (Hebrew), (Tel-Aviv: Shazar Center, 2009).

Inbari, A. "Between one concealment to the next, the abyss flickers" (Hebrew), in *Hadarim* 13, ed. H. Yeshurun, (Tel Aviv, Winter 1999).

Inbari,A. "On the language of revelation" (Hebrew), in: *Hadarim 14*, ed. H. Yeshurun (Tel Aviv, Winter 2002)

Lahover, F. *Bialik, His Life and Works* (Hebrew), (Tel Aviv: Dvir, 1956).

Libes Y. "De Natura Dei" in *Studies in Jewish Myth and Jewish Messianism* (1993), pp. 1-64, 151-169.

Luz, Z. and Shamir, Z. ed., *On Bialik's "Revealment and Concealment in Language"* (Ramat Gan: Bar-Ilan UP, 2000).

Mansbach, A. *Existence and Meaning: Martin Heidegger on Man, Language, and Art* (Hebrew), (Jerusalem: Magnes press, 1998).

Mendeley Mokher Sefarim, *Kol Kitvey* (Hebrew), (Tel Aviv: Dvir, 1958).

Miron, D. *Farewell to the Poor "I"* (Hebrew), (Tel Aviv: Open University Press, 1986).

Moses, S. *Walter Benjamin and the Spirit of Modernity* (Hebrew), (Tel-Aviv: Resling, 2003).

Noor, A. ed. *W. Benjamin, the Metaphysics of Youth* (Hebrew), trans. D. Dotan (Tel-Aviv: Resling, 2009).

Ofrat, G. "The Philosophical Miss and the Religious Chance" (Hebrew) in *Studio Art Magazine*, 115 (July 2000).

Bibliography

Ophir, A. "The Political" (Hebrew), in *Mafteakh, Lexical Review of Political Thought*, vol. 2, summer 2010, http://mafteakh.tau.ac.il/wp-content/uploads/2010/08/2-2010-06.pdf

- Pedaya, H. "The Mute Language of Sights and the Speech of Darkness" (Hebrew), in *An offering to Menachem*, ed. H. Amit, A. Hacohen & H. Be'er (Jerusalem: Hakibbutz, 2007), pp. 427-442.

Pimentel, D. "The Gift of Place" (Hebrew), *Bezalel History and Theory Protocols*, Vol. 10, October 2008, http://aleph.nli.org.il:80/F/?func=direct&doc_number=000485353&local_base=RMB01

Roi, B. "Shechina", in *Devarim Ahadim 8* (Jerusalem: Hartman Institute, June 2010), http://www.hartman.org.il/Research_And_Comment_View.asp?Article_Id=517&Cat_Id=324&Cat_Type=Research_And_Comment

Sandbank, S. trans. *Frederich Holderlin: Selected Poems* (Hebrew), (Tel-Aviv: Hargol, 2005).

Sandbank, S. trans. *Frederich Holderlin: Hyperion or the Hermit in Greece,* (Hebrew), (Tel-Aviv: Babel, 2003).

Salhov, S. "That Could Not Be Chained" (Hebrew), *Studio Art Magazine* 118, (February 2001).

Schweid, E. "Myth and Judaism in Kaufmann, Buber and Baeck", *Eshel Beer Sheva* vol. 4 (BG University, 1995), pp. 342-365.

Schweid, E. "Myth and Historical memory in Jewish Thought" in D. Ohana and R. S. Wistrich, ed. *Myth and Memory* (Jerusalem: Van Leer - Hakibbutz, 1996), pp.41-72.

Schweid, E. "The Language of the Renewed Prophecy" in *Prophets for Their People and Humanity* (Hebrew), (Jerusalem: Magnes Press, 1998).

Schweid, E. *History between Myth and Narrative*, Israel vol.1 (2002).

Shamir, Z. "To compile Sparkles Amidst the Broken Vessels" (Hebrew), in *Sadan, Studies in Hebrew Literature,* vol. 4, A. Holtzman ed. (Tel Aviv: Tel Aviv UP, 2000), pp. 75-113.

Bibliography

Shavit U. and Shamir Z., ed., *On the Edge of the Pond* (Tel-Aviv: Hakibbutz, 1994).

Sluhovsky, M. "The Beauty of Failure" (Hebrew), *Amirot,* February 2012, http://amirot.blogspot.ch/2012/02/blog-post_55.html

Urbach, E. E. *Hazal* (Hebrew), (Jerusalem: Magnes, 1982).

Yadgar Y. "Masortiut" (Hebrew), *Mafteakh, Lexical Review of Political Thought*, vol. 5, summer 2012, http://mafteakh.tau.ac.il/wp-content/uploads/2012/06/5-2012-

Think Media: EGS Media Philosophy Series

Wolfgang Schirmacher, *editor*

A Postcognitive Negation: The Sadomasochistic Dialectic of American Psychology, Matthew Giobbi

A World Without Reason, Jeff McGary

All for Nothing, Rachel K. Ward

Asking, for Telling, by Doing, as if Betraying, Stephen David Ross

Memory and Catastrophe, Joan Grossman

Can Computers Create Art?, James Morris

Community without Identity: The Ontology and Politics of Heidegger, Tony See

Deleuze and the Sign, Christopher M. Drohan

Deleuze: History and Science, Manuel DeLanda

DRUGS Rhetoric of Fantasy, Addiction to Truth, Dennis Schep

Facticity, Poverty and Clones: On Kazuo Ishiguro's 'Never Let Me Go', Brian Willems

Fear and Laughter: A Politics of Not Selves 'For' Self, Jake Reeder

Gratitude for Technology, Baruch Gottlieb

Hospitality in the Age of Media Representation, Christian Hänggi

Itself, Robert Craig Baum

Jack Spicer: The Poet as Crystal Radio Set, Matthew Keenan

Laughter and Mourning: point of rupture, Pamela Noensie

Letters to a Young Therapist: Relational Practices for the Coming Community, Vincenzo Di Nicola

Literature as Pure Mediality: Kafka and the Scene of Writing, Paul DeNicola

Media Courage: ImpossiblePedagogy in an Artificial Community, Fred Isseks

Metastaesthetics, Nicholas Alexander Hayes

Mirrors triptych technology: Remediation and Translation Figures, Diana Silberman Keller

Necessity of Terrorism political evolution and assimilation, Sharif Abdunnur

No Future Now, Denah Johnston

Nomad X, Drew Minh

On Becoming-Music: Between Boredom and Ecstasy, Peter Price

Painting as Metaphor, Sarah Nind

Performing the Archive: The Transformation of the Archive in Contemporary Art from Repository of Documents to Art Medium, Simone Osthoff

Philosophy of Media Sounds, Michael Schmidt

Polyrhythmic Ethics, Julia Tell

Propaganda of the Dead: Terrorism and Revolution, Mark Reilly

Repetition, Ambivalence and Inarticulateness: Mourning and Memory in Western Heroism, Serena Hashimoto

Resonance: Philosophy for Sonic Art, Peter Price

Schriftzeichen der Wahrheit: Zur Philosophie der Filmsprache, Alexander J. Klemm

Scratch & Sniff, Peter van de Kamp

Shamanism + Cyberspace, Mina Cheon

Sonic Soma: Sound, Body and the Origins of the Alphabet, Elise Kermani

Sovereignty in Singularity: Aporias in Ethics and Aesthetics, Gregory Bray

The Art of the Transpersonal Self: Transformation as Aesthetic and Energetic Practice, Norbert Koppensteiner

The Ethics of Uncertainty: Aporetic Openings, Michael Anker

The Image That Doesn't Want to be Seen, Kenneth Feinstein

The Infinite City: Politics of Speed, Asli Telli Aydemir

The Media Poet, Michelle Cartier

The Novel Imagery: Aesthetic Response as Feral Laboratory, Dawan Stanford

The Organic Organisation: freedom, creativity and the search for fulfilment, Nicholas Ind

The Suicide Bomber; and her gift of death, Jeremy Fernando

The Transreal Political Aesthetics of Crossing Realities, Micha Cárdenas

Theodore, Sofia Fasos

Trans Desire/Affective Cyborgs, Micha Cárdenas

Trans/actions: art, film and death, Bruce Barber

Transience: A poiesis, of dis/appearance, Julia Hölzl

Trauma, Hysteria, Philosophy, Hannes Charen

Upward Crashes Fracture's Topoi: Musil, Kiefer, Darger, Paola Piglia-Veronese

Other books available from Atropos Press

5 Milton Stories (For the Witty, Wise and Worldly Child), Sofia Fasos Korahais

Che Guevara and the Economic Debate in Cuba, Luiz Bernardo Pericás

Grey Ecology, Paul Virilio

heart, speech, this, Gina Rae Foster

Follow Us or Die, Vincent W.J., van Gerven Oei

Just Living: Philosophy in Artificial Life. Collected Works Volume 1, Wolfgang Schirmacher

Laughter, Henri Bergson

Pessoa, The Meaphysical Courier, Judith Balso

Philosophical Essays: from Ancient Creed to Technological Man, Hans Jonas

Philosophy of Culture, Schopenhauer and Tradition, Wolfgang Schirmacher

Talking Cheddo: Teaching Hard Kushitic Truths Liberating PanAfrikanism, Menkowra Manga Clem Marshall

Teletheory, Gregory L. Ulmer

The Tupperware Blitzkrieg, Anthony Metivier

Vilém Flusser's Brazilian Vampyroteuthis Infernalis, Vilém Flusser

www.ingramcontent.com/pod-product-compliance
Lightning Source LLC
Chambersburg PA
CBHW081833170426
43199CB00017B/2716